SHINGON

Red Fudō. Painted scroll on silk, Heian period
(12th century), Kōyasan.

Shingon

Japanese Esoteric Buddhism

TAIKŌ YAMASAKI

Translated and adapted by
RICHARD and CYNTHIA
PETERSON

Edited by YASUYOSHI MORIMOTO
and DAVID KIDD

SHAMBHALA
Boston & London
1988

Shambhala Publications, Inc.
Horticultural Hall
300 Massachusetts Avenue
Boston, Massachusetts 02115

9 8 7 6 5 4 3 2 1

FIRST EDITION

Printed in the United States of America
Distributed in the United States by Random House
and in Canada by Random House of Canada Ltd.

Library of Congress Cataloging-in-Publication Data
Yamasaki, Taikō, 1929–
Shingon: Japanese esoteric Buddhism / Taiko Yamasaki ; translated
and adapted by Richard and Cynthia Peterson ; edited by Yasuyoshi
Morimoto and David Kidd.—1st ed.
p. cm.
Based on the author's: Mikkyō meisō to shinsō shinri and Mikkyō meisoho.
Bibliography: p.
Includes index.
ISBN 0-87773-443-7 (pbk.)
1. Shingon (Sect) . I. Morimoto, Yasuyoshi. II. Kidd, David.
III. Yamasaki, Taiko, 1929– Mikkyō meisō to shinsō shinri.
IV. Yamasaki, Taiko, 1929– Mikkyō meisoho. V. Title.
BQ8965.4.Y36 1988
294.3'92–dc19 87-28619
CIP

Contents

Foreword by Carmen Blacker   ix
Editor's Preface   xiii
Translators' Note   xv
Author's Introduction: *The Creative Will of the Universe*   xvii

1   *Origins and Development of Esoteric Buddhism in India and China*   3

Indian Origins   4
The Rise of Mahayana and Esoteric Buddhism   6
The Middle Period   10
Later Development and Decline in India   13
Introduction of the Esoteric Teaching to China   15
The Age of the Great T'ang Patriarchs   17

2   *Historical Background of Shingon Buddhism in Japan*   23

The Introduction of Esoteric Buddhism to Japan   23
Kūkai and the Establishment of Shingon   26
The Status of the Esoteric Teachings after Kūkai   33
Developments in the Shingon Sect   37
Shingon from the Feudal Period to the Present   42
Mountain Worship, Pilgrimage, and Popular Beliefs   49

3   *Mikkyo: The Esoteric Teaching*   56

The Precepts   57
Four Major Characteristics of the Esoteric Teaching   57
Dainichi Nyorai: The Central Deity   62
The Universal Body of the Six Great Elements   64
The Mikkyo Affirmation of the Self and Human Desire   72
The Magic of Mantra   75
The Originally Unborn   79
The Suprahistorical Nature of the Esoteric Sutras   81
The *Dainichi-kyō*   83

The *Kongōchō-gyō*   85
The Dharma Lineage and the Legend of the Iron Tower   86

4   *The Ten Levels of Mind*   90

The Eight Levels of Consciousness   90
The Ninth, Tenth, and Innumerable Levels of Consciousness   92
The Ten Levels of Mind   95
The Three Layers of Delusion   98
The Stages of Samadhi   99
Wisdom and Skillful Means   103

5   *The Secret Activities of Body, Speech, and Mind*   106

Esoteric Practice Based on Form   108
The Mystery of Empowerment   110
The Secret of Body: The Esoteric Mudra   112
The Secret of Speech: Esoteric Mantra Practice   116
The Secret of Mind: Internal Visualization   119

6   *The Dynamic Mandala*   123

Types of Mandala   126
Outline of the Tai-zō Mandala   128
The Concentric Structure of the Tai-zō Mandala   132
Outline of the Kongō-kai Mandala   138
The Nine Assemblies of the Kongō-kai Mandala   140
The Spiral Movement of the Kongō-kai Mandala   145
The Dual Taizō-Kongōkai Mandala   147

7   *The Scope and Complexity of Shingon Ritual*   152

Representative Mikkyo Practices   153
Basic Visualization Techniques   154
The Concentration Points   159
The General Format of Esoteric Ritual   162
Ritual Implements and Offerings   163
The Preparatory Fourfold Enlightenment Practice   168
Shingon Initiation   175

8   *Concentrated Three-Secrets Practices*   182

The Morning Star Meditation   182
Celestial Bodies and Meditation on the Universe   184
The Practice of the Morning Star   185

An Experience with the Morning Star Meditation   188
The A-Syllable Visualization   190
The All-Encompassing Symbolism of the A-Syllable   192
Techniques of the A-Syllable Visualization   195
The A-Syllable Visualization and the Dual Mandala   198
The Nine-Layered A-Syllable Practice and the Tai-zō   206
Seizon's Text on the A-Syllable Visualization   210
Meanings of the A-Syllable and Moon Disk   212
Kakuban's *A-Syllable Visualization*   215

Editor's Postscript   217
Notes   219
Appendix: Japanese Names and Terms with Sanskrit or Chinese
    Equivalents   229
Index   237

Foreword

A consensus of tradition has always told us that "esoteric" teachings are kept secret and reserved because they transcend the limited capacities of ordinary men. A cordon must be thrown around them to protect them from abuse or distortion at the hands of those too ignorant to comprehend their meaning. Until shortly after the Second World War, Shingon was one such school. It is a late school of Buddhism, which originated in India sometime during the seventh century and was carried eastward to China and Japan in the course of the next two hundred years. Another branch of the doctrine went north to Tibet during the eighth century. At the time of its origin it was a completely new school of Buddhism, which taught that man could recover his innate but lost Buddha nature "in this very body." No longer was it necessary to wait until after death or after the passage of countless rebirths. By performing certain disciplines of body, speech, and mind, and by undergoing certain initiatic consecrations, the disciple could realize, in this life, his fundamental identity with the Buddhahood of the whole world.

This school, known variously as esoteric or Tantric Buddhism, has always drawn a distinction between its exoteric and its esoteric teachings. For the world at large it offered a brilliant art and iconography, a pantheon of divine protectors from worldly ills, a doctrine of the ultimate Buddhahood of all sentient beings, and a corpus of magic spells whereby ordinary people could be helped to heal their sicknesses, vanquish their enemies, bring rain during a drought, and ensure an abundant harvest.

The spiritual practices leading to the various initiations, on the other hand, were always treated as esoteric; they were reserved for those disciples who were undergoing the prescribed training toward the requisite consecration. Such teachings, known as *mikkyō* in Japanese, were never committed to writing. They were transmitted by word of mouth to those qualified to receive them.

The *mikkyō* doctrines were brought to Japan by Kūkai at the beginning of the ninth century. For some eleven hundred years they remained esoteric, handed down in an initiatic chain from master to pupil. They were never recorded or published. Some forty years ago, however, this carefully guarded secrecy, this strict distinction between exoteric and esoteric, began to break down. Accounts of doctrine and practice, never before written down, began to be published in Japan for all to read.

Comparatively little of this wisdom has so far been made available to Western readers. Works on Shingon art and iconography have appeared in English; treatises in French have been published on the fascinating subject of the Two Mandalas, so prominent in the rituals and meditations of *mikkyō;* some invaluable monographs have been given us by authorities such as Kiyota Minoru. By and large, however, this important school of Buddhism, which has immeasurably enriched the cultural and spiritual life of Japan, has been neglected in the West. Compared with the immense literature on Zen, and the substantial writing on Tibetan *vajrayāna,* works on Shingon *mikkyō* have been scarce. Details of the spiritual exercises, published so comparatively recently in Japan, have been especially inaccessible.

This book is the first comprehensive study of Shingon—treating its history, its doctrines, and its practical disciplines—to appear in any Western language. It will be warmly welcomed by all Western students of Buddhism. Much of it is based on two books by Professor Taikō Yamasaki, *Mikkyō meisōhō* (1974) and *Mikkyō meisō no shinsō shinri* (1981). Both are practical guides to Shingon meditation methods. A Shingon priest of high rank, a pupil of the celebrated Kanayama Bokushō, a student of Indian yoga and of depth psychology, an adept in all the various forms of esoteric meditation, Professor Yamasaki is admirably fitted to introduce these complex teachings to Western readers. His books were published in Japan in the hope that practical instructions in these well-tried meditation techniques might prove a useful corrective to the psychological ills of the age.

His work has been translated and edited by a dedicated team of scholars, both American and Japanese. Always working in close collaboration with Professor Yamasaki, they have nevertheless thought right to broaden the scope of the book for the needs of an English readership. They have accordingly drawn on a wider range of Shingon sources than those provided by Professor Yamasaki alone.

The resulting study is a true overview of the subject. Here for the first time the English reader can follow the history of the school, from its mysterious origin in India to its introduction and development in Japan. We can read of the remarkable men who carried the teachings from India to China in the course of the eighth century, who translated the texts—let us never forget the appalling difficulties of translating from the Sanskrit to the Chinese—and who continued the initiatic chain of teaching in the capitals of T'ang China. Here too is the life of the brilliant genius Kūkai—calligrapher, sculptor, and spiritual master—who brought the teachings from China to Japan in the early ninth century and who systematized both doctrine and practice in such a way that they have survived virtually unchanged to this day. Here too are the metaphysical doctrines of the school, its founding scriptures, its views on levels of consciousness and stages of *samādhi.* Here too is the whole range of Shingon practice, its meditations and exercises, hitherto virtually unknown in the West.

Nor is this all. We can also find guidance to the mysteries of the Two Mandalas and their use in ritual and meditation. These mandalas may be familiar to us as icons on the walls of temples. But of their construction, of the correct progression through the multitudinous figures that inhabit them, of their function in ritual, little has so far been divulged in English.

How welcome, therefore, is the full description given here of the Taizōkai, or Womb World Mandala, with its central Buddha, its twelve rectangular "halls," its 409 divinities, its orientation to the east, its eight red petals, its five gates. We are guided through each "hall," with its resident divinities, and shown how the construction of the mandala follows prescriptions in the *Mahāvairocana Sūtra*.

Here also are described the intricacies of the Kongōkai or Diamond World Mandala, with its nine squares, its orientation to the west, its 1461 divinities, and its interior spiral movement toward the center.

Of special interest to Western students of Buddhism, however, will be the account here given of the spiritual exercises practiced in Shingon, whereby the disciple can recover his lost Buddha nature. Fully described are the *sammitsu*, the three secret modes of "symbolic mimesis" by which the disciple can identify his bodily actions, his speech, and the operations of his mind with those of the Buddha Vairocana.

We shall find that the exercise comprises a period of a hundred days, in which the disciple must enact a symbolic drama by means of mudras of the hands, mantras, and visualizations. The place of the rite is sealed off by golden walls and nets, the Buddha and his retinue are brought to the place in a jeweled carriage, invited inside, feasted, entertained, and worshiped. At the climax of the rite the disciple's Buddha nature is released and fused into a mystic unity with the Buddha. Thereafter the magic walls and nets are "untied" and the divine guests sent back to their world with flowers strewn under their feet. It is a complex and difficult practice, which requires the personal supervision of a teacher.

The reader will likewise find here a fascinating account of some of the supplementary meditations of Shingon. Professor Yamasaki is thoroughly versed in the *ajikan*, or recitation and visualization of the Sanskrit letter *A*, a sound that is held to encapsulate all the wisdom of the *Mahāvairocana Sūtra* and to speak directly to a deep layer of our consciousness. Professor Yamasaki is, further, one of the few people alive to have completed the extremely arduous practice known as the *kokūzō gumonji-no-hō*, here called the Morning Star Meditation because the disciple by this practice hopes to achieve mystic union with the deity Akashagarbha in the form of the planet Venus. Professor Yamasaki's account of his personal experiences in undergoing this grueling fifty-day discipline makes fascinating reading. He lived in a small temple on the top of Mount Misen, open on three sides to the landscape and surrounded by huge trees. In fifty days he had to accomplish a million times the recitation of the mantra *Nō bō Akyasha kyarabaya on ari kyamari bori sowaka*. Every day, therefore, with a rosary to help him count, and facing east in full view of the morning star, he had to recite the mantra 21,600 times. As the days went by he reported visions and phenomena of unusual intensity, which required courage and wisdom to withstand. Toward the end of the practice these diminished in force, to give way to a heightened and crystalline clarity of consciousness and perception.

In Japan today, despite the headlong pace of modernization during the last forty years, much of a more ancient world has survived, on a level of the mind that seemingly remains untouched by modern gadgetry. Shingon has been lost to India and has long vanished from China. Only in Japan has this old and mysterious school of Buddhism survived. Some there may be who deplore the "release" of hitherto esoteric knowledge, who believe that such an opening of the gates can result only in misuse and spiritual impoverishment. Others may reply that it is better to record than to lose, better that such knowledge be made available to all than lost to all. Be that as it may, the release of Shingon esoteric doctrine has been a fact in Japan for several decades. It is surely good, therefore, that Western readers should be given an overview of this school by a qualified and initiated authority. Our gratitude goes to Professor Yamasaki and to the devoted team who have given us this valuable book.

Carmen Blacker
Cambridge University 1987

Editor's Preface

This book was first conceived by Yasuyoshi Morimoto, the codirector with me of The Oomoto School of Traditional Japanese Arts, as a combined translation into English of two books in Japanese by his friend, Taikō Yamasaki, dean of the Department of Esoteric Buddhist Studies at Shuchi-in University in Kyoto. The first of these books, *Mikkyō Meisō-hō* (Secret Meditation Techniques of Shingon Buddhism), was published in 1974 by Nagata Bunshōdō, Kyoto; and the second, entitled *Mikkyō Meisō to Shinsō Shinri* (Shingon Meditation Techniques and Psychological Theories of Mind), was published in 1981 by Sōgen-sha, Kyoto.

The author is a scholar of traditional Shingon doctrine and ritual practice, head priest of Joko-in temple in Kobe, and holder of the Shingon title of *dento dai ajari*, "great master of the transmission of the light." His two books describing Shingon thought and meditation practices were written for Japanese readers who, if not Shingon followers, nevertheless knew a great deal about Shingon and Japanese Buddhism in general.

Since this book in English is intended for Western readers, it has become, by necessity, a general introduction to Shingon history, doctrine, and practice, seen both as Shingon has traditionally seen itself, and as it is viewed today by a modern Shingon practitioner and scholar. Keeping intact the Shingon view is one of the aims of this book.

The all-suffering and hard-working translators, Richard and Cynthia Peterson, both born in Japan, produced this English version over some four years whenever they were not otherwise engaged with me and Mr. Morimoto in operating the Oomoto school. Mere translation hardly sufficed, since some portions of Professor Yamasaki's original two books were not used, while other information was incorporated into an entirely new and reorganized English text.

For our part, Mr. Morimoto and I have labored to ensure that the book, exotic though it be, makes at least some sense to an interested Western reader.

The rest is up to Shingon.

David Kidd, Director
The Oomoto School of Traditional Arts
Kujoyama, Kyoto, 1986

Translators' Note

Many passages from Shingon sutras and texts are quoted in this book. They are translations from Japanese texts or from Japanese versions of the source texts. Their sources are identified in the notes at the back of the book. When first named, Shingon texts are identified by their titles in Chinese (in the Japanese transliteration) or in Japanese. Titles of most texts are also followed by English equivalents, and these are thereafter identified by English title. As a rule, the titles of sutras and Sanskrit or Chinese commentaries are not translated into English (with some few exceptions, e.g., the *Lotus Sutra* and the *Commentary on the Dainichi-kyō*); neither are Sanskrit titles of Shingon sutras given.

Since Shingon is a Japanese form of Buddhism, most terms, names of deities, and titles of texts are given in their Japanese pronunciation, with some exceptions in sections dealing with the history of esoteric Buddhism in India. Symbolic syllables are given in upper case in Japanese pronunciation (e.g., A, BA, RA). Chinese, Sanskrit, and Tibetan names of people remain in the romanized forms of those languages; Japanese equivalents are also given where appropriate. Japanese names of people in the preface are given in the order of personal name followed by family name; in the text, this order is reversed. A romanized list of some Japanese words and names with equivalents in Sanskrit (and a few in Chinese) is appended.

Most Japanese terms in the text, except for proper names, are printed in italics, and, when occurring alone, are not otherwise identified as Japanese. Sanskrit words are ordinarily not specially identified as such, except by context. Where confusion seems likely, Sanskrit words are identified by the abbreviation *Skt.*, Chinese by *Ch.*, and Japanese by *Jap.* The following are treated as English words: bodhicitta, bodhisattva, Buddha, Dharma, karma, Mahayana, mandala, mantra, mudra, nirvana, samadhi, sangha (samgha), samaya, stupa, sutra, tantra, Theravada, vajra. They appear in the text without diacritical marks.

AUTHOR'S INTRODUCTION

The Creative Will
of the Universe

The intellectual and experiential system of Shingon esoteric Buddhism offers valid techniques for realizing the universal creative will. It is high time that the esoteric tradition, secretly maintained in an unbroken line of transmission for over a thousand years, become part of the legacy of all mankind.

Today advanced sciences and disciplines—such as physics, mathematics, history, Western philosophy, physiology, psychology, and so forth—exist in such profusion that no single person can any longer follow their continuing development. Shingon today is unrelated but complementary to these bodies of human knowledge, and new knowledge does not lessen the value of the esoteric teachings. For its part, the Shingon "experiential science" of human potential is the repository of a profound philosophical tradition that embraces all aspects of the material world and the immeasurable inner self, expressing the union of the human being and the universe, the microcosm and macrocosm.

Research into esoteric Buddhism is carried on in terms of history, bibliography, linguistics, philosophy, and art, but these tend to be strictly analytical studies that ignore the subject of the entire tradition, the self. In order to see Shingon objectively in historical perspective, it is of course necessary to look at it from the outside. But at the same time, we need a discipline that allows understanding of its practices from within, to clarify the profound significance of the truth expressed in the texts, and to incorporate all this correctly as part of one's whole self.

If the former is objective Shingon study in terms of history and logic, then the latter is subjective and suprahistorical, dealing with the experiential knowledge and wisdom of Shingon and its practices. Without a balance of both approaches, contemporary understanding of esoteric Buddhism can be neither sound nor profound. This is the original spirit of traditional Shingon study, and this book is an attempt to contribute to such an approach by introducing the Shingon Buddhist system of inseparable doctrine and practice.

It should be understood, therefore, that no study of Shingon Buddhism can be complete without the understanding that comes from experience. The esoteric practices have always been transmitted exclusively within the Shingon priesthood, held secretly for initiates alone. Although it is not possible to disclose all of Shingon's secrets in this book, it seems equally impossible to withhold whatever might be of value to a wider audience.

It is one of the characteristics of Shingon doctrine that extremely complex truths can also be expressed with extreme simplicity, and conversely, that the simplest doctrines can have endless ramifications. One must not cling to either the simplicity or the complexity. In the practices, too, there is tremendous range and variety. Whether concise or expanded in form, however, they all aim toward realization of that to which the esoteric teachings lead: knowing one's own mind as it truly is.

SHINGON

ONE

Origins and Development
of Esoteric Buddhism
in India and China

Shingon is the form of esoteric Buddhism brought from China to Japan by the priest Kūkai (posthumously given the title Kōbō Daishi) near the beginning of the ninth century. This form of Buddhism in general is known in Japanese as *mikkyō* (hereafter Mikkyo), meaning "secret teaching" or "secret Buddhism." This term properly refers as well to the esoteric teachings included as part of Tendai Buddhism, founded in Japan by Saichō (also known by the title Dengyō Daishi), a contemporary of Kūkai. The history and doctrine of Tendai, however, are beyond the scope of this book.

One of several currents within the broad Mahayana tradition, Mikkyo developed gradually in India as a synthesis of doctrines, philosophies, deities, religious rituals, and meditation techniques from a wide variety of sources. Assimilation of Hindu deities and rituals, for example, was especially marked in the Buddhism that became Mikkyo. Such diverse elements came together over time and, combining with Mahayana philosophical teachings, formed a coherent Buddhist system of thought and practice.

Shingon traditionally classifies esoteric Buddhist teachings as being of either the "pure" (*shōjun*) or "miscellaneous" (*zōbu*) category Mikkyo. The pure teachings are those based on the *Dainichi-kyō* and the *Kongōchō-gyō,* the fundamental sutras of Shingon. Probably written during the last half of the seventh century in India, these sutras contain the first systematic presentation of Mikkyo doctrine and practice as incorporated by Shingon. The miscellaneous teachings comprise the esoteric Buddhist texts and practices predating these two sutras. The miscellaneous category includes many elements also found in the pure category, but the latter teachings represent a comprehensive synthesis of ritual and philosophy that were not yet systematized in the former.

The name Shingon is a transliteration into Japanese of the Chinese Chen-yen, which means "true word," referring to the incantations of central importance in Mikkyo. The teachings brought together in Japan under the name of Shin-

3

gon are said to represent the middle period of esoteric Buddhist development in India. This, extending from the seventh into the eighth century, was the time when the *Dainichi-kyō* and *Kongōchō-gyō* were compiled. Further doctrines and practices were produced during the latter perid of Indian Mikkyo, which lasted until the early thirteenth century. Although these were important in the development of Tibetan Buddhism, they had little influence on Shingon in Japan.

The full range of esoteric Buddhist history is vast in time and geography, reaching from India to Central Asia, Ceylon, China, Korea, Japan, Mongolia, Nepal, Southeast Asia, and Tibet. The Mikkyo tradition survives in Japan today, but in other lands where the Indian source-tradition developed in varying ways, the esoteric Buddhist teachings have mostly declined, some to the point of extinction.

This chapter will trace the outline of Mikkyo history from India to China. It will touch only very briefly on developments in the latter period in India, which had little influence on Shingon. Chapter Two will describe the historical background of Shingon in Japan. The meditative techniques, religious doctrines, and important terms brought up in these two chapters in connection with Mikkyo history will be described more fully in later sections.

INDIAN ORIGINS

Esoteric Buddhism places strong emphasis on ritual, especially that involving incantations. Much of this ritual was assimilated from other religious systems. Some of the origins of esoteric Buddhism can be traced as far back as the culture of pre-Aryan India, thought to have flourished sometime from the mid-third to mid-second millennium B.C.E. in such centers as Mohenjo-daro and Harappā. These pre-Aryan peoples worshiped numerous gods and seem to have practiced a kind of religious yoga as well as magical incantation.

The Aryans who invaded India around 1500–1200 B.C.E. also included magical incantation as an important part of their religious ritual. The religion of these Aryans is known as Brahmanism (*baramon-kyō*), whose priests, the Brahmin caste, performed rituals of praise, offering, and entreaty to the gods. Among their scriptures is the *Ṛg Veda,* the first literary product of Indo-Aryan culture. Probably written not long after the Aryans' arrival, this text was followed over some five centuries by three further Vedas.

The texts of Brahmanism record many ritual practices that are now regarded as seeds of later esoteric Buddhist ritual. The Brahmanistic fire ritual, for example, was taken directly into esoteric Buddhism, which adapted the ritual to its own aims and thought. Various deities described in the *Ṛg Veda,* such as Indra (Jap., Taishaku-ten), Varuṇa (Jap., Sui-ten), and Agni (Jap., Ka-ten), were absorbed into the esoteric Buddhist pantheon. The universal Buddha of Shingon, Dainichi Nyorai (literally "Great Sun"; Skt., Mahāvairocana), may have originated in the lesser deity known in the Vedas as Asura (Jap., Ashura), which in turn seems to be related to the Zoroastrian Ahura Mazda, god of light.

After the first millennium B.C.E., the nomadic Indo-Aryans began to lead a more settled life based on agriculture, mixing more closely with the pre-Aryan peoples. The *Atharva Veda,* written during this time, shows an increasing importance being placed on incantations, used for such purposes as healing, prolonging life, increasing benefits, subduing enemies, and so on.

In general, magical incantation of this kind is known in Sanskrit as mantra, the term whose Chinese translation was the origin of the name Shingon. In the Vedas these magical practices are classified in various types according to their purpose, and the same classifications appear later in esoteric Buddhist sutras. Although it is difficult to trace direct historical connections between Brahanism and esoteric Buddhism, many such parallels exist. Texts recording ritual procedures offer another example. Brahmanism gave rise to a body of such literature, associated with the Vedas, of styles called *vidhi* and *kalpa.* As esoteric Buddhism developed its own ritual texts, these were also called *vidhi* or *kalpa* (and later tantra), all of which Shingon refers to as *giki.*

The sixth and fifth centuries B.C.E. were a time of transition in India. The appearance of new religious and philosophical teachings, among them Buddhism, reflected a general tendency away from Brahmanism and its rigid social order. In the cities, wealth and power were being accumulated by a new merchant class, which presumably felt less need for the magic and ritual associated with the old nomadic and agricultural cultures. Śākyamuni Buddha (hereafter Shakyamuni), addressing his teachings primarily to this social class, forbade Brahmanistic ritual practices and mantric magic as being oriented toward secular benefit rather than the proper goal of Buddhism, which was spiritual liberation through self-awareness.

Nevertheless, some incantations were implicitly allowed to Buddhists from Shakyamuni's time. The type of incantation recorded in early Buddhist texts in the Pali language is known as *paritta.* One such incantation was the Khanda Paritta, used for protection from poisonous snakes. By the use of this spell, the reciter manifested compassion toward snakes, thus averting their danger. Other magically oriented *parittas* also came into use by Buddhists, and the mantric literature continued to grow. A spell said to have protected a peacock from a hunter was recited to avert disaster, while another conquered fear. A *paritta* to arouse faith was said to have been used by the Brahmanical deity Indra to convert a warlike evil spirit to Buddhism. Other mantric practices adopted by Buddhism and found in its early scriptures include incantations used to worship the seven Buddhas of the past (Shakyamuni and the six Buddhas considered to have preceded him).

As the Buddhist order grew, it reached from the cities into outlying farming villages, where it was influenced by older religious and magical traditions surviving from pre-Aryan times. The Buddhist religion spread conspicuously under King Aśoka, who unified India under the Maurya dynasty in the third century B.C.E. After the fall of the Mauryas around 180 B.C.E., several Greek kingdoms were established in North and Northwest India, where nomadic tribes from the north also established communities. Indian society and beliefs were influenced by exposure to these foreign cultures. Shamanistic beliefs brought by the nomads probably strengthened tendencies to incorporate ritual magic into Buddhism. Under such influences, Buddhism tended to take on an increasingly magical coloring, especially at its geographical fringes.

This tendency continued under the Kuṣāṇa (hereafter Kushana) dynasty, founded by a group of Aryans who entered North India around the end of the first century B.C.E. and beginning of the first century C.E. From the second to third century, the third Kushana ruler, King Kaniṣka, expanded his kingdom to extend from Central Asia as far as Persia. Indian culture was stimulated by resulting contact with Central Asian and Mediterranean civilizations. It was during these times of transition and ferment that the form of Buddhism called Mahayana came into being, building on teachings developed in earlier Buddhism. Under the Kushana dynasty, Buddhism spread in Central Asia, and, communicated along the silk road, reached China in the later Han dynasty (25–220 C.E.).

THE RISE OF MAHAYANA AND ESOTERIC BUDDHISM

Around the turn of the millennium, a new movement arose within Buddhism which added to the earlier canon further texts dealing with incantations and the newly developing doctrine of the bodhisattva. The concept of the bodhisattva, who vowed to seek enlightenment not only for himself but for all beings, represented an important development in Buddhism. This was the beginning of Mahayana (daijō), or "Great Vehicle" Buddhism, which offered salvation to lay followers as well as to the priestly order. The complicated development of Mahayana involved the coming together of many preexisting elements which coalesced as a more or less separate form of Buddhism probably around the end of the first century C.E.

Mahayana from the beginning included important ritual and devotional aspects that contributed to the formation of esoteric Buddhism. From the second century B.C.E. to the second century C.E., there was a general revival of Brahmanism that also affected Buddhism. Tribal faiths and folk beliefs were assimilated into Brahmanism, resulting in the rise of a popular religion, Hinduism, that stimulated the further development of ritual elements already present in Mahayana and earlier Buddhism.

Important in this regard were new conceptions of the Buddha as an anthropomorphic object of worship. During Shakyamuni's lifetime people employed rituals to worship the Buddha's person. These included offerings, worship, and Buddha visualization techniques—all of which are considered characteristic of esoteric practice. The Buddha was, however, thought of as a transcendent being too sacred to be portrayed except indirectly in such forms as the stupa (tō), or reliquary mound. As a memorial and reliquary, the stupa was early regarded as a symbol of the Buddha, and worship of stupas was popular even before Mahayana.

At some time near the end of the first century B.C.E., sculptured Buddha images closely resembling Greek sculpture came to be made in the Gāndhāra region in Northwest India. These were influenced by Hellenistic culture, and possibly inspired by an earlier Indian tradition of Buddhist imagery. At about the same time, more characteristically Indian images of Buddhas and bodhisattvas were being created in the Mathurā region. Such sculptures, appearing more or less contemporaneously with Mahayana, indicate a trend toward deification of the Buddha, who began to take on the aspect of a transcendental being of which the historical Shakyamuni had been only an earthly manifestation.

Among the earliest Mahayana sutras is one, written around the time that the Buddhist sculpture of Gāndhāra was being made, describing practices by which the bodhisattva practitioner could cause Amida Buddha to manifest.[1] The sutra describes these meditations in conjunction with the creation of Buddha-images. Such images seem to have been closely linked with worship ritual, including internal visualization of a Buddha. The concept of Buddhas as anthropomorphic objects of worship thus stimulated the development of ritual forms of worship, and Mahayana incorporated Brahmanic religious ritual formats, myths, and mystic disciplines into its own growing devotional practice.

Around the second century C.E., simple Buddhist rituals were being performed in which incense, flowers, and light were offered before a Buddha-image. As an aid to reaching meditative absorption, the meditator would also recite mantric verses called dhāraṇī (hereafter dharani) while holding the hands in a gesture known as gasshō (palms together at the breast) to show prayerful homage. Another early proto-esoteric sutra, centered on a dharani, describes a ritual of material offering for use by lay bodhisattva practitioners and an internally visualized offering ritual for priestly practitioners.[2] This sutra also describes such rituals as offering of incense and flowers to a Buddha reliquary stupa (said to be of equal value to making an offering to the living Shakyamuni); remembering the appearance of the Buddha while reciting dharani; and offering of incense, flowers, and light to a Buddha-image while reciting dharani. Esoteric Buddhism particularly stressed ritual practices of these kinds.

As Mahayana grew, it gave birth to a tremendous literature. Among the first Mahayana sutras written were the early Wisdom (Skt., Prajñāpāramitā) sutras. Although sutras are difficult to date with certainty, these were probably written sometime between the first and third centuries C.E. The Wisdom literature is vast. Its texts best known in the West (through English translations by Edward Conze) are probably the *Heart Sutra* (*Hannya Haramita Shin-gyō*, translated into Chinese in the early fourth century) and the *Diamond Sutra* (*Kongō-kyō*, trans-

7

lated also in the early fourth century). Other important Mahayana sutras are the *Lotus Sutra* (*Hokke-kyō,* first translated in 286) and the *Flower Garland Sutra* (*Kegon-kyō,* first translated ca. 418–420).

All of these sutras taught some form or other of "secret" incantation, whether dharani (a long mantra), the shorter *vidyā* (hereafter vidya), or mantra. These incantations were intended to unify body and mind in religious meditation, or were considered symbols of Buddha-enlightenment. Some, however, remained the same magical incantations they had always been, and Mahayana sutras also include mantras used for nonreligious purposes, such as averting misfortune. Early Mahayana sutras (including the *Lotus Sutra* and Wisdom sutras) relate instances of misfortunes escaped by copying, hearing, or reciting sutras.

An individual who played a major part in the establishment of Mahayana was Nāgārjuna (Jap., Ryūmyō, also Ryūju), who was born of Brahmin caste in southern India sometime between the mid-second and mid-third centuries. He distinguished himself for scholarly learning before becoming a Buddhist priest. Nāgārjuna (hereafter Nagarjuna) founded the Mādhyamika school, which taught the middle way between the extremes of believing in either the reality or unreality of things. His commentaries on the sutras created the philosophical foundation of Mahayana and all later schools of Buddhism.

Nagarjuna is also a figure of legendary dimensions in the traditional view of Shingon history. Named the third patriarch in the Shingon lineage, he is the first human listed in line of descent from the archetypal bodhisattva Kongō-satta, recipient of the esoteric teaching directly from the cosmic Buddha, Dai-nichi Nyorai. According to Mikkyo legend, Kongōsatta, after having been initiated by Dainichi Nyorai into the deepest mysteries of Buddhism, hid himself within an iron tower in southern India. There the bodhisattva concealed himself for centuries, until Nagarjuna opened the Iron Tower and, according to one version of this legend, received from Kongōsatta the two major sutras of Shingon Buddhism, the *Dainichi-kyō* and the *Kongōchō-gyō*. (In terms of historical chronology, these sutras are not known to have appeared until centuries later.)

Works attributed to Nagarjuna were very important in Chinese and Japanese Buddhism. He is said to have written the *Daichido-ron* (Treatise on the Attainment of Great Wisdom), for example. Composed as a commentary on the *Maka Hannya Haramitsu-kyō* (*Great Wisdom Sutra*), this text systematically presents the central Mahayana concept of wisdom, with reference to many earlier Mahayana sutras. It classifies wisdom in various types, one of which is called incantation (*jumon*). Some writings on Mahayana philosophy attributed to Nagarjuna, though considered forgeries by other Buddhist sects, are valued as fundamental texts of Shingon Buddhism.

An important current of Mahayana thought, founded in the Wisdom sutras, had to do with the view that all things are empty of permanent reality, in other words, void. In this approach, ultimate truth can only be described as void (*kū*), and the goal of wisdom can be attained by a process of negating all incorrect views of reality. The school founded by Nagarjuna further elucidated voidness as a mystical experience transcending language and the duality between worldly and transcendental truth.

This, the Mādhyamika (*chūgan*) school, represents one of the two main philosophical currents within Mahayana. The other was the Yoga (*yuga*) school, founded on meditative practice with the goal of transforming ordinary consciousness into wisdom. The yoga practitioners turned their efforts to penetrating the nature of worldly delusions. This school is also known as Consciousness-Only (*yuishiki*) because it denied the objective reality of all phenomena, explaining them to be no more than transformations of the perceiving consciousness.

The above presents a much-simplified view of religious doctrines too complex and sophisticated to do justice to here. Shingon, setting these developments within the framework of Mikkyo history, tends to see Mahayana thought as representing an increasingly philosophical, academic superstructure of Buddhism. In contrast, the evolving esoteric substream of Buddhism is understood as representing the concerns of the common people.

Even the sutras coming out of the priestly academies, however, all dealt with some type of incantation. On the popular level, esoteric texts were increasingly concerned with devotional ritual and magical practices for worldly benefit. Techniques to cause and stop rain, for example, had become an important part of Buddhist ritual by the fourth or fifth centuries. When these two currents of Buddhism, the philosophical and the magical (whose separation is somewhat overstated here), were systematically combined in the seventh century, esoteric Buddhism came into its flowering.

About 320 C.E., King Chandragupta I founded the Gupta dynasty, which would unite northern and southern India. Under this dynasty Brahmin culture again came to dominate India, beginning the so-called Hindu period. During this period Sanskrit became the common language of Buddhism, which incorporated much Brahmin terminology. The Gupta dynasty supported Hinduism, but did not suppress Buddhism, whose main patrons were merchants and members of the court. Although the Mahayana schools continued to develop during this period, they seem to have been active mostly within the confines of their temple compounds.

Esoteric Buddhism seems to have maintained its strong appeal among the populace, and Buddhist ritual continued to be elaborated during the Gupta dynasty. One sutra of this period, for example, describes worship rituals to be performed for various Hindu deities in order to fulfill a petitioner's particular wish. It records detailed techniques for establishing a sacred space in which the practitioner invited the deity to manifest himself and receive the offering, methods for constructing altars, techniques for making entreaties to the deities, and rituals for offering incense, flowers, and light to different deities.

From around the time of Chandragupta I, too, esoteric Buddhist ritual texts (*giki*) were written prescribing the rules and forms of ritual. Modeled after similar texts in Brahmanism, these were related to specific sutras, whose doctrinal import they expand on in terms of actual practice. Already by the fourth century, therefore, Buddhism had a wealth of magical rituals. As well as the above worship and meditation practices, techniques existed for summoning the powers of particular deities to achieve such purposes as making and stopping rain, healing, and so on.

The fire ritual (Skt., *homa;* Jap., *goma*) is another example of Brahmanistic ritual taken into esoteric Buddhism. This practice, adopted whole, appears as a Buddhist form of offering around the third century. Later sutras describe three types of fire ritual (for averting misfortune, increasing good fortune, and subduing baneful influences), illustrating how it had become established as an important esoteric Buddhist practice. Although the fire ritual's Brahmanistic format remained more or less intact, the practice was given Buddhist symbolic significance.

In early Buddhist sutras, most Hindu deities who appear are depicted as hearers of the Buddha's preaching. With the development of Mahayana, these gods came to be seen as protectors of Buddhism. In esoteric sutras, deities of Hindu origin were considered as manifestations of the Buddha, and had associated incantations and worship rituals. Before the seventh century, however, a comprehensive system unifying the growing multitudes of Buddhas, bodhisattvas, and other deities had not yet been developed. The esoteric Buddhist mandala, which would graphically illustrate such a system, and which would be a basic component of Mikkyo ritual, had yet to appear.

THE MIDDLE PERIOD

The Gupta dynasty, which had enjoyed commerce and communication over a vast area reaching to the Mediterranean on the west and China on the east, began to fail in the late fifth century. The end of trade with the collapsing Roman Empire damaged the Gupta money economy, and the dynasty was also weakened by an invasion of Huns in Northwest India. The schools of Buddhism patronized by the court and merchants lost much of their support, while Brahmanism, Hinduism, and magical practices grew in popularity.

Esoteric Buddhism also continued to grow. A transition was gradually taking place, however, that resulted in a new phase of development sometime around the seventh century. Shingon historians see this as the passage from early-period to middle-period Mikkyo. The first produced the miscellaneous and the second produced the pure category teachings. The pure teachings evolved into the tantric teachings characteristic of the latter period of esoteric Buddhism.

Texts of esoteric Hinduism and Buddhism written from sometime around the beginning of the seventh century began to be called tantras. The Sanskrit word *tantra,* meaning "warp," was used to refer to texts dealing primarily with ritual practice. In contrast, the sutras were the woof, setting forth basic religious principles. Because of its emphasis on tantras, later esoteric Buddhism (and sometimes esoteric Buddhism in general) is often termed Tantric Buddhism.

These tantras were classified in various ways in Indian and Tibetan esoteric Buddhism. One fourfold system partly parallels the Shingon miscellaneous–pure division. The first of these four types of tantra comprises the early esoteric texts (*kriyā tantra*) produced by early-period Mikkyo. This corresponds to the miscellaneous category of Shingon. The second type (*caryā tantra*) combines ritual with Mahayana philosophy, and refers to the texts related to the *Dainichi-kyō*. The third type of text (*yoga tantra*), based on yogic practice, further combines ritual with Mahayana thought, as in the early *Kongōchō-gyō*. The second and third types are what Shingon places in the category of pure teachings, the product of middle-period Mikkyo. The fourth type (*anuttarayoga tantra*), mostly growing out of the *Kongōchō-gyō* lineage, comprises the texts of later Indian esoteric Buddhism.

Texts written around the sixth and seventh centuries suggest a rapid development in esoteric practices. Ritual was becoming standardized, as were the iconographic forms of a variety of deities. Many complex rituals existed, centered on different deities. The prescribed postures of body and hands known as mudras had become systematized, together with complex visualizations of deities and mantric syllables. Particular Sanskrit syllables and objects had come into use as symbols of deities. The primary aim of early esoteric Buddhism had been to ward off misfortune and bring about good fortune. In approaching the middle period, however, practices originating as magical rituals for worldly benefit were gradually reoriented to the aims of Mahayana doctrine. The focus of esoteric ritual was shifting toward the purpose of attaining Buddhahood, which in the middle period would become the explicit, immediate aim of practice.

This is illustrated in the mid-seventh-century compendium of practices known as the *Darani Jikkyō,* the most systematized of the miscellaneous category texts. This sutra refers to a greatly increased number of deities, each with its own mudra, mantra, and detailed offering ritual. Although the aim of such ritual is still primarily avoidance of misfortune, this sutra also deals with such Mahayana doctrines as the void nature of things and the attainment of enlightenment. Dharani sutras of this period in general treat the attainment of wisdom as one purpose of dharani recitation. Such changes point to the transition from early- to middle-period esoteric teachings.

At the beginning of the seventh century, King Harṣa of a later Gupta dynasty unified northern India under his rule. Buddhism thrived in his kingdom, particularly at the temple center in eastern India known as Nalanda, which had been founded by a Gupta king in the early fifth century. Here the Mahayana teachings of void and consciousness-only were elaborated, providing a natural background for the further development of esoteric Buddhism. By the mid-seventh century, Nalanda had become a large complex with some ten thousand priests, described by the great Chinese priest and translator Hsüan-tsang (Jap., Genjō; 602–664), who journeyed to India in 629 to obtain sutras, staying until 645.

One esoteric practitioner active at Nalanda and noted for mystical attainments was Dharmagupta (Jap., Darumakikuta). Sometime near the beginning of the seventh century, he taught Śubhakarasiṃha (Jap., Zenmui; hereafter Shubhakarasimha), an important figure in the Shingon lineage. Another Shingon patriarch, Vajrabodhi (Jap., Kongōchi; 671–741), also studied at Nalanda, as did the priest Prajñā (Jap., Hannya; 734–810), who later passed on esoteric teachings to Kūkai in Ch'ang-an in the early ninth century.

The appearance of middle-period esoteric Buddhist teachings is not clearly established as to time and location. The syntheses of ritual practice and Mahayana thought characteristic of these teachings, however, are represented by the two fundamental Shingon sutras. The legend of Nagarjuna and the iron tower notwithstanding, the first of these, the *Dainichi-kyō,* was probably written in the mid-seventh century somewhere in western or central India. The series of texts commonly referred to in Shingon as the *Kongōchō-gyō* probably began to be written in the late seventh century in South India.

These sutras are of great significance in the development of esoteric Buddhism. Both name Dainichi Nyorai as the fundamental Buddha, and describe mandala systems that portray this central Buddha as the source of many different Buddha-manifestations, each an independent deity in itself. As to practice, the two sutras systematize the ritual activities of body (mudra), speech (mantra), and mind (visualization), and present them as inseparable aspects of symbolic activity leading to rapid attainment of enlightenment.

A major figure for Mikkyo during this period was Nāgabodhi (Jap., Ryūchi), the fourth patriarch in the Shingon lineage, about whom, however, little is known. In the traditional Shingon history, he is said to have been the direct disciple of Nagarjuna; if so, Nāgabodhi would have had to be several hundred years old. No names of individuals who carried on Nagarjuna's teaching over the preceding five or six centuries are known, but Shingon reveres them symbolically under this fourth patriarch's name. In the early eighth century Nāgabodhi passed on his teaching to Vajrabodhi, who introduced the *Kongōchō-gyō* to China. The succeeding Shingon patriarch, Amoghavajra, is also said to have studied under Nāgabodhi in Ceylon sometime after 741.

It is the esoteric Buddhism of this middle period that was taken to China by the above patriarchs and from there to Japan. After the eighth century, the teachings set forth in the *Dainichi-kyō* seem not to have been developed further in India. The *Kongōchō-gyō* teachings, however, continued to evolve, and further sub-sutras were written. One significant related text is the *Hannya Rishu-kyō* (*Wisdom-Truth Sutra*), which also belongs in the line of Mahayana Wisdom sutras. This esoteric sutra, of great importance to Shingon, affirms all human desire as a source of energy that can be used to realize Buddhahood.

LATER DEVELOPMENT AND DECLINE IN INDIA

Esoteric Buddhism continued to prosper in southern and central India from the end of the seventh and into the eighth century. In Northwest India, however, where the Rajputs were coming into power, Buddhism did not flourish. In southern India, the Pallava dynasty, which had supported the esoteric teachings, was overthrown by the Shiva-worshiping Chola dynasty in the ninth century, and esoteric Buddhism shifted up to Orissa in eastern India. There it enjoyed the support of King Indrabhūti, said to have been a patriarch of later esoteric Buddhism, author of many texts, and father of the great priest Padmasambhava.

Beginning in the early eighth century, increasing areas of India came under the threat of Muslim conquest and the consequent destruction of non-Islamic religions. In eastern India, however, esoteric Buddhism continued to thrive, especially under the Pāla dynasty, established in the mid-eighth century when it overthrew the Brahmin Guptas. This dynasty, which lasted until the twelfth century, supported Buddhism at a time when Hinduism was on the ascendant elsewhere in non-Muslim India. This was the final period of esoteric Buddhism in India, and it was this later flowering that had the greatest influence in Tibet.

Pāla esoteric Buddhism seems to have been centered in institutions. Sutras and ritual manuals were being written in great numbers at Nālandā, for example, and at Odantapurī, which was founded at the dynastic capital by Gopāla (r. 750–770), the first Pāla king. The great center of Vikramaśilā was founded by Dharmapāla, the second Pāla king, who ruled into the ninth century. Vikramaśilā, laid out in the form of a cosmic diagram, became the preeminent center for esoteric study, and its destruction by Muslim conquerors in 1203 marks the end of esoteric Buddhism in India.

During this latter period, various schools arose centered on different tantras, each with distinctive systems of practice. Those texts from this period that were carried over the vast distances to China and then to Japan arrived well after Shingon's formative period and, consequently, had little influence there. From the eighth century on, yoga tantras in the lineage of the *Kongōchō-gyō* saw great development in India.

During the latter half of the eighth century a distinct body of esoteric Buddhist literature began to develop known as the anuttarayoga (Jap., *mujōyuga*) tantras. These teachings, which in many ways closely resemble Hindu tantrism, involved practice of meditative union with the female consorts that had come to be identified with each deity.

This school brought together two different lineages of esoteric practice that appeared during the late eighth century. The first comprised the "father" (Jap., *fu*) tantras (known in Sanskrit as *yoga, mahāyoga,* or *uttarayoga* tantras), identified with the teachings of skillful means and the void. This body of teachings was centered on visualization of the essential Buddha's differentiation into the myriad phenomena of this world. The second comprised the "mother" (Jap. *mo*) trantras (known in Sanskrit as *yoginī* or *ḍākinī* tantras), identified with the teachings of wisdom and great bliss (*tairaku*). This lineage emphasized union, using psychophysiological yoga, of the practitioner with the universal Buddha. The anuttarayoga tantras treated these two lineages as forming an inseparable unity.

The representative text of the father tantras is the *Guhyasamāja Tantra,* which enjoyed great popularity in India and Tibet, where many commentaries on it were written. Such was not the case in China, however, and this text was not transmitted to Japan. Where the mandalas of middle-perid Mikkyo were centered on Dainichi Nyorai, the line of father tantras developed mandalas with other deities, such as Ashuku, at their center. There were also mandalas having only peripheral Buddhas accompanied by female consorts.

An important text representative of the mother tantras is the *Hevajra Tantra.* This line of esoteric Buddhism shows many similarities with Hindu tantrism in practice and terminology, but is nevertheless distinctly Buddhist in orientation. The mother tantra lineage produced mandalas in which the central deity could be either male or female, and in which the surrounding four Buddhas were given female form. The peripheral deities were also different from those in the father tantra mandalas.

Although other forms of Buddhism had been introduced earlier, esoteric Buddhism was first taken to Tibet in the latter half of the eighth century when Padmasambhava was summoned there from India. Known for his magical attainments, Padmasambhava is said to have subdued the local Tibetan gods and demons at his will, thus proving the supremacy of Buddhism. The first Tibetan priests subsequently took their vows, and translations began to be made of sutras considered acceptable by the rulers. Incorporating, to a greater or lesser extent, elements of the indigenous shamanistic religion (Tib., Bon-po), early Tibetan Buddhism took form as a religion serving the court.

Orthodox Buddhism was suppressed in central Tibet for a short period in the mid-ninth century, and its priests fled to eastern regions. From the east, a group of twenty-one priests was sent to study in India. One of the two who returned was Rin-chen bzaṅ-po (958–1055), who began a new cycle of sutra translation. No longer restricted by court sponsorship, Tibetan Buddhism took in new esoteric teachings from India, brought by a succession of masters that included Atīśa, a renowned tantric master from Vikramaśīla. The Tibetan Buddhism that resulted, which tended to form into discrete sects following the teachings of different founding masters, is often called Vajrayāna.

Indian esoteric Buddhism was early transmitted to Ceylon, from where it was taken by sea to Sumatra and Java. This southern sea route was one of the ways by which Buddhism entered China. During the Pāla dynasty the esoteric Buddhism of Vikramaśila in India was transmitted to Java, inspiring construction of the great stupa at Borobodur. In the early eleventh century Atīśa is said to have studied in Java for several years before taking his teachings to Tibet. Despite such indications of the importance of esoteric Buddhism in ancient Java, it declined there after the thirteenth century, probably as a result of competition with Hinduism and spreading Islam.

In India, the Muslims continued to increase their territory, and by the early eleventh century they had occupied the north. Where they advanced, Buddhist and Hindu temples and images were destroyed. Around this time the *Kālacakra Tantra* was written. This text contains Hindu elements distinguishing it from the father and mother tantras. The *Kālacakra Tantra* urges all the various Hindu sects to join with esoteric Buddhism against the encroaching Muslims. The calendrical science in this text's astrology shows influences from Islamic culture.

The *Kālacakra Tantra,* the final development of Indian esoteric Buddhism, unites the two preceding streams of tantras, as indicated even in its title: *Kāla* refers to the skillful means of the father tantras, and *cakra* to the wisdom of the mother tantras. This later text also built on preceding esoteric concepts to set forth a "primal Buddha" (Skt., Ādibuddha) considered to be the origin of all Buddhas.

In the early thirteenth century the Muslims reached eastern India, where they slaughtered Buddhists, destroyed temples, and burned sutras. The Buddhists who survived fled to Tibet, Nepal, southern India, and Java. Buddhism in India virtually ended, although a combined form of Buddhism and Hinduism, with an admixture of Islam, survived as a popular religion in Bengal and Orissa.

INTRODUCTION OF THE ESOTERIC TEACHING TO CHINA

Buddhism was early carried by traders and then by missionaries from India by sea to Ceylon and Southeast Asia, and by land into West and Central Asia, Nepal, Tibet, and Mongolia. Buddhism spread to China by both the southern sea route and overland through Central Asia along the silk route. Esoteric Buddhist teachings, however, were first taken to China, along with general Buddhism, from Central Asia, where they enjoyed considerable popularity, probably in great part because their strong magical element fit well with the shamanistic beliefs of the nomadic tribes. Sutras of the miscellaneous category dealing with incantations for prosperity and avoidance of disaster entered China in the third century, brought by such Central Asian peoples.

Five centuries passed between the first exposure to Buddhist incantations and the transmission of the pure category esoteric Buddhist teachings to China in the mid-T'ang dynasty. During these years, many miscellaneous category texts were brought and translated into Chinese. This was a period of turmoil and change in China, marked by the rise and fall of numerous kingdoms and dynasties, the growing political and cultural influence of nomadic peoples in northern China, and the growth of Taoism. Taoist practices for divination, healing, and gaining immortality were widely popular, as was faith in a growing Taoist pantheon. In this situation Buddhist ritual and magic were well received, and the esoteric element in Chinese Buddhism reinforced.

In 222, Dharmakāla (Jap., Donkakara), a priest from central India, arrived at Lo-yang and became the first to transmit the Buddhist precepts to China. He was also accomplished in the arts of astrology and divination. The first esoteric sutras to be taken to China were translated in the Three Kingdoms period (222–280) by the lay practitioner Chih-ch'ien (Jap., Shiken) of Wu. Taken along with Theravada and Mahayana texts, these were sutras dealing with incantations. Dharmarakṣa (Jap., Chikuhōgo or Chikudonmara), who came from Tun-huang to Ch'ang-an during the Western Chin (265–316), translated many incantatory sutras dealing mostly with avoidance of disaster.

During this troubled time a number of foreign Buddhist priests gained popularity due to their magical powers. Fo T'u-ch'eng (Jap., Buttochō), for example, who came from Central Asia, converted the leader of the Hu tribe in northern China, who was impressed by the priest's abilities in ritual magic. It appears that the Chinese in general were interested at least as much in such magic as in the doctrines of Buddhism.

Probably the first transmission of the esoteric Buddhist teachings to southern China took place through Śrīmitra (Jap., Hakushirimittara; d. 342), who arrived at the city of Chien-k'ang near the beginning of the fourth century. He performed incantatory magic and translated sutras showing the increasing Buddhistic element in such practices. Another important early figure in this regard was Dharmarakṣa (Jap., Donmuran), who in the later fourth century came to the Eastern Chin kingdom in southern China. He translated esoteric sutras describing rituals for healing eyes and teeth and for making and stopping rain.

A notable figure in the spread of Buddhism to China was the Central Asian Kumārajīva (Jap., Kumarajū or Rajū; 344–413). He arrived in Ch'ang-an in 401, and over the next twelve years produced translations of important Mahayana texts, including some esoteric sutras. A slightly later arrival was Dharmakṣema (Jap., Donmushin or Donmusen; 385–433), a Central Indian who came to the kingdom of the Northern Liang (397–439). Like Kumārajīva, he was famous both for his translations, which include important esoteric sutras, and for his attainments in incantatory practice.

T'an-yao (Jap., Don'yō), a fifth-century Chinese priest of the Northern Wei dynasty, is known for his activities to preserve Buddhism, which was persecuted around 446, and for his contribution to the creation of the Yün-kang caves. Among the translations to which he contributed is that of a sutra (the *Dai Kichigi Jinshu-kyō*)[3] relating magical techniques for rain-making, treasure-finding, self-concealing, and so on.

During the sixth century the number of such texts being translated into Chinese increased. A sutra appearing around this time in southern China treats ritual for worldly benefit, the practice of mudras, the fire ritual, and depiction of deities in an early form of mandala.[4] An interesting figure from this period is the Indian Bodhiruci (Jap., Bodairushi), who arrived in Lo-yang in 508 and became famous for his magical powers. By the year 535 he had translated some thirty texts in one hundred volumes.

As esoteric Buddhism flourished in India during the seventh century, the number of texts coming to China increased correspondingly in the Sui (581–618) and early T'ang (founded in 618) dynasties. This period marked the reunification of China under the T'ang, its subsequent expansion, and the flourishing of Buddhism. This was the time, too, when Hsüan-tsang returned from his long journey to India bringing a large number of Mahayana sutras. Among these were a few esoteric texts as well, including an early form of the *Wisdom-Truth Sutra*.

In the mid-seventh century Chih-t'ung (Jap., Chi-tsū) translated a sutra which dealt not only with the usual ritual for worldly benefit but also stressed the efficacy of praying to Kannon, bodhisattva of compassion, for immediate enlightenment.[5] This text shows the coming together of ritual magic and Mahayana philosophy. In 652 the Indian priest Atikūṭa (Jap., Ajikuta) arrived in Ch'ang-an bringing many Sanskrit texts, and shortly thereafter performed the first esoteric initiation in China. He is said to have translated the *Darani Jikkyō*, the sutra containing the most systematized of miscellaneous category practices.

I-ching (Jap., Gijō; 635–713), a native of Shantung, travelled by the southern sea soute to India, where he made pilgrimage to holy sites and studied sutras and incantation at Nalanda. After many vicissitudes he returned to Lo-yang in 695 with four hundred Buddhist texts, and his translations include several esoteric sutras. Between the years 680 and 710 there were several other priests in China working contemporaneously on translation of esoteric sutras.[6] This activity in seventh-century China indicates how esoteric Buddhism was developing in India at the time, and presages the coming of the pure category esoteric teachings.

THE AGE OF THE GREAT T'ANG PATRIARCHS

The T'ang dynasty, when China was actively embracing new things and ideas from foreign lands, reached a peak of cosmopolitan glory remarkable in world history. Under the emperor Hsüan Tsung (r. 712–756) Taoism and Buddhism both flourished, their magical rituals finding great favor at the court. In 714

Hsüan Tsung ordered a reform of Buddhism, which had become involved in power struggles within the court. The emperor then showed a protective interest in the new esoteric teachings, reputed to contain the most efficacious of Buddhist rituals. These were being introduced to China around that time by the three great masters Shubhakarasimha, who brought the *Dainichi-kyō*, Vajrabodhi, who brought sutras in the *Kongōchō-gyō* lineage, and Amoghavajra, who further spread the esoteric teachings in China.

Shubhakarasimha (Jap., Zenmui; 637–735) arrived in China in 716, just before Vajrabodhi, bringing with him the *Dainichi-kyō*. Born into royalty in India, Shubhakarasimha at the age of thirteen almost became king, but renounced the throne and entered the priesthood instead. Studying esoteric Buddhism under Dharmagupta at Nālandā, he quickly became a master. Shubhakarasimha took copies of the sutras and travelled through Central Asia to China, reaching the T'ang capital of Ch'ang-an in 716. Preceded by his fame, he was welcomed by emperor Hsüan Tsung and installed in a temple where he began translating sutras. In 724 he moved to Lo-yang, the eastern capital, where, with his disciple I-hsing, he completed the Chinese version of the *Dainichi-kyō*, followed by a major commentary on that sutra and translations of further texts.

Warmly received by the emperor upon his arrival in China, Shubhakarasimha was frequently summoned to the court to perform rain-making and other rituals. Although he requested the emperor's permission to return to the West, his request was not granted and he died in China in 735. Subhakarasimha and I-hsing, though greatly honored in Shingon, are not placed in the direct Dharma lineage of eight patriarchs (*fuhō hasso*) originating with Dainichi Nyorai. These two are, however, included between Amoghavajra and Hui-kuo in another listing of eight Shingon patriarchs who transmitted the Mikkyo teachings (*denji hasso*).

I'hsing (Jap., Ichigyō; 683–727) was learned in various forms of Buddhism. Before meeting Shubhakarasimha, he had studied meditation (Ch., Ch'an; Jap., Zen), the precepts (Ch., Lü; Jap., Ritsu), and the doctrines of T'ien-t'ai (Jap., Tendai) Buddhism, which unified various teachings on the basis of the *Lotus Sutra*. He became Shubhakarasimha's disciple in 716, and four years later also met Vajrabodhi, who initiated him into further secret mantra and mudra practices. I-hsing is thus seen as an important figure in the history of the Japanese sects of Zen, Ritsu, Tendai, and Shingon.

I-hsing was well known for his abilities in other areas as well. He studied mathematics and calendrical science at Mount T'ien-t'ai, and gained fame for his important contribution to the creation of a new calendar. He was well versed also in Taoist star divination and magic. The T'ang court was particularly interested in Taoism, and I-hsing's learning in this area no doubt aided him in his activities.

For Shingon, I-hsing's most important work was the *Dainichi-kyō Sho* (Commentary on the Dainichi-kyō), a work in twenty volumes explaining the seven-

volume original sutra. This, written as a record of Shubhakarasimha's teachings, I-hsing expanded on the basis of his own broad knowledge, incorporating
many quotes from the *Lotus Sutra,* for example, as well as other Mahayana
sutras. The commentary reformulates the teachings of the *Dainichi-kyō* within
the framework of Chinese Buddhism, and in Shingon it remains a primary text
for study of those teachings. I-hsing died in a temple in Ch'ang-an, and Hsüan
Tsung, bestowing on him the title of "great wisdom meditation master," per-
sonally wrote I-hsing's funerary inscription. He left no direct successor.

Vajrabodhi (Jap., Kongōchi; 671–741) was born in India (conflicting accounts have him either a prince from central India or a Brahmin from southern
India). At the age of ten he took Buddhist orders at Nalanda, where he studied
Mahayana teachings. He later studied the doctrine of the *Kongōchō-gyō* under
Nagabodhi for seven years. Legend has it that Vajrabodhi was inspired by the
bodhisattva Kannon to journey to China. After first crossing to Ceylon, he
made a difficult three-year sea voyage to China, where he arrived in Lo-yang
around 720.

Under the patronage of Hsüan Tsung, Vajrabodhi was active in Ch'ang-an
and Lo-yang, performing esoteric rituals to marvellous effect and translating
numerous sutras and commentaries. He introduced important texts in the lineage of the *Kongōchō-gyō* and laid a strong foundation for esoteric Buddhist
teachings in T'ang China. Around the same time that Vajrabodhi was translating *Kongōchō-gyō* texts, Shubhakarasimha was engaged in introducing the
Dainichi-kyō to China. The transmission of these two fundamental sutras was of
central importance in the formation of Chinese esoteric Buddhism, but it is not
known whether Shubhakarasimha and Vajrabodhi ever actually met. In 741 Vajrabodhi set out to return to India, but fell ill and died in Lo-yang. He was named
the fifth Shingon patriarch, and his chief disciple, Amoghavajra, the sixth.

Amoghavajra (Jap., Fukū; 705–774) was born in Central Asia of a Brahmin
father from northern India. He lost his father while still a child, and was taken
east by his mother, arriving in China in 714. Later, in Ch'ang-an, he met the
recently arrived Vajrabodhi, who became his master. Entering the priesthood,
Amoghavajra remained with Vajrabodhi and studied teachings in the lineage of
the *Kongōchō-gyō.*

The year after Vajrabodhi's death, Amoghavajra, determining to seek further teachings from India, set out for the port of Canton. From there, accompanied by disciples, he took the sea route by way of Java and eventually reached
Ceylon. There he received teachings and practices in the *Kongōchō-gyō* lineage.
In 746 he returned to Ch'ang-an with five hundred volumes of Sanskrit texts.
Thereafter, Amoghavajra was often summoned before the emperor, whom he
initiated into the esoteric teachings along with many court officials. He is said
to have performed various magical rituals with impressive results.

Two years later, in 755, the revolt of general An Lu-shan began. Emperor
Hsüan Tsung fled the capital, and a new emperor, Su Tsung, regained the

throne with the aid of foreign troops. At Su Tsung's request Amoghavajra performed rituals to subdue the rebels, thus gaining the emperor's trust. In the tumultuous years that followed he strove to reestablish the stability of the dynasty, in recognition for which he was given exalted title and rank. The next emperor, Tai Tsung, quelled the revolt completely, restoring peace in 763, but the T'ang dynasty had been struck a blow from which it never fully recovered.

Amoghavajra thereafter built an esoteric Buddhist temple on Mount Wu-t'ai, sacred to Monju, the bodhisattva of wisdom, and spread the practices of Monju throughout China. When Amoghavajra died in 774 the emperor suspended all court activities for three days of mourning. Amoghavajra had served the three successive T'ang emperors Hsüan Tsung, Su Tsung, and Tai Tsung. The number of Buddhist texts he translated is uncertain. He himself listed 77, but as many as 172 have been attributed to him, among which some seem to be Amoghavajra's own compositions. He is recognized (together with Kumārajīva, Paramārtha (Jap., Shintai), and Hsüan-tsang) as one of China's four great Buddhist translators. Noted for having played an important role in the sinicization of esoteric Buddhism, he is said to have been in large part responsible for the spread of the esoteric teachings in China. Amoghavajra was named the sixth Shingon patriarch.

Amoghavajra left a large number of important disciples. The youngest and eventually the most important of these was the Chinese Hui-kuo (Jap., Keika; 746–805), the seventh Shingon patriarch. Hui-kuo entered orders at the age of nine at Ch'ing-lung Temple (Jap., Shōryū-ji) in Ch'ang-an and became Amoghavajra's disciple at seventeen. Hui-kuo received esoteric initiation about three years later, with auspicious results. Shortly thereafter he received further initiations into Kongō-kai Mandala practices from Amoghavajra and then Tai-zō Mandala practices from a top disciple, himself thus becoming a teacher in the esoteric tradition.

The year after his master's death, Hui-kuo was installed by imperial decree in the Eastern Pagoda Hall at Ch'ing-lung Temple. Esteemed by emperor Tai Tsung, Hui-kuo was also assigned to ritual duties at court. His reputation spread, and many disciples, some from other countries, came to study under him. In 789 a rain ritual he performed so impressed the new emperor, Te Tsung, that Hui-kuo was summoned to court to perform rituals for the preservation of the dynasty over a period of about seventy days. During a great drought in 798 Hui-kuo again held a rain-making ritual in the palace, with desired effect. The next year he successfully held a healing ritual for the crown prince.

In the fifth month of 805 Hui-kuo was aged sixty, ill, and near death (he had already conveyed his last testament) when he met Kūkai, then an unknown Japanese priest studying in Ch'ang-an. Teaching him the doctrines and practices of both mandalas (symbolizing the teachings of both major sutras) in the short space of three months, Hui-kuo proclaimed Kūkai, his last disciple, as a Dharma successor. In the twelfth month of that year Hui-kuo died. He was buried beside Amoghavajra's pagoda outside Ch'ang-an. Some one thousand disciples gathered for the funeral, and the honor of writing a funerary inscription on their behalf was given to Kūkai. Hui-kuo had been proclaimed master by three successive emperors, Tai Tsung, Te Tsung, and Shun Tsung.

Hui-kuo is credited with gathering together the still scattered elements of Chinese esoteric Buddhism into a coherent system (though in China it was never considered a separate, independent sect as it later was in Japan). Although he wrote some texts on ritual practice, no translations or commentaries on sutras or doctrinal matters by Hui-kuo survive, so it is difficult to know how much of this period's teaching originated with him. It seems that he was, however, learned in general Mahayana Buddhism as well as the esoteric teachings, and was probably the first master to have systematically combined the teachings of the two main esoteric sutras. One of Hui-kuo's Chinese disciples, I-ts'ao (Jap., Gisō), carried on the Dharma succession at Ch'ing-lung Temple, and Kūkai carried the teachings back to Japan, where he founded the Shingon sect.

Some new texts and teachings were still being introduced to China from India at this time. Among other esoteric Buddhist figures then present in China was the Indian priest Prajñā (Jap., Hannya; 734–810), who had studied at Nalanda. He travelled to China by the southern sea route, arriving in Ch'ang-an in 782. He translated several sutras, which in 806 he passed on, with other teachings to Kūkai.[7] These were important in the establishment of Shingon in Japan.

After Hui-kuo, teachings based on another sutra, the *Soshitsuji-kyō,* became prominent. This text came to be seen as a separate presentation of the dual teachings of the *Dainichi-kyō* and *Kongōchō-gyō* united in one. According to this development, which was incorporated into Tendai esoterism, there were three major sutras, the first two separate and the third joining them. (Shingon, considering the two sutras sufficient in themselves, did not follow this system.) The *Kongōchō-gyō* teachings themselves seem not to have been widely studied in China at this time.

Among Hui-kuo's many disciples, I-ts'ao was active in passing on teachings to numerous disciples. Of these, an outstanding figure was I-chen (Jap., Gishin), who became master of initiation at Ch'ing-lung Temple as well as a practitioner of ritual at the court. I-chen and his disciples were important sources of teaching for several Japanese priests, including some priests of the Tendai sect, who went to China after Kūkai.[8]

Mikkyo teaching was also being carried on at other temples located away from the capital. After Hui-kuo's time, however, the court came to favor Taoism, and the esoteric Buddhist teachings gradually declined in influence. Mikkyo of the period was shifting its emphasis away from Buddhist liberation toward magic for worldly benefit. Texts stressing this type of ritual, with influence from popular beliefs, were written and attributed to preceding patriarchs. At the same time, many Buddhist institutions and priests had grown extremely wealthy and sometimes corrupt. The state, deprived of revenue from the tax-free temples and urged on by Taoists, reacted.

In Ch'ang-an, Japanese priests witnessed the persecutive reform of Buddhism that began in 841 under emperor Wu Tsung. The emperor decreed the destruction of Buddhist institutions and confiscation of their property. Large numbers of clergy were forcibly returned to lay status. Buddhist ritual magic was forbidden. Dealt a crippling blow, Buddhism was saved from destruction by the death of Wu Tsung in 845, and although the next emperor, Hsüan Tsung, enacted favorable policies, Buddhism did not fully recover.

After Wu Tsung's persecutions the esoteric teachings declined, and Buddhism underwent another persecution from 955 to 959 under the later Chou dynasty. Buddhism revived, however, during the Northern Sung dynasty (960–1126). In 971 the emperor Sung T'ai Tsu ordered the printing of a full edition of the sutras, which was completed in 983. In 982 emperor Sung T'ai Tsung established a sutra translation institute at a temple in the capital, and translation of numerous Buddhist texts was begun. As the dynasty exerted its control on border areas, communication with Central Asia and India recommenced, and new Buddhist texts were brought into China.

One figure known to have been active during this period is Shih-hu (Jap., Sego). An Indian who arrived in China around 980 (and whose original name is unknown), he translated a large number of Buddhist texts, including Indian tantras of later-period Mikkyo. Another, Dharmabhadra (Jap., Hōken, also Hōten; d. 1001), came from Nalanda to Sung China in 973 and translated a large number of texts, both general Mahayana and esoteric. He worked with Shih-hu and T'ien-hsi-tsai (Jap., Tensokusai; d. 1000), from Kashmir, who came to China with Shih-hu.

The works of these individuals, however, appear not to have resulted in a long-lasting revival of esoteric Buddhism. In the mid-eleventh century the esoteric teachings became popular under the Liao dynasty in northern China, but they seem to have been appreciatd mostly for their magical aspects, which were joined with folk beliefs. The Mongols, who rose to power and established the Yüan dynasty in 1271, adopted the esoteric Buddhism of Tibet, and this form of esoteric Buddhism continued to exist in China up to modern times.

TWO

Historical Background of Shingon
Buddhism in Japan

THE INTRODUCTION OF ESOTERIC BUDDHISM TO JAPAN

Although no doubt known ear- lier in Japan, Buddhism was officially introduced in the mid- sixth century from the Korean
kingdom of Paekche. Elements of miscellaneous category esoteric teachings probably first ar- rived around the same time. The
powerful aristocratic clans of Japan were concerned with Buddhism primarily
as a new and potent magic paralleling shamanistic beliefs and practices already
used to achieve prosperity and perpetuate their rule. As in China, the new religion was not valued for its religious thought as much as it was for the secular benefits promised by its ritual. The magic-oriented miscellaneous category
teachings were, therefore, easily adapted to Japanese circumstances, and their
presence prepared for the later establishment of the pure category esoteric
teachings.

At the time that Buddhism was first introduced, Japan was entering a major
era of transition. The various clans were being united and political power was
gradually being centralized in a government with the emperor (or, infrequently,
empress) as its head. A bureaucratic system and laws on the Chinese model
were instituted. Chinese culture was being assimilated on a large scale, with
Buddhism serving as a primary means of introducing new language, art, and
thought. After many vicissitudes Buddhism was established by the eighth century as an official religion with the function of performing rituals for pacification of the realm and protection of the state (*chingo kokka*).

By the Nara period (710–784) there were many esoteric sutras and works of
Buddhist art in Japan. It seems likely that esoteric forms of practice were also
carried on there even before the Nara period. Such practices included incantation, rain-making, averting misfortune, bringing good fortune, healing, and
prolonging life. Devotional practice of incantation had already become widespread within the framework of Japanese Buddhism in general.

Many esoteric deities, such as the Thousand-Armed Kannon, the Eleven-
Headed Kannon, the Horse-Headed Kannon, and the Five Great Power Bodhisattvas, were sculpted following Chinese models. Out of the approximately

150 Buddhist sculptures remaining today from the Nara period, about forty pieces are of esoteric deities.[1] No sculptures of Dainichi Nyorai or the fierce deity Fudō Myō-ō had yet been made, however, nor were the major mandalas known in Japan.

The elements of Mikkyo then present were an integral part of Japanese Buddhism, which the court and noble clans sponsored in expectation of the same benefits offered by preexisting ritual, such as healing, prosperity, and victory over foes. To these ends, temples and pagodas were erected, Buddha-images made, and sutras copied and recited. Priests installed in grand temples carried on purificatory practices of confession (keka) and held rainy-season retreats (ango) devoted to healing illness among the ruling class and assuring good harvests.

The magical, this-worldly benefits spoken of in the esoteric sutras early introduced to Japan were especially well received. Esoteric sutras provided a basis for prominent state-oriented magical rituals held in the imperial palace and at temples, and these were also performed as agricultural rites belonging to the regular palace rituals to ensure good harvests and to ward off disaster. The Mikkyo texts brought to Japan in the Nara period dealt with dharani, and faith in the miraculous efficacy of these incantations was widespread. A sutra of the deity Fukūkenjaku Kannon, for example, lists twenty immediate benefits of reciting this bodhisattva's dharani, including the avoidance of illness, immunity to disaster by fire or water, and safety from bandits, war, and harmful insects.[2]

This and the other esoteric texts were brought from China, along with general Buddhist sutras, by a succession of individuals such as Dōshō, who returned from China in 661, and Dōji, who returned in 718. Many of the texts they brought back had only very recently been translated from Sanskrit into Chinese. Among the Japanese priests who made the often dangerous sea voyage to China to bring back sutras, Gembō is prominent. After spending nearly twenty years in China, Gembō returned to Japan in 735 with some five thousand sutras and texts. The records of the Shōsō-in, an imperial treasure house built in Nara in 756, include a list of titles of sutras copied in Japan up to that time. The esoteric texts listed there, all but a few of which belong in the miscellaneous category, total some one-fourth of the texts included in the present Shingon canon.[3] Although some texts in the pure category had been brought to Japan by this time, they were merely a few among thousands, and no particular attention seems to have been paid to them.

The Dainichi-kyō was copied by Japanese priests in 737, only twelve years after Shubhakarasimha translated it in China. Records show that further copies were made during the Nara period, and one copy dating from 766 is still extant. The Shakumakaen-ron (Treatise Explaining Mahayana), a work attributed to Nagarjuna, was brought to Japan in 778. Its authorship became a matter of dispute almost immediately, although Kūkai later considered it authentic. Though not strictly an esoteric text, it is highly valued by Shingon.

Lectures on the Dainichi-kyō were held in 772. Even in China, however, it was not until the time of Amoghavajra that these pure category sutras received the particular emphasis given them in the Shingon system. It is only natural, therefore, that understanding of the esoteric texts already in Japan in the eighth century was anything but complete, or that Kūkai later felt it necessary to go to China to study the Mikkyo teachings.

Study of Buddhist doctrine and philosophy was not neglected during the Nara period, but such study seems to have been mostly scholastic in nature. Although Nara Buddhism is said to have consisted of six schools, these were by no means rigidly separated. Their study was ordinarily combined, and priests of different schools lived and worked together in the same temples. These priests (mostly members of aristocratic families) were also expected to be accomplished in ritual. Buddhist scholarship was thus carried on in tandem with ritual practice directed to immediate, material benefit for the state and the temples' noble patrons.

By the late Nara period, the practice of dharani recitation had gained wide favor, giving rise to tales of miracles brought about by the faithful chanting of incantations to various deities. In order to enter the priesthood, Buddhist novices studied prescribed subjects that, apart from general Mahayana texts, included esoteric texts and ten types of dharani incantation. An early group of esoteric practitioners was called the school of Natural Wisdom (*jinenchi-shū*, not included among the six major Buddhist schools). Composed of priests from Nara, its members withdrew to mountain retreats to practice austerities and concentrate on developing magical powers.

One practice said to bring about this result, as well as a vastly increased memory useful in taking the examination for the priesthood, was the Morning Star meditation (*gumonji-hō*), an esoteric practice centered on incantation to the bodhisattva Kokūzō. The text of the Morning Star meditation was brought to Japan in 718 by the prominent Nara priest Dōji, who had received it from Shubhakarasimha. This meditation was taught by an anonymous Japanese priest to the young Kūkai, on whom it made such an impression that Shingon traditionally considers it to have been this practice that brought Kūkai his first experiential insight into Mikkyo.

Apart from the Buddhism sponsored by the court for its own purposes, popular Buddhism also developed in the Nara period. Some priests, transgressing official restrictions, left their temples to teach and work among the populace. Perhaps the best known of these was the priest Gyōgi (668–749) of the Hossō school. Various mountain practitioners also had close ties to the common people, who called on the supranormal abilities in healing and prophecy these practitioners were believed to have. Prominent among the mountain hermits was the seventh- or eighth-century figure known as En-no-Gyōja, around whom a body of legend continued to grow for centuries. Although often associated with Mikkyo, such early practitioners did not belong in the orthodox line of teachings transmitted from master to disciple.

The officially ordained priesthood was strictly regulated by the state. Increasing numbers of common people, however, left their livelihoods to become lay Buddhist practitioners. Such practitioners (the men known as *ubasoku,* women as *ubai*) attached themselves to temples or joined the mountain ascetics, while others wandered in the cities and countryside. Despite state opposition, this phenomenon of unofficial Buddhists grew, and came to be perceived as a threat to the central bureaucratic system. The popular movements in Nara Buddhism were not stopped, however, but continued to develop over succeeding centuries. From the early ninth century they would increasingly come under the influence of the new sects of Tendai and Shingon.

KŪKAI AND THE ESTABLISHMENT OF SHINGON

The beginning of esoteric Buddhism in Japan is dated to the first decade of the ninth century, when Saichō, the founder of the Tendai sect of Buddhism in Japan, and Kūkai, the founder of Shingon, brought their respective teachings back from T'ang China. This was not long after the capital was moved from Nara, first to Nagaoka and then in 794 to the city of Heian (today known as Kyoto), modelled after the T'ang capital of Ch'ang-an.

An important factor in the imperial court's move away from the old capital of Nara seems to have been the intention of lessening the influence of the Nara Buddhist priesthood on court politics. The Heian court therefore encouraged new schools of Buddhism, first Tendai and then also Shingon, both to weaken the power of the priesthood in Nara and to serve the court and its new capital. Tendai and Shingon both were enabled to grow by the patronage of the successive emperors and important aristocratic families. The establishment of Shingon must have been in large part due to Kūkai's abilities, both secular and religious, but there is no doubt that early Heian politics also played a role.

The move to Heian marked the beginning of a historical period, named after the new capital, that lasted until the late twelfth century. The Heian period saw the flowering of an aristocratic culture, the rise and fall of great noble families, and the assimilation of Buddhism into the mainstream of Japanese culture. The ritual, art, and doctrines of esoteric Buddhism were taken up with particular enthusiasm and came to exert a broad influence over religious practices and beliefs, both aristocratic and popular.

Many details of Kūkai's life are uncertain, including the year of his birth, probably 774. He was born into the aristocratic Saeki family in a place now known as Zentsūji in the Sanuki region of the island of Shikoku. His given name seems to have been Tōtomono; he took the Buddhist name Kūkai, meaning Sea of Void, later in his life. Kūkai studied under a maternal uncle who was an influential scholar and tutor to the crown prince, and then as a young man he entered the university in the capital. The course of study there, Confucian in orientation, ordinarily led to entry into the court bureaucracy. Kūkai abandoned this study, however, and entered on a different course.

At about the age of twenty-four, Kūkai wrote a text called the *Sangō Shiiki* (Indication of the Basis of the Three Teachings), declaring the superiority of Buddhism to Taoism and Confucianism. In the introduction to this work, he relates how as a student he met a priest who gave him instruction in the esoteric Morning Star meditation. After immersing himself for some time in this rigorous practice, he determined to devote himself to Buddhism. Kūkai probably took formal Buddhist vows in 804, at the age of about thirty-one.

Relatively little is known of the events of Kūkai's life before he went to China in 804. It is clear, however, that the forms of Buddhism then dominant in Japan did not satisfy him. The exoteric teachings, at least as they were known to the Nara sects, seemed to indicate that enlightenment was virtually impossible to attain in one lifetime, coming, if at all, only after many rebirths. Buddhist study was primarily exegetical, while Kūkai, though himself a brilliant scholar, was inclined to value the intuitive insights gained through ritual practice. His experience of the Morning Star meditation in the solitude of natural settings seems to have shaped his approach to Buddhism, and though he must have studied the doctrines then available at temples in Nara, Kūkai wrote about various remote mountainous regions as places where he was accustomed to spending much time in meditative practice. In his own words (from his collected literary works, the *Shōryō-shū*):

> Kūkai is not known for his talents, and his words and actions are nothing to speak of. Sleeping in the snow with only his arms to pillow his head, and eating wild plants on the cloudy peaks—that is all he knows.[4]

He no doubt searched arduously for teachings explaining how Buddhahood was actually to be achieved. A traditional account has it that Kūkai, guided by a prophetic dream, found a copy of the *Dainichi-kyō* in a pagoda at the Kumedera Temple in Nara. This sutra stresses immediate attainment of enlightenment, and it was this sutra, he said, so profound that no one in Japan could explain it to him, that determined him to go to China for instruction.

On the sixth day of the sixth month in 804, Kūkai set off by ship from Kyushu with an official delegation. Saichō, travelling on a separate ship, was a member of the same expedition, though his destination was Mount T'ien-t'ai, the center of Tendai teaching. (Also in this expedition was the priest Ryōzen, who would go to Mount Wu-t'ai-shan and there end his life having achieved distinction as the only Japanese to be given the exalted title of Sanzō, signifying great accomplishment in Buddhism.) The ship carrying Kūkai reached the Fukien coast of China about a month and a half later. After some delay in receiving official permission for his group to proceed, Kūkai travelled overland to Ch'ang-an, where he arrived in the twelfth month of 804.

Kūkai's own writings are the major source of information on events of his stay in the Chinese capital. He moved into the Hsiming Temple, and it was probably at this time that he met the Indian Prajñā; another Indian priest Kūkai met during his stay in Ch'ang-an was Muniśrī (Jap., Munishiri). Under these two priests he studied Sanskrit and Indian Buddhist teachings.

In the fifth month of 805, while visiting Ch'ing-lung Temple, he had a dramatic first meeting with Hui-kuo, who declared that he had long been awaiting Kūkai's arrival. Kūkai was soon initiated into the teachings of both mandalas, and shortly thereafter received the Dharma succession. Before his death on the fifteenth day of the twelfth month of that same year, Hui-kuo instructed Kūkai to carry the esoteric teachings to Japan.

Within a brief period of two years Kūkai had succeeded to the esoteric Buddhist lineage. Another of Hui-kuo's disciples had been assigned to carry on the teachings in China. Although he had come to China expecting to stay for twenty years, Kūkai did not tarry in carrying out his master's instructions. Arriving back in Kyushu in the tenth month of 806, he sent the emperor Heizei (r. 806–809) a memorial reporting on his activities in China and listing the items he had brought back with him, which included 142 sutras in Chinese translation, 42 books of Sanskrit incantations, 32 commentaries, 10 mandalas and paintings, 9 ritual implements, and various relics of Mikkyo masters.

In this text, the *Goshōrai Mokuroku* (List of Items Brought from China), Kūkai declares the nature of the new teachings of the two fundamental sutras and his position as a legitimate successor to Hui-kuo. As he would continue to do in later writings, he also explains how the esoteric teachings differ from those of exoteric Buddhism. There was no immediate response to his memorial, however, and it seems that he did not go to the capital for some time. Kūkai's activities over the next two or three years are not definitely known.

At that time the court was interested in the new teachings of Tendai brought back from China the year before by Saichō, who had enjoyed court patronage under the preceding emperor, Kammu (r. 781–806). Of special interest were the teachings of Mikkyo, then reaching their height of popularity in the T'ang capital. It was in 805, by imperial command, that Saichō performed the first esoteric initiation in Japan at a temple near the capital. The Tendai sect received state recognition in 806, when authorization was given for two Tendai priests to be included in the limited number of official priests ordained each year, one of whom was to devote himself to studying the teachings of the *Lotus Sutra,* and the other to the teachings of esoteric Buddhism.

Perhaps for such reasons, some years passed before Kūkai could proceed to the capital, and it was not until after the installation of the emperor Saga (r. 809–823) that he worked publicly to further the cause of Shingon in Japan. The date of Shingon's establishment as an independent sect of Japanese Buddhism is unclear but is often set at ca. 812–813, when Kūkai was about thirty-nine years of age.[5] It was probably in his capacity as an accomplished calligrapher that Kūkai first met the emperor Saga, who was a connoisseur and practitioner of that and other arts. In 809 he presented the emperor with a two-panelled screen of his calligraphy, and again, two years later, with poetic texts and calligraphy-related items he had brought back from China. Kūkai seems to have developed a close relationship with Saga and his successor, Emperor Junna.

A short-lived rebellion broke out against the newly installed Emperor Saga in 810. (As a result of this turmoil, the crown prince was deposed, and later, under the name of Shinnyo, became one of Kūkai's disciples). That same year, Kūkai requested and received imperial permission to perform an esoteric ritual for the pacification of the state based on new sutras he had brought back from China. This ritual was held at Takaosan-ji (also known as Jingo-ji), the temple north of the capital where Saichō had performed his Mikkyo initiation ritual only five years before.

Kūkai and Saichō probably first met in 809 or 810. Saichō, who had studied Mikkyo during the short period of a month and a half while waiting for a return ship to Japan at the end of his stay in China, was eager to further his knowledge, and began to borrow texts from Kūkai. In the eleventh month of 812 Kūkai gave esoteric initiation in the Kongō-kai Mandala to a small group, including Saichō, at Takaosan-ji. The next month, he performed a similar initiation in the Tai-zō Mandala for a group of some 145, among whom were Saichō and some of his top disciples as well as high-ranking priests from Nara. These events mark the beginning of Kūkai's rise to prominence as a religious leader.

When Saichō requested the higher initiation that would qualify him as a master, Kūkai replied that further study and Shingon practice would first be necessary. Saichō sent several disciples, including his favorite, Taihan (778– 837), to study with Kūkai at Takaosan-ji. Although Saichō later sent many letters requesting Taihan to return to the Tendai center being built on Hiei-zan, Taihan stayed on as Kūkai's disciple.

The main difference between these two towering figures of Heian Buddhism, however, probably lay in their approach to Mikkyo. Saichō considered Mikkyo to be one aspect of the complete Tendai teaching, which was to comprise the *Lotus Sutra* (*en*), Mikkyo (*mitsu*), meditation (*zen*), and the precepts (*kai*). Kūkai, on the other hand, considered Mikkyo to be the fulfillment of all Buddhist teachings, a necessary and sufficient approach in itself. When Saichō later requested the loan of an esoteric sutra commentary, Kūkai refused on the ground that Mikkyo could not be learned by simply reading its texts, and some texts in particular required preparation by esoteric practice to be understood correctly.

Shingon subsequently had considerable influence on the esoteric aspects of Tendai. The esoteric teaching of the Tendai sect brought to Japan by Saichō and his successors (primarily Ennin, Enchin, and Annen) came to be called *taimitsu* (a contraction of Tendai Mikkyo). This is distinguished from the Shingon teachings, brought by Kūkai, called *tōmitsu* (a contraction of Tō-ji Mikkyo, referring to the central Shingon temple of that name). *Taimitsu* was considered an addition to the already-existing doctrine of the Tendai sect. The Mikkyo brought to

Japan by Kūkai was further systematized by him and given the coherent doctrinal basis on which Shingon Buddhism has continued as an independent sect.

In 816 Kūkai requested imperial permission to found a center for meditative practice on Kōya-san, the sacred mountain of Kōya, located on the Kii Peninsula in present-day Wakayama Prefecture. Then some days' travel from the capital, this was a high, gently sloping valley, 828 meters above sea level, bounded by several peaks. Permission came quickly, and Kūkai immediately dispatched two disciples to survey the mountaintop. Two years later, Kūkai climbed Kōya-san himself, at which time he is said to have met the local god of the mountain in the person of a hunter accompanied by two dogs, black and white. Several such legends exist, and native deities associated with Shingon are enshrined at various places on and around the sacred mountain. Kūkai did in fact invoke the protection of local deities when he performed an esoteric ritual to establish a sacred realm of practice on the mountaintop. This consecrated area was named Kongōbu-ji.

Kūkai commenced actual construction there in 819. The temple compound was to have pagodas and various other buildings in a mandala-like arrangement of his own design that would provide an ideal environment for Shingon practice. The management of Kōya-san was his own private responsibility, and work progressed slowly, interrupted by lack of funds and pressing duties in the distant capital. Spending as much time as he could on the mountain, Kūkai would receive letters urging him to return to Heian. He quotes one such letter from a friend, the Imperial Councillor Yoshimine no Ason Yasuyo, who wrote: "The master has entered the cold and uncomfortable mountain of Kōya, and has perhaps forgotten to return to the capital. What pleasure can there be in the mountains?" In reply, Kūkai wrote:

A cupful of mountain river water in the morning sustains my life. The evening mist nurtures my mind. The dawn moon and the morning wind wash away all impurities.[6]

This was to be the character of Kūkai's Kōya-san, a place of practice away from the secular world and the immediate supervision of the court where Shingon could develop in its own way. In his poem "Playing in the Mountains and Following the Mountain Sage," Kūkai expressed the Shingon view of the natural universe:

> The three secrets fill the world.
> Space is the sublime meditation hall.
> The mountain is the brush and the sea the ink,
> Heaven and earth the case that holds the sutras.[7]

The symbolic activities of body, speech, and mind (the three secrets) are present throughout the entire cosmos, which is their sphere of activity. Natural phe-

30

nomena such as mountains and seas express the truth described in the sutras, and that which embodies all teachings is the universe.

Kūkai's ambitious plans for Kōya-san were not to see completion during his lifetime. In 823, however, in an important step forward for the new sect, the emperor Saga put Kūkai in charge of Tō-ji, the "Temple of the East." Founded under imperial patronage to be one of the new capital's great state institutions, it remained only partly built next to the main south gate of the capital. Kūkai exercised his artistic and architectural talents in bringing it to completion.

Temples at that time were ordinarily used by priests of the various Buddhist schools together. With imperial permission, however, Kūkai made Tō-ji an exclusively Shingon temple, renamed Kyō-ō Gokoku-ji (Nation-Protecting Temple of the King of Teachings). By court decree, fifty Shingon priests (and none of other sects) were to reside there and follow a special course of study outlined by Kūkai. This was the first major center for Shingon study and practice. Both Tō-ji (as it is still popularly called), a major landmark in the present city of Kyoto, and Kōya-san, with its large mountaintop complex of temples far from the busy world, continue today as vital Shingon centers.

In 823 the emperor Junna (r. 823–833) succeeded Saga, and Kūkai continued working with the new emperor's support. It is said that by the end of his life he had performed some fifty esoteric rituals of various kinds for the court. He gave emperors Heizei, Saga, and Junna initiation into Mikkyo practice. Increasingly elevated official Buddhist rank was bestowed on him. Near the end of his life, a Shingon temple was built within the palace grounds. There, under the emperor Nimmyō (r. 833–850), Kūkai instituted the tradition of an annual ritual for the peace of the nation that is practiced today, though at Tō-ji rather than the palace.

Buddhism of the Heian period was generally typified by the idea of pacification and support of the nation (*chingo kokka*), and Shingon in particular has often been viewed as a religion oriented to the benefit of the aristocracy. The Buddhist concept of benefiting the ruler, however, also traditionally included the sense of benefit to the ruled. For Kūkai, the idea of pacifying the realm signified the establishment of peace rather than the quelling of opposing forces, and the Shingon rituals he performed for the court invariably included the aim of benefit for all the people of the nation.

In 828 Kūkai founded a school near Tō-ji. While Japanese education at the time was for the nobility alone, Kūkai intended the new institution to be for clergy, laymen, nobility, and commoners alike. It was named Shugei Shuchi-in, in double allusion to a passage in the *Dainichi-kyō* stating that the Mikkyo master should combine all the learned arts, and another passage in the *Great Wisdom Sutra* stating that all things can be known through the seed of all-wisdom. Founded on the Buddhist basis of compassion toward all beings, this school was to teach all the religions, arts, and sciences of the day. Little is known about how the school fared, and it did not survive long as an institution. It closed its doors in 845, and the property it occupied was sold by Tō-ji to finance the education of Shingon priests. The tradition of learning it established is carried on in the present Shuchi-in ("Wisdom-Seed") University, located adjacent to Tō-ji and still bearing the name of its predecessor, as well as by Kōya-san University.

Many of the commentaries and ritual manuals fundamental to Shingon doctrine and practice were written by Kūkai, and his importance in Shingon history can hardly be overestimated. One major work fundamental to the establishment of Shingon doctrine was the *Jūjūshin-ron* (Treatise on Ten Levels of Mind), which he completed around the year 830. The emperor Junna had required the major schools of Buddhism to produce summaries of their teachings; Kūkai's response was this text in ten volumes, containing some six hundred quotations and allusions to sutras and other works. In it Kūkai classifies the development of the individual human being in successive stages associated with the teachings of the major religions of the time. The tenth stage, embodied by Shingon, expresses the fulfillment of the preceding.

At about the same time, Kūkai wrote the *Hizō Hōyaku* (Precious Key to the Secret Treasury). In three volumes this text summarized the teaching of the ten stages, eliminating many of the quotations found in the *Treatise on Ten Levels of Mind*. Kūkai had earlier written certain other important works known jointly as the three writings (*sanbu-sho*). The first of these three one-volume texts was the *Sokushin Jōbutsu-gi* (The Meaning of Becoming a Buddha in This Body), expounding the central Shingon teaching of attaining enlightenment within one's present lifetime. The second was the *Shōji Jissō-gi* (The True Meaning of the Voiced Syllable), which deals with the use of language as a symbolic expression of universal reality in order to attain enlightenment. The third was the *Unji-gi* (The Meaning of the UN-Syllable), which shows how all truth can be encompassed within a single Sanskrit syllable. These texts thus explain, respectively, the ritual activities of body, speech, and mind, the three secrets that are combined in Shingon practice.

Kūkai is remembered for his contributions to culture and society in general as well as to religion. Counted among the most renowned calligraphers in Japanese history, he was also a master of literary expression. Many paintings and sculptures were created under his supervision (and perhaps directly by his hand) as artistic embodiments of the esoteric teachings, and those that still exist, now in museums as well as temples, are recognized as treasures not only of Japanese but of world art. He introduced new medical practices from China. His ability even in civil engineering, perhaps also learned in China, is attested by the major irrigation reservoir he built in Shikoku. A list of Kūkai's accomplishments, even excluding the many that are obviously legendary, would be impressive.

In the fifteenth day of the third month of 835, Kūkai gathered his disciples together on Kōya-san and conveyed his last testament. Six days later he passed away, and a popular belief arose that Kūkai had not died but had entered an eternal state of meditation on Kōya-san. In 921 the emperor Daigo bestowed on him the posthumous title of Kōbō Daishi, Dharma-Spreading Great Master, by which he is commonly known today.

THE STATUS OF THE ESOTERIC TEACHINGS
AFTER KŪKAI

Kūkai left a number of important disciples who carried on leadership of the Shingon sect.[8] Jichie (also Jitsue; 786–847), for example, was among Kūkai's early disciples, and was one of those first dispatched to Kōya-san. Kūkai later put him in charge of Tō-ji, from which position Jichie contributed to the establishment of Shingon, receiving official permission to increase the numbers of student priests there, and obtaining financial support for Kōya-san. The property of the school established by Kūkai was sold by Jichie, who used the funds to establish a course of Shingon instruction at Tō-ji. Kūkai's lineage of teachings was passed on primarily through his disciples Jichie and Shinga, who transmitted them in turn to disciples of their own.

Shinzei (800–860), who had earlier been head of Takaosan-ji, became head of Tō-ji after Jichie. In 836 he and another Shingon priest (Shinzen) had attempted the passage to China, but failed because of a typhoon. Due to his many accomplishments, in 856 Shinzei became the first Shingon priest to be awarded the high priestly title of *sōjō*. He appealed to the court, saying that the honor should have gone to his master, whereupon the higher title of *daisōjō* was posthumously awarded to Kūkai.

Shinga (801–879), Kūkai's younger brother, was put in charge of various temples and also entrusted with the sutra repository at Tō-ji. He came head of Tō-ji after Shinzei. Shinga was especially accomplished in ritual practice, and enjoyed close relations with the court. Among his disciples was Shinzen (804–891). Although he had studied under his uncle Kūkai, Shinzen was the direct disciple of Shinga. Kūkai's last testament gave Shinzen charge of Kōya-san, and for fifty-six years he devoted himself to carrying on the difficult task of completing Kongōbu-ji, in the meantime also being appointed to important positions at Tō-ji. In 876 Shinzen borrowed certain important texts in the Tō-ji sutra repository from Shinga and took them to Kōya-san, where they were passed on to his successors. This was the origin of a famous conflict between the two Shingon centers.

After the failed attempt by Shinzen and Shinzei to travel to China, the ex-crown prince Shinnyo reached Ch'ang-an in 864. From there he attempted to go on to India, but died along the way. There were four Shingon priests, however, who went to China after Kūkai and returned with further texts and teachings.[9] The last official delegation from Japan to the T'ang court departed in 838, and among its members were the Shingon priests Jōkyō (d. 866) and Engyō

(799–852), as well as the important Tendai priest Ennin. Both Jōkyō and Engyō returned to Japan in 839, after studying and receiving advanced initiations in China.

E-un (798–869), Jichie's disciple, travelled to China in 842 on a merchant ship, and after study in Ch'ang-an and pilgrimages to various places returned to Japan in 847, bringing texts, images, and ritual implements. Shūei (809–884), who had first studied Tendai on Hiei-zan before turning to Shingon, went to China in 862 with Shinnyo and studied Mikkyo under Chinese and Indian teachers. He returned to Japan in 865, bringing 134 texts and some 50 images and implements. He was appointed the fifth head of Tō-ji, carried on Mikkyo activity at the court, and was highly esteemed for his knowledge and character. Shūei transmitted the lineage from Kūkai and Jichie on to several disciples of his own.

The direct influence Chinese culture had exercised on Japan was on the wane by the late ninth century, when another official delegation to the T'ang court was planned but then cancelled. Japan seems to have turned inward, as though digesting and adapting what it had taken in from the continent, and Mikkyo priests ceased trying to obtain new teachings from China as they had in the decades after Saichō and Kūkai. Commercial and intellectual traffic between Japan and China was carried on more or less continuously, despite the lapse in official diplomatic relations, but Mikkyo in China did not see any conspicuous development.[10]

In the different cultural conditions of China (and India before it), Mikkyo had not been made into a separate sect of Buddhism. It is considered characteristic of Buddhism in Heian times that separate sects were established, beginning with Tendai and Shingon, each with its own priesthood and organization. Even in Japan, however, though more emphasis was placed on sectarian differences, these were not always rigidly maintained. The various earlier schools of Japanese Buddhism actively took up Mikkyo, by means of whose rituals they could more readily secure the patronage of wealthy nobles. Shingon and Tendai, too, though stressing mutual differences, had no little influence on each other. Some Shingon priests studied Tendai, and during the lifetimes of Kūkai and Saichō many Tendai priests studied Shingon, so that the lines of transmission of the esoteric teachings intersect at many points, and their Dharma lineages merge as they go back to the source in China.

The new Mikkyo texts and practices brought back from China by the Shingon priests mentioned above did not necessarily stimulate further development of the doctrinal system established by Kūkai. Rather, they probably reinforced a growing Shingon emphasis on ritual. Later Tendai priests, however, returned from China with further teachings and practices not known to Shingon, and the line between the two sects became somewhat more distinct. In the last half of the ninth century, in fact, the prestige of Shingon seems to have paled somewhat before the vigorous activity seen in Tendai.

The eminent Tendai leader Ennin (794–864) became influential when in 847 he returned from long study in China bringing such new Mikkyo teachings. Ennin initiated the emperor Montoku (r. 850–858), the powerful regent Fujiwara Yoshifusa (804–872), and many other members of the aristocracy into the Tendai Mikkyo. Amother important Tendai priest, Enchin (814–891), returned from China in 858 after about five years of study, and similarly gave esoteric initiation to Emperor Seiwa (r. 858–876) and to Yoshifusa, who gave him their support. Tendai thus increased greatly in influence.

Ennin and Enchin placed Mikkyo at increasingly higher levels within the systematization of Tendai teachings begun by Saichō. Mikkyo was given its highest position in Tendai by Annen (841–ca. 915), in whose reevaluation of Tendai teachings Mikkyo was made superior to the *Lotus Sutra*. Annen, in fact, proposed that the Tendai sect should be named Shingon because of the importance of the esoteric teachings. This was not done, however, and the Tendai Mikkyo known as *taimitsu* is recognized as distinct from the Shingon *tōmitsu*. The two underwent parallel but separate developments.

One point on which Shingon and Tendai Mikkyo are clearly distinguishable, for example, is in their view of the *Soshitsuji-kyō*, a sutra Shingon considers to be in the lineage of the *Dainichi-kyō*. It was brought to Japan by both Saichō and Kūkai, as well as earlier by Genbō. Shingon considers the teachings of its two fundamental sutras, expressed symbolically in the two mandalas, to be "two yet not-two" (*nini funi*). In other words, they are inseparable dual aspects of a single, all-embracing reality.

Tendai Mikkyo, in an elaboration on this concept, considers the *Soshitsuji-kyō* to be an expression of the union of the two sutras. The *Dainichi-kyō* and *Kongōchō-gyō* are in themselves two (*nini*), while the *Soshitsuji-kyō* separately represents their nonduality (*funi*). Although Shingon includes this text among its important sutras, it differs from Tendai in not considering it of central importance. As to practices of the two major mandalas, Shingon has two general types, each associated with one of the mandalas, and each of which is considered to contain the expression of the other. Along with these, however, Tendai has a third, separate practice (the *soshitsuji-hō*) expressing the nonduality of the two main mandalas. Different schools of thought on the expression of the nonduality of Mikkyo teachings later arose within Shingon as well.

Further developments in Shingon also had to do with the relationship between doctrine and practice. Esoteric Buddhism in general stresses the mutual interdependence of doctrinal study and meditative practice. Exclusive study of doctrine not grounded in practice is described as being no more than empty theory, while ritual practice not founded on doctrinal understanding is described as a degeneration of the teachings that cannot lead to realization. On the other hand, esoteric Buddhism closely associates ritual for the religious purpose of enlightenment with ritual for immediate secular benefit, and vice versa.

Although Kūkai had clearly placed equal value on doctrinal study, he also emphasized the rich variety of ritual practice as one of Shingon's major strengths. After Kūkai, Shingon came often to be regarded one-sidedly as a sect devoted to magical ritual and techniques for material benefit in this world. This view was not entirely unfounded, as there were abuses, and a reaction was inevitable.

While Tendai saw considerable doctrinal development, therefore, Shingon after Kūkai experienced a period of relative inactivity in this respect that lasted about a half-century. The main concern in Shingon during these years was performance of rituals to bring about worldly benefits, particularly for aristocratic supporters. Priests were called on, for example, to vanquish the vengeful spirits (*onryō*) commonly thought to be responsible for illness and misfortune. Unable to add significantly to Kūkai's sophisticated doctrinal system, and with scholarly learning not in great demand in any case, Shingon groups concentrated on developing special characteristics of ritual practice by which to establish their own authority. The ultimate effect would be to split Shingon into groups centered on powerful temples.

The late ninth century saw a continuing shift of political power away from the bureaucracy and into the hands of great aristocratic families, particularly the Fujiwara, whose wealth was in large agricultural estates. Buddhist temples depended increasingly on contributions and grants of their own income-producing land from the imperial family and the wealthy nobility. As the restrictions on construction of private temples were relaxed, certain nobles made their private villas into temples, which they endowed with farmlands. Certain temples thus grew economically powerful, but in the process were sometimes drawn into the political struggles of their patrons.

The number of important Shingon temples, each with its own patrons, increased. As well as Tō-ji, Kongōbu-ji, and Takaosan-ji, for example, there was the temple of Daikaku-ji, in the northwest sector of the capital, founded in 876 with an imperial prince at its head. Later, in the thirteenth and fourteenth centuries, several retired emperors made their headquarters there, and, though it was periodically destroyed during times of war, it otherwise flourished as a temple with imperial connections. Similarly, the Kajū-ji temple was established by the wish of emperor Daigo's mother in a family palace in the Yamashina district east of the capital. It grew influential under imperial patronage, though like other temples its fortunes rose and fell during periods of war and turmoil.

The restoration of Shingon prestige after its half-century of eclipse came about largely under the emperor Uda (867–931; r. 887–897), who is closely connected with Ninna-ji, a temple in the northwest sector of the capital. Uda built Ninna-ji in 887 by order of the previous emperor (Kōkō, r. 884–887), founding it first as a Tendai temple. In 899, however, after retiring, the ex-emperor Uda entered priestly orders at Ninna-ji under the Shingon priest Yakushin (827–906), then head of Tō-ji. In 904 the retired emperor established his own quarters at Ninna-ji, where he exercised authority in both Shingon and government affairs. Many subtemples were subsequently built in the Ninna-ji complex, which soon became a major Buddhist center with close ties to the imperial family.

Another figure active in reestablishing Shingon was Shōbō (832–909), who was known as an accomplished practitioner of esoteric ritual as well as a scholar in Mikkyo and other Buddhist teachings. Shōbō is linked with the important temple of Daigo-ji, which he is said to have founded in 874. Located in the Yamashina district, this temple rose to prominence under the patronage of various emperors, primarily Daigo (r. 897–930), and became famous as a center for study of Shingon ritual.

DEVELOPMENTS IN THE SHINGON SECT

Although firmly established as a sect of Japanese Buddhism, Shingon was by no means totally unified. This is clearly shown by the appearance of subschools (or "styles," *ryū*). In the esoteric tradition masters communicated their teachings directly to disciples who in turn initiated their own disciples, in this way preserving the sanctity of the line of Dharma transmission. Most masters established in their own temples would pass on their temples and teachings, influenced by individual differences of style and interpretation, to their most promising disciples.

With time, the inevitable differences between the teachings of individual masters tended to crystallize as differences between one temple and another. This process was influenced, too, by factional politics. The major temples thus were the nuclei of what took form as subsects and branches of Shingon. The first development of such schools within Shingon can be traced back to Ninna-ji and Daigo-ji. The Shingon lineage established at Ninna-ji, where Yakushin passed on his teachings to the retired emperor Uda, came to be called the Hirosawa school, which was known for having many members of the imperial family among its leaders.

The lineage originating with Shōbō at Daigo-ji was carried on through various disciples to Ningai (951–1056), also known as the Rain Priest (Ame no Sōjō) because of his abilities in esoteric ritual. Under Ningai, this lineage came to be known as the Ono school, from the location of a temple he founded, later known as Zuishin-in. The Daigo-ji group, though also enjoying imperial support, was not as closely associated with the nobility.

The Ono school had the reputation of being oriented toward the less exalted social classes, the Hirosawa of being oriented toward the nobility. The former is said to stress oral transmission, while the latter stresses the sutras and texts. It appears, however, that there were actually few clear-cut differences between them, at least in their early years. The Ono and Hirosawa schools did not appear as such distinct movements until the eleventh or twelfth centuries, and various formulations of differences between them were no doubt made from that time.

Shingon thus never became a monolithic unity administered from a single center. The Ono and Hirosawa lineages later split into twelve further sub-schools founded on minor differences in master-to-disciple transmission, especially regarding points of ritual. Under conditions of social and political disharmony, the twelve had become thirty-six around the beginning of the thirteenth century, and by the fifteenth century seventy or more teaching "styles" existed. The existence of these schools complicates any study of Shingon, but their differences are mostly in relatively minor points of doctrine or ritual. On substantial issues, they are not mutually exclusive. (The descriptions of Shingon practices given in this book will conform to the ritual of the Chū-in school, headquartered on Kōya-san.)

The course of events on Kōya-san was somewhat different. Efforts to complete Kūkai's plans there were carried on by Jichie and, after his death, by Shinzen. Work did not progress easily on that isolated mountain, however, especially at a time when the central bureaucracy was losing power and other major temples were competing for support. Differences arose between Kongōbu-ji and Tō-ji over the official allotment of priests to be ordained annually, and over the training and qualifying of these priests. Another conflict was centered on the *Sanjūjō Sakushi* (Thirty-Volume Copybook), a precious relic containing notes Kūkai had made on Mikkyo teachings during his time in China. When Shinzen was head of Tō-ji, he had removed this set of texts from the sutra repository and taken it to Kōya-san. There it passed into the hands of Mukū (d. 918) when he became head of Kongōbu-ji in 894.

Around this time, Kangen (853–925) was active in building up the Shingon sect. Becoming head of Tō-ji, in 912 Kangen requested that Mukū return the *Thirty-Volume Copybook*. Mukū adamantly refused, however, and when an imperial order arrived commanding their return, he left the mountain, taking the texts and his disciples with him. Kangen was then appointed simultaneous head of Tō-ji, Kongōbu-ji, and Daigo-ji, putting him in a position to unify Shingon somewhat under the authority of Tō-ji. He managed to gather the texts together in the sutra repository there in 919. Control of Kōya-san thus passed into the hands of Tō-ji, which thereafter tended to neglect the mountain. Kōya-san entered a bleak phase that lasted for about a century. The doctrinal training program (*denpō-e*) begun there by Shinzen sixty years before came to a stop, not to be reinstituted for some two hundred years.

It was also Kangen who urged the court to bestow on Kūkai the title of Kōbō Daishi. His repeated petitions finally succeeding in 921, Kangen immediately made the journey to Kōya-san to make a report at Kūkai's tomb. There were reports that the crypt was opened and Kūkai's body found unchanged, and from about this time, the popular belief that the great master had not died began to spread. Although periodic attempts were made to repair the temple buildings there and construct new ones, Kōya-san was, however, repeatedly struck by lightning and the buildings there were destroyed in the resulting fires. At times the mountain was virtually abandoned.

Efforts to revive Kōya-san gained new impetus under the priest Jōyo (also Kishin Shōnin; 958–1047). After a life of study and pilgrimage, at the age of sixty he desired to learn where his parents had been reborn, and in meditation had a vision of Kōya-san. Climbing the mountain around 1016, he found desolation. Thereafter he lived on Kōya-san, working to restore it, and the priestly population gradually grew again. In 1023 the powerful statesman Fujiwara Michinaga (966–1027) made a pilgrimage to Kōya-san. Signifying the support of the Fujiwara family, this was an important step forward for Kōya-san, whose fortunes began to rise as pilgrimage to the mountain beame increasingly popular.

Certain widespread beliefs played a large part in the restoration of Kōya-san, among them the growing faith in recitation of the name of Amida Buddha in the formula NAMU AMIDA BUTSU. By invoking the saving power of this Buddha with faith and sincerity, the believer hoped to be reborn in the Western Paradise of Amida, where enlightenment could be attained with ease, thus escaping the ills and misfortunes of this world forever. Such recitation, known as *nembutsu,* was a practice accessible to all, regardless of intellectual sophistication or doctrinal training. Faith in the efficacy of this kind of recitation grew at Hiei-zan from around the middle of the ninth century, and from there spread throughout Japan.

Growth of *nembutsu* faith took place against a background of political and social instability that lent credence to a widespread belief that the world had entered an evil, degenerate age (*mappō,* "the end of the Dharma"). In times when war, poverty, famine, and pestilence seemed almost commonplace, people turned away from this fleeting life to an eternal world of bliss waiting beyond the grave. Kōya-san, like certain other sacred mountains, was coming to be seen as a Pure Land on this earth, one visit to which would remove all impediments to rebirth in Amida Buddha's paradise. This was an important reason for the growing popularity of pilgrimage there, and no doubt the belief that Kūkai was still alive in eternal meditation on the mountain also played a part in these developments.

At this time in Japan there were many wandering lay practitioners who were variously involved with mountain worship and ascetic practices as well as *nembutsu* recitation. They were generally called *hijiri,* meaning saints, sages, or wise men, though they were not necessarily known for their saintly qualities. Travelling throughout the land chanting and performing rituals, these itinerant practitioners gained fame and favor among the populace. *Hijiri* associated with Kōya-san joined Amida invocation with devotion to Kūkai, against a general background of Shingon teachings, and were instrumental in spreading the cult of Kūkai as well as raising funds to build new temples on Kōya-san. Jōyo had probably been involved with some part of the *hijiri* movement before going up to the mountain.

In the latter half of the Heian period, therefore, Kōya-san flourished. Various groups of lay *nembutsu* practitioners established a permanent presence on the mountain from around the eleventh century and came to be known as Kōya "wise men" (*kōya hijiri*). Pilgrimage became increasingly popular among nobles and commoners. Retired emperors, who were making a practice of ruling from their retirement, began to make their way to the mountain regularly. New temple buildings were constructed, ranging from simple hermit huts to grander imperial palace-temples, and Kōya-san became a center for pilgrimage from all over Japan, as well as a place of refuge for displaced aristocrats and war-weary soldiers.

The last years of the Heian period were a time of turmoil and transition in which the warrior class rose to power, eventually establishing a new government at the city in eastern Japan that gave the Kamakura period (1185–1333) its name. Several new forms of Buddhism rose to prominence during this time. The Pure Land movement was established as the Jōdo sect by the priest Hōnen (1133–1212) and enjoyed great popularity. Jōdo Shin (True Pure Land), a related sect, was begun by Shinran (1173–1262). Zen Buddhism also gained favor, particularly with the warrior class; the Rinzai Zen sect was founded by Eisai (1141–1215), the Sōtō sect by Dōgen (1200–1253).

All of these leading Buddhist figures had originally been associated with Tendai, as had the charismatic Nichiren (1222–1282), who studied Mikkyo before founding his own movement, the Hokke (Lotus) or Nichiren sect. He was later to make ferocious attacks on Tendai and Shingon. Ippen (1239–1289) founded a travelling group of *nembutsu* practitioners that eventually came to be known as the Ji sect. This sect attained widespread popularity, and large numbers of Ji followers centered their activities on Kōya-san, eventually becoming the predominant group of Kōya *hijiri*.

From the late Heian period and into Kamakura, Kōya-san's wealth and prestige increased as it continued to receive support from members of the court and populace while forging links as well with the military class. The Kōya priests were also not averse to establishing connections with the new Buddhist sects, which came to have some influence on Shingon. Many halls for Amida invocation were built on Kōya-san, and most of the religious leaders of the time are said to have made pilgrimages there. Some Zen priests also carried on their own practice as well as Shingon study on the mountain.

In this way, as popular Buddhism grew, Shingon influence also spread, and new temples were established in different parts of the country. The new Buddhist sects also stimulated doctrinal study in Shingon. Although there were excesses of scholastic enthusiasm, minute study and analysis of old texts led to some advances in understanding. By the Kamakura period, Kōya-san had become an important center of doctrinal study. The priest Kakuban was an important figure in this regard.

Kakuban (1095–1143) first came to Kōya-san when he was about twenty years old, having already studied at several places, including Ninna-ji as well as temples of the Tendai and various Nara sects. He immersed himself in rigorous Shingon practice, and worked to reinvigorate doctrinal study as well. In 1130, with the support of the retired emperor Toba (r. 1107–1123; d. 1156), Kakuban founded a new institute of Shingon study on Kōya-san. This proving too small for the numbers of student priests, in 1132 he built a larger institute, the Daidenpō-in, as well as a temple for *nembutsu* practice called the Mitsugon-in. Having been endowed with sufficient estate lands, that year Kakuban reinstituted the Dharma transmission lectures (*denpō-e*) that had lapsed since the early tenth century. The ex-emperor Toba attended celebratory festivities on the mountain.

In the interest of reform, Kakuban sought instruction in the various Shingon schools as well as Tendai Mikkyo. These he united in a new lineage of practice called the Denpō-in school. In doctrinal study, too, Kakuban was innovative, incorporating Pure Land teachings into Shingon. He developed a doctrinal basis for Mikkyo-style *nembutsu,* explaining, for example, that Amida Buddha is none other than Dainichi Nyorai. In line with Shingon emphasis on attaining enlightenment within one's lifetime, he taught that the Pure Land actually exists in this very world, where the transition of rebirth can take place in this body. He sought also to restore the balance between ritual practice and doctrinal study.

Unfortunately, the newly prominent Daidenpō-in with its reform-oriented leader came into conflict with the preexisting subtemples of Kongōbu-ji. As well as the matter of prestige, there was a dispute over title to certain estate lands. In 1134 Kakuban was appointed chief abbot (*zasu*) of Kongōbu-ji, a position that since the early tenth century had customarily been held by the corresponding head priest of Tō-ji. Placed in authority over all Kōya-san institutions, Kakuban found himself opposed by priests of both Kongōbu-ji and Tō-ji. These priests, fearing loss of their own power, joined together in petitioning for Kakuban's dismissal. Under intense pressure, Kakuban yielded up his offices and secluded himself in the Mitsugon-in for a thousand-day meditation.

The conflict between Daidenpō-in and Kongōbu-ji priests, however, worsened. In 1140 the opposing Kōya priests assaulted the temples allied with Kakuban and burned them to the ground. Kakuban, together with hundreds of scholar-priests, fled the mountain for a branch temple he had established earlier at nearby Negoro. There he died three years later. The posthumous title of Kōgyō Daishi was bestowed on him in 1690.

The priestly factions of Kongōbu-ji and Daidenpō-in made peace and then came into conflict several times again in succeeding years. Finally a later Daidenpō-in leader, the priest Raiyu (1226–1304), withdrew entirely from Kōya-san in 1288, and made Negoro-ji the headquarters for the teaching lineage originated by Kakuban. This geographical separation furthered the doctrinal split, and abstruse differences between the two parties began to be emphasized. The Negoro faction came to be called the "new teachings" sect (*shingi-ha*) by the Kōya priests in contradistinction to their own "old teachings" sect (*kogi-ha*).

These names took hold, seeming to point to considerable doctrinal differences, but such differences as actually did exist had to do, for example, with subtle points concerning the origin of the Mikkyo teachings. It is established Shingon doctrine that the source of the esoteric Buddhist teachings is the Dharma Body (*hosshin*), the Buddha in the aspect of perfect universal self-enlightenment, which is personified as Dainichi Nyorai. Different aspects of this Dharma Body were elaborated, however, with the result that various ideas existed as to which level of universal self-enlightenment was actually the source of Shingon Mikkyo.

As refined by the "old teachings" school on Kōya-san, this source was considered to be the "essential ground" (*honji-shin*) of the Dharma Body. According to the "new teachings" school at Negoro, the source was the "empowerment body" (*kaji-shin*) of the Dharma Body. These doctrines do not alter fundamental Shingon positions, however, and it is likely that the split between Kōya-san and Negoro actually grew out of the maneuverings of various priestly factions.

The Negoro doctrine was further established by Raiyu, and firmly systematized by Shōken (1307–1392). On Kōya-san, Kakukai (1142–1223) was an important scholar-priest active in study and clarification of Shingon teachings. Among his many disciples were several who influenced the doctrinal revival on the mountain, but particularly important were Hosshō (d. 1245) and Dōhan (1178–1252), whose individual teachings differed on fine distinctions concerning the nature of the Dharma realm. Both these priests were exiled from Kōya-san in 1243 for their part in the conflict betweeen Kongōbu-ji and Daidenpō-in. Dōhan eventually was allowed to return, but Hosshō died in exile. The teachings of these two priests were later further refined on Kōya-san.

SHINGON FROM THE FEUDAL PERIOD TO THE PRESENT

While Kōya-san and Negoro-ji came to flourish as centers for doctrinal study, the temples of Tō-ji, Ninna-ji, and Daigo-ji continued to focus on ritual practice. The movement to unite doctrinal study and meditative practice continued, however, and important scholar-priests also appeared in these latter temples, which came to be established as doctrinal centers as well.

During the later Heian period Tō-ji had been weakened by civil unrest, fires, and loss of its income-producing estates. The temple's fortunes were not restored until the late thirteenth century, when the emperor Go-Uda (1267–1324; r. 1274–1287) began to study Shingon under Tō-ji masters. In 1307 he entered the priesthood, and after living at Tō-ji for some time moved into Daikaku-ji. Renouncing the usual political role of the retired emperor, he devoted himself to the moral and financial support of Shingon. Through Go-Uda's efforts both Tō-ji and Daikaku-ji were revitalized. Daikaku-ji, however, was completely burned in 1336 during the turbulent transition from Kamakura into Muromachi.

In 1331 the emperor Go-Daigo (r. 1318–1339) rose up against the Kamakura government, which had attempted to force his abdication in favor of a rival, more tractable imperial line. Japan entered a time of open conflict among feudal factions that saw the end of the Kamakura rulers. This was known as the period of Southern and Northern courts (1336–1392), when there were two contending imperial courts, that of Go-Daigo in Yoshino, near Nara, and that of another imperial line in Kyoto. The result of complicated maneuverings and military clashes was the rise to power of the Ashikaga shoguns, under whom the imperial line was reunified in Kyoto in 1392. The time of Ashikaga rule, when the seat of government was returned to the capital, is known also as the Muromachi period (1392–1568).

During the period of Southern and Northern courts, Kōya-san did not ally itself with either of the two courts. Priests at other temples did become involved in the struggle, however, and rivalries occurred within Shingon, partly along political and partly along doctrinal lines. The priest Kōshin (1278–1357), a supporter of Emperor Go-Daigo, gained influence and became head of Daigo-ji and then Tō-ji, but was denounced as a heretic by opposing priests at Tō-ji and Kōya-san. Another lineage at Daigo-ji supported the Ashikaga faction, eventually rising with them to a position of influence, and this temple's fortunes thus flourished.

Daikaku-ji was also restored and, like Ninna-ji, continued to be prominent as a temple associated with the imperial family (*monzeki*). At Tō-ji, Shingon doctrinal study came to thrive during this period under a series of priests known as the "three treasures of Tō-ji" (*tōji sanpō*).[11] On Kōya-san, too, the establishment of the Muromachi period was accompanied by considerable vitality in Shingon study. The line of teaching earlier elaborated by Dōhan was carried on by Chōkaku (1340–1416). In contraposition to this lineage (which was also esteemed at other Shingon temples, including Tō-ji, Daigo-ji, and Negoro), the teachings of Hosshō were carried on by Yūkai (1345–1416).

The tension between these two lines of teaching resulted in a vigorous doctrinal development known as the "great systematization of Ōei" (*ōei no taisei*). Named for the reign of Go-Komatsu (r. 1392–1412), the first emperor in the Muromachi period, this is said to mark the flourishing of orthodox Shingon doctrine on Kōya-san. The two lines of teaching were to be united in the early twentieth century. In the meantime, however, their debates became a traditional forum for doctrinal study.

Yūkai exercised great decisiveness in seeking to unify Shingon doctrine. Renowned as a scholar, practitioner, and author of important Shingon texts, he is known too for driving *nembutsu* practice off the mountain. By Yūkai's time, the majority of Kōya *hijiri* were those associated with the Ji sect. Not only were this group eliminating Mikkyo aspects from their *nembutsu* recitation practice, but they had become particularly unruly, dancing about the mountain ringing bells and chanting in loud voices. The Kongōbu-ji priests had repeatedly forbidden such practices, and Yūkai succeeded in driving them off.

Yūkai also played an important role in purging what was known as the Tachikawa school. The origin of the Tachikawa school has been attributed to the eleventh–twelfth century Ninkan, a Shingon priest who was exiled in 1113 for his part in a court intrigue. Before committing suicide the next year, it is said, he transmitted heterodox Mikkyo teachings to a Taoist from the town of Tachikawa in the Musashi region, near present-day Tokyo. This student of Ninkan's combined Taoism and Mikkyo with folk beliefs to form a cult considered heretical by Shingon.

The Tachikawa teachings (probably named after the town of Tachikawa) were particularly influenced by Taoist *yin–yang* beliefs (*on'yō-dō*). The use of sexual symbolism to express the indivisibility of Shingon's two sutras, two mandalas, truth and wisdom, and so forth, was not particularly rare. The Tachikawa school, however, apparently promoted the actual practice of ritual sex. Although in this it resembles certain teachings developed in Tantric Buddhism of the later period in India, the Tachikawa school is thought to have arisen in Japan without Indian influence through a combination of Taoist, Mikkyo, and popular beliefs.

Systematization of the Tachikawa teachings was attributed, perhaps falsely, to the controversial Kōshin (1278–1357), who started his career in Tendai, also studied in Nara, and is said to have become adept at numerology before being initiated into Shingon at Daigo-ji. He apparently received mixed orthodox and heterodox esoteric teachings from his masters. Becoming close to the emperor Go-Daigo, Kōshin was appointed head of Daigo-ji but was sent into exile for performing ritual magic against the regent Hōjō Takatoki (1316–1333), then head of the Kamakura government against which Go-Daigo was asserting imperial independence.

Kōshin was called back to the capital after the overthrow of the Kamakura government, and was appointed head of Tō-ji. Kōya-san priests denounced Kōshin for his dissolute lifestyle, and he was exiled again, then reinstated, but left the capital when his patron emperor Go-Murakami (r. 1339–1368) moved the court south to Yoshino, where Kōshin died. Kōshin was thereafter portrayed as an evil priest, but it is uncertain whether he actually deserved this reputation. Rather, it seems likely that he was deliberately defamed by priests of opposing factions. The Tachikawa teachings were extirpated by orthodox Shingon: Yūkai burned all the writings of the Tachikawa school at his temple on Kōya-san, saving only a list of the texts destroyed.

During the Muromachi period, Japan experienced economic growth, while the arts saw new development. The Zen Buddhist sect, whose priests introduced important Chinese influences, rose to new prominence. At the same time, however, the feudal lords were increasing their power and central authority was weakening. A conflict known as the Ōnin War, beginning in 1467 and lasting until 1477, resulted in the Muromachi government's final collapse, and Japan entered a century of unremitting war known as the Sengoku period (1482–1588).

Kyoto was ravaged in a succession of battles, and Shingon's temple complexes suffered greatly during the civil wars. The government lacked the power to prevent repeated destructive incursions into the capital city, and most of the temples there (of all Buddhist sects) were burned, their income-producing lands reduced, and their priests impoverished and scattered. Much of Daigo-ji, Daikaku-ji, and Ninna-ji were burned down in battles, while Tō-ji lost most of its buildings to fire during a peasants' uprising. Since income-producing estates held by the temples were being taken over by local feudal lords, the temples did not have the means to rebuild.

On the isolated mountains of Negoro and Kōya-san, not directly threatened at this time, the temples felt compelled to build up a force of armed monks to prevent the loss of their lands. For some time the scholar-priests on Kōya had left administrative and financial affairs to what became a separate class of priests. It was these administrative priests (*gyōnin*) who controlled the warrior monks. Unfortunately, the defensive forces went out of control and sought to expand Kōya-san's land holdings by military might, eventually entering into the political conflicts that continued throughout feudal Japan up to the early seventeenth century. Other temple centers, too—at times, no doubt, of necessity—were taking political sides.

In the second half of the sixteenth century the feudal lord Oda Nobunaga (1534–1582) began to consolidate power in the area of the capital. After his assassination this power was extended over Japan by Toyotomi Hideyoshi (1536–1598). The half-decade or so of their activity is frequently called the Azuchi–Momoyama period, following which Tokugawa Ieyasu (1542–1616) established his government in the city of Edo in 1603. The time of the Tokugawa family's dynastic regime is known as the Tokugawa or Edo period (1603–1868).

In order to establish his authority Nobunaga sought to eliminate the military power of the great Buddhist temples. In 1571, for example, Nobunaga invaded Hiei-zan in force, burning all the temples and killing thousands of the residents, many but not all of whom were warrior monks. In 1580 he subdued the fortress-like Hongan-ji temple, center for a powerful True Pure Land group, after years of campaigning. Nobunaga also moved against Kōya-san, but did not mount a full-scale attack. Hideyoshi carried on a similar strategy.

The Shingi school at Negoro, which by then was experiencing its own internal

45

divisions, was attacked by Hideyoshi's forces and destroyed in 1585. Hideyoshi then turned toward Kōya-san, threatening it with the same fate if its warrior monks did not lay down their arms. After debate, the priests wisely decided to submit. Although the mountain's influence and land holdings were greatly reduced, Kōya-san was at least saved from destruction, and this was in part due to the mediation of the priest Ōgo (1537–1608).

Originally a warrior, Ōgo had withdrawn to Kōya-san after the downfall of his lord. There entering orders, he practiced severe austerities, subsisting only on nuts and berries, and came to be known as the Wood-Eating Saint (Mokujiki Shōnin). Hideyoshi's respect for Ōgo, who went to him and pleaded on behalf of the mountain, no doubt had much to do with his sparing of the Kongōbu-ji temple complex. Ōgo went on to raise support for the restoration of Kōya-san's fortunes, and in 1594, amid great ceremony, Hideyoshi made a visit to the mountain. When Hideyoshi died in 1598, Ōgo supervised the building of his mausoleum in Kyoto. Ōgo is said to have been responsible, under Hideyoshi's orders, for the construction of twenty-five temple buildings on Kōya-san as well as the restoration or rebuilding of some eighty structures at temples elsewhere.

When peace finally came in the early seventeenth century, Kōya-san was virtually the only major Shingon establishment that remained intact. Most temples elsewhere had been destroyed in earlier conflicts or in Nobunaga's and Hideyoshi's efforts to put an end to the meddling of Buddhist sects in political affairs. This accomplished, both Hideyoshi and the Tokugawa government that followed aided in restoration of the destroyed temples, though the regime maintained close control over all sects, and in fact over all members of society. Hideyoshi supported the rebuilding of Tō-ji and Daigo-ji, for example, while Ninna-ji was similarly restored under the Tokugawa regime.

Before Hideyoshi destroyed the Mount Negoro temple, two main lineages had developed there, led by Sen'yo (1530–1604) and Gen'yū (1529–1605). These two fled with some of their followers to Kōya-san, but were prevented by the old conflict and Hideyoshi's orders from staying on. After spending some time in hiding, Sen'yo was given the temple of Hase-dera by Hideyoshi's half-brother Hidenaga in 1587. This temple he made headquarters of the new Buzan school. Gen'yū went to Daigo-ji, but was not allowed to teach there, so he set up his own quarters outside Kyoto and there gathered numbers of students. In 1600 Ieyasu gave him property where Hideyoshi's mausoleum had been built in Kyoto. There Gen'yū founded the Chishaku-in temple, which became headquarters of the new Chizan school. These two schools are not divided by major doctrinal differences, and both belong to the Shingi sect of Shingon.

The Tokugawa regime exercised strict control over all institutions, including those of Buddhism. Previously, most large temples had evolved loose systems of self-government based on priestly consensus, but these began to change under Nobunaga and Hideyoshi. As soon as its power was assured, the Tokugawa government began to issue a series of regulations (*jiin hatto*) on administration and ecclesiastical affairs to the various temples and sects.

As regards Shingon, these regulations established rigid hierarchical arrangements in which Tō-ji, Ninna-ji, Daigo-ji, Takaosan-ji, and Kongōbu-ji were named central temples responsible for lesser temples under them. This centralization of administrative authority was intended to strengthen government control. A similar system was applied to branch temples in the area of the new capital of Edo. Procedures were regularized for initiation, training, wearing high priestly robes, granting ecclesiastical titles, and so on. The influence of imperial-related temples was limited. In general, the government encouraged scholarly activity, making it the basis for advancement in priestly rank, but supervised study and controlled scholarship funds. Such regulations were later unified and applied to all Buddhist institutions.

Against this background of increasing government control, scholarly study of Shingon flourished, while further reform movements and factions also made their appearance. Both centers of the "new teachings" Shingi school became important centers for Shingon study; Hase-dera in particular became renowned for broad learning in other sects of Buddhism and secular learning as well. The scholar priests on Kōya-san began to regain authority from the administrative priests, and learning was promoted there also. The Ji-sect *hijiri* were reinstated on the mountain and officially absorbed into the Shingon system. Conflicts between these three groups broke out into the open, and were only settled by government action in the late seventeenth century, when some one thousand rebellious administrative priests and *hijiri* were expelled from the mountain and over nine hundred of their temples destroyed.

In general, Shingon study became rigidly systematized, and since contact between opposing schools of thought more or less ceased, no developments of fundamental importance to doctrine took place during the Tokugawa period. Efforts were made to spread practice of the precepts around the end of the sixteenth century. The priest Jōgon (1639–1702), for example, was a scholar who actively taught the precepts and built up a following among feudal lords and commoners alike. He also founded a new school of ritual practice that united all such preceding lineages in one.

Even more renowned was Onkō (1718–1804), also known as Jiun Sonja. As a young man he travelled here and there studying the many teachings of Buddhism as well as Confucianism and Shinto. Urging a return to the Buddhism of Shakyamuni's time, he spread practice of the precepts. Onkō was an important scholar of Sanskrit, and among his many works is a thousand-volume compilation and study of sutras and texts in that language. His disciples numbered in the hundreds.

Throughout the Tokugawa period there were numerous Shingon priests active in general scholarship as well as sectarian doctrinal study. Many also composed religious and moral texts directed to the populace, relating Mikkyo teachings to secular life. This type of activity and the emphasis on precepts was probably at least partially in reaction to growing criticism of Buddhism. Such criticism came first from Confucian scholars who became prominent beginning in early Tokugawa, and then was taken up by proponents of the National Learning movement, who sought to restore native Japanese cultural and religious traditions. Buddhism was attacked less on doctrinal grounds than because its priests were widely viewed as degenerate and unfairly privileged, while its institutions, with their large land holdings, were considered socially unproductive.

In 1868 the Tokugawa regime ended with the reinstitution of imperial rule in what is known as the Meiji Restoration. The anti–Buddhist sentiment that had developed earlier in Tokugawa swelled into a widespread movement to root out Buddhism (*haibutsu kishaku*) that continued for several years, unopposed by the Meiji government. Thousands of temples throughout Japan were destroyed or ransacked, their ritual implements melted down, and texts and images of deities burned. The government itself relaxed the rules of conduct for priests, encouraging them to return to secular life, and issued a series of anti–Buddhist directives.

An early policy of the new government was the thorough sundering of all connections between Shinto and Buddhism (*shinbutsu bunri*). This was done in order to restore Shinto to the native purity it had enjoyed in ancient times, when religion and imperial government were one. The result was creation of a "State Shinto" that channelled religious devotion to the needs of the state and worship of the emperor. To this end, shrines were forbidden to employ Buddhist implements, images, or names. Amalgamated shrine-temples were declared Shinto shrines, and their Buddhist priests returned to lay status. Connections with the imperial family traditionally enjoyed by certain temples were severed, and the imperial court purged of Buddhist elements.

The anti–Buddhist policies of the Meiji period came as especially hard blows to Shingon and Tendai, which had been most closely amalgamated with Shinto and folk beliefs. The majority of shrine-temples had belonged to the Shingon sect. These sects had also been accustomed to holding their own income-producing estates; when their lands were lost, their temples lost their economic base. They therefore followed the example of other Buddhist sects and turned to religious activity among the populace, something new in the history of Shingon institutions (though not on the part of individual priests). From the late nineteenth century, Shingon concentrated on the cult of Kūkai as its basis for popular support.

Under these trying circumstances the various schools of Shingon united, divided, and recombined in different groupings, then reseparated to recombine yet again in different ways over the years, changing names and leaders. Today the major "new teachings" subsects remain the Buzan at Hase-dera in Nara prefecture and the Chizan at Chishaku-in in Kyoto. The larger "old teachings" subsects are headquartered variously at the following temples: Kongōbu-ji on

Kōya-san, and Kajū-ji, Daigo-in, Ninna-ji, Tō-ji, Sennyū-ji, and Daikaku-ji, all within the city of Kyoto.

Another major school is the Shingon Ritsu (Precepts) sect, centered at Saidai-ji temple in Nara. Incorporated into Shingon by government edict in the nineteenth century, it became independent again as a separate subsect under its present name in the twentieth century. There are many other subsects as well, numbering some forty in all, including new ones that came into being after the Second World War.

Shingon now has some eighteen major headquarter temples (*honzan,* or "original mountains") throughout Japan, each the center of one or another school. These subdivisions of Shingon Buddhism have altered many times over the centuries, merging, separating, changing names, remerging and subdividing due to reform movements, doctrinal differences, and secular political circumstances. The existence of so many factions may give the misleading impression of a Shingon entirely divided against itself, but this is not the case. All subsects have in common the fundamental esoteric teachings and practices, and all are valid expressions of an ancient, dynamic tradition that is broad enough in scope to accommodate their differences. There are many important activities in which various branches act together. Shuchi-in University and other Shingon educational institutions are examples. The annual ritual for the welfare of Japan and the world held at Tō-ji (the *goshichinichi mishu-hō,* among the largest and most important of esoteric practices) continues with the participation of the whole of Shingon.

Because of the fluid nature of religious belief in Japan, it is difficult to arrive at a precise accounting of Shingon's numerical strength. Shingon today is estimated to have some ten million followers. Some of these may count themselves concurrent followers of other sects as well. The priesthood numbers about sixteen thousand, distributed among approximately eleven thousand Shingon temples in Japan. The influence on Japanese culture and society of the esoteric teachings and practices, at many different levels of understanding, was strong in the past and continues today.

MOUNTAIN WORSHIP, PILGRIMAGE, AND POPULAR BELIEFS

Shingon is sometimes characterized as an aristocratic form of Buddhism, particularly in contrast to the Pure Land and Nichiren sects, which grew with strong popular support during the Kamakura period. Founded in a time when Buddhism was officially sponsored to perform ritual for the state, Shingon developed under the patronage of the court nobility. Its economic base lay in the income-producing farmlands bestowed on temples by the court and then by wealthy aristocrats. As Buddhist institutions, these temples were mainly concerned with training priests in the elaborate rituals and complex doctrines of Mikkyo. It is not surprising, therefore, that Shingon has been criticized as being aloof from the common people.

It is true that Shingon has been aristocratic in the sense that its inner teachings were fully transmitted to relatively few individuals in any historical period, and those individuals were, of necessity, qualified priests. Furthermore, its complex teachings would naturally appeal far more to literate members of the nobility than to uneducated lower classes. No doubt Kūkai had this in mind when he founded the school that was to plant the "seed of wisdom" in all levels of society. The Shingon teachings are, however, rooted in the fundamental Mahayana concept of compassion, while Mikkyo rituals are properly performed for the benefit—both material and spiritual—not just of priest or petitioner but of all living beings. The life and work of Kūkai exemplify this concern.

The same type of concern is also clearly evident in the activities of priests in a collateral movement in Shingon that emphasized practice of the priestly precepts (*ritsu*). An important figure in this movement was Jitsuhan (d. 1144). Having studied Hossō, Shingon, and Tendai teachings, Jitsuhan searched for a master from whom to receive the legitimate lineage of the precepts. He went to the famous Nara temple of Tōshōdai-ji, where the great Chinese priest Ganjin (Ch., Chien-chen; 688–763) had established an orthodox precepts lineage some three hundred years earlier, but he found it in ruins. Meeting a priest from whom to receive this lineage, Jitsuhan afterward devoted himself to its teaching as well as to Shingon practice. This kind of activity led eventually to formation of the Shingon Ritsu sect.

Among those who spread the teaching of the precepts was Shunjō (1166–1227), who studied Mikkyo at both Hieizan and Kōya-san, and then went to China in 1199. He returned in 1211, bringing great learning and quantities of texts on various subjects. Shunjō established the temple of Sennyū-ji in Kyoto under court patronage, and there combined the teachings and practices of Tendai, Shingon, Zen, Pure Land, and the precepts. After him, Eison (1201–1290), who studied at Daigo-ji, Hiei-zan, Kōya-san, and the Nara schools, travelled throughout the country preaching practice of the precepts. Eison restored the Saidai-ji temple in Nara, which later became the center of the Shingon Ritsu schol. Among the many activities he is known for is his performance of esoteric rituals to preserve the nation when Japan faced the threat of Mongol invasions.

Priests who worked to spread the precepts were also often involved in work for social welfare, and Eison was particularly active in this regard. On his teaching travels, he also built bridges and established hostels for travellers and clinics for the ill, as well as distributing food and money to the poor. His disciple Ninshō (1217–1303) carried on similar activity, as well as Shingon ritual to ward off the Mongols, thus achieving renown. Ninshō built bridges and roads, dug wells, and established sanctuaries within which it was forbidden to kill living things. He also established baths, hospitals, hostels for the poor, and even a clinic for horses.

Later Shingon priests, following a tradition set by priests of the Kamakura sects, began to write texts explaining doctrine in language easily read by laymen. This type of literature (*kana hōgo*) became increasingly popular. Shingon temples, particularly on Kōya-san, were also involved in printing and publication of various texts on Mikkyo and other subjects. Through such activities Shingon together with the other Buddhist sects helped to disseminate both Buddhist and secular culture and knowledge of the written Japanese language throughout the country.

On another level, the various groups of *hijiri* also did good works among the populace as they traveled about the country spreading *nembutsu* practice and collecting donations for the building of temples. Not only did they effect the assimilation of Buddhist beliefs into popular culture, but they also built bridges, extended roads, and dug wells, in part as a practice of purification and atonement for sins. The orthodox lineage of Mikkyo doctrine and practice was carried on by the priesthood, while the role of the *hijiri* for Shingon was to disseminate popular faith in Kūkai and Kōya-san. In addition, the splendor of the Kōya-san temple compound is in large part due to the efforts of these "wise men" of the mountain.

Esoteric Buddhism, of course, had traditionally been open to the influence of beliefs and concerns of the common people. In India, the Mahayana movement had originated in large part from a popular reaction to the increasingly abstract concerns of older, then dominant forms of Buddhism. Esoteric Buddhism further developed by uniting Mahayana teachings with folk beliefs and practices. Thus the constellation of Buddhas and bodhisattvas found in Shingon, for example, incorporates Hindu gods and goddesses commonly worshiped by the Indian people. It is difficult to trace how native beliefs may have influenced Shingon in Japan; Mikkyo, however, had much to do with the shapes taken by Japanese religion.

Mikkyo influence on popular belief is illustrated in *shugendō,* a form of lay religious practice carried on by various groups throughout Japan. This movement is rooted in the ancient Japanese worship of mountains as supernatural realms where agricultural gods and ancestral spirits dwell. Native beliefs of this kind were influenced by Taoism and Buddhism, some of whose followers sought out numinous mountain sites for meditation or incantation practice. The founding of *shugendō* is attributed to a semi-mythical ascetic called En-no-Gyōja, who was active around Mount Katsuragi in the Nara region sometime during the seventh to eighth centuries. Little is known about him, however, not even whether he was a Buddhist, though legends abound.

By means of rigorous practice in the wilds, hermits and ascetics were thought to take on some of the supernatural power present there. Some practitioners of miscellaneous category Mikkyo in the Nara period, such as the Natural Wis-

51

dom priests at Yoshino, favored mountains as places for meditation. Other Buddhist precursors of *shugendō* include early *hijiri* and *Lotus Sutra* practitioners. One prominent example is the self-ordained priest Taichō (682–767), who underwent mountain austerities from an early age, experienced many manifestations of spiritual power, and gathered a large following.

Natural Wisdom priests regularly performed the Morning Star meditation, the practice of which was so significant to Kūkai. Folk and Buddhist elements in mountain worship seem to have been inextricably tangled at that time, however, and it is not clear whether the founder of Shingon was actually associated with the Natural Wisdom school. In any case, Mikkyo elements were present early in mountain-related practices.

Shingon and Tendai valued remote mountain areas for their proper Buddhist practice, as is evident from the creation of extensive temple compounds on Kōya-san and Hiei-zan. Both sects played important parts in the growth of *shugendō,* with which many Mikkyo priests are associated. Shōbō, for example, who founded Daigo-ji, is considered the patriarch of one line of *shugendō.* This Shingon priest is said to have established Kinbu-sen, a sacred mountain in the Nara area, as a place of practice, improving access for pilgrims by starting a ferry service and building roads.

During the Heian period the spiritual powers of mountain ascetics came into demand for warding off evil influences, telling fortunes, healing illness, ensuring safe childbirth, and so on. Further sacred sites were opened up, and *shugendō's* popularity grew. Practitioners who were also Shingon or Tendai followers gave it an increasingly Buddhistic format, freely incorporating Mikkyo elements into their ritual and adapting Mikkyo concepts to create their own doctrinal framework. By the early Kamakura period two main lines of *shugendō* had formed: the Honzan school, centered on the sacred moutains of Kumano, was associated with Tendai; the Tōzan school, centered on the peaks in the area of Mount Kinbu, was associated with Shingon.

Known as *yamabushi* ("those who repose in the mountains"), the distinctively-dressed *shugendō* practitioners perform pilgrimages from peak to peak in sacred mountain areas. Following routes related to the patterns of Mikkyo mandalas, on each peak they perform secret rites and austerities. The spiritual power thus attained, considered efficacious in divination and magical ritual, is put to the service of the community. Historically, these practitioners are considered to have made important contributions to the development of remote regions of Japan.

The development of *shugendō* was closely bound to the assimilation of native Japanese religious beliefs with the imported teachings of Buddhism in a process known as "merging gods and Buddhas" (*shinbutsu shūgō*). As early as the Nara period, for example, Buddhist temples came to be built at shrines to worship the local gods, which were often given Buddhist names. Those gods were invoked as guardian deities of Buddhism. As the counterparts of such shrine-temples (*jingū-ji*), Shinto shrines to local gods were also built in the precincts of some Buddhist temples, especially those of the Tendai and Shingon sects. Kōya-san enshrines such protective gods (*chinju* or *garanjin*) as Niu Myōjin, for example, and the great Shinto deity Hachiman is worshiped at Tō-ji with Buddhist ritual.

The association of Shinto and Buddhist deities grew ever closer. From local allies, the gods came to be seen as divine converts to Buddhism who were on the way to enlightenment. During the Heian period Buddhas came to be regarded as the original essence of which the Shinto gods were manifestations. In other words, the Shinto gods were local emanations of the Buddhas, the two being inseparable in essence. The sun goddess Amaterasu worshiped at the grand shrine of Ise, for example, was said to be essentially identical to Dainichi Nyorai. This concept (called *honji suijaku*) established the assimilation of Buddhist and Shinto deities.

The popular tendency to unite Shinto and Buddhist deities into a single (however vague) system of faith underwent considerable elaboration from the middle of the Heian period on. Gradually increasing consciousness of a national identity during the Kamakura period contributed to a strengthening of Shinto, particularly the practice of worship at the Ise shrine. As a result, the so-called Dual (*ryōbu*) Shinto took form. Named from the Shingon term for the dual mandala, Dual Shinto identified the inner and outer shrines at Ise with the two main Shingon mandalas. This was also called Kūkai-style (*daishi-ryū*) Shinto because of a legend that he had founded it. A corresponding Mikkyo–Shinto school (known as *sannō ichijitsu shintō*) developed in affiliation with Tendai.

Texts systematizing the doctrines of these schools were written and attributed to Kūkai and Saichō. The result of such movements was both to popularize Mikkyo and to add a strong Buddhistic element to folk beliefs. In the Muromachi period leaders of Shinto shrines began to assert their independence from Buddhism, and the idea gained currency that the native gods were the essence of which Buddhist deities were lesser manifestations (*jinpon butsujaku*). The Yoshida school of Shinto, for instance, stated that both Confucianism and Buddhism had originated in the native Japanese religion. Many of the practices and doctrinal arguments employed by this type of school were Buddhist, particularly esoteric Buddhist, in origin.

Around the end of the eighteenth century the Shingon priest Onkō promoted a form of Dual Shinto. He taught that Shinto was the proper Japanese Way, which, however, cannot be properly explained except by Mikkyo doctrine. On this basis he founded the Unden school, which combined Buddhism and Shinto and incorporated Mikkyo ritual practices.

In general, Japanese religious practices developed through the merging of folk faiths and social customs with Buddhist beliefs and practices. Various Buddhist deities, such as Kannon, became objects of popular faith. Mikkyo deities figure prominently in this regard, as witnessed by the stone figures of Jizō, a compassionate bodhisattva linked especially with travellers, women, chidren, and childbirth, which can be found by roadsides and in temples throughout Japan. The fierce, evil-subduing bodhisattva Fudō Myō-ō likewise became a focus of folk beliefs.

Much of the Buddhist, and Mikkyo, influence in Japan has to do with rituals directed to spirits of the departed. The *urabon-e,* which was originally a Buddhist feast given to priests after their summer period of seclusion, came to be linked with festivals for the ancestors. Recitation of an esoteric mantra called the *kōmyō shingon* became popular during the Heian period for healing, subduing evil influences, driving away insects, and so forth, as well as for removing all impediments to salvation. The same incantation was used in a ritual empowerment of earth (*dosha kaji-hō*) which, when sprinkled on a grave or on a corpse, was said to result in the immediate rebirth of the departed in the Pure Land. This and other Mikkyo rituals were incorporated into common Japanese funeral customs and ancestor practices.

The practice of pilgrimage, from early times a strong element in popular faith, developed together with mountain worship and related beliefs. As described earlier, many sacred mountains of Japan came to be seen as the earthly paradises of certain gods or Buddhas. This was linked to the rise of Pure Land beliefs stressing rebirth in the paradise of Amida Buddha. There were popular beliefs, too, associated with the bodhisattva Miroku, the future Buddha, who will some day descend from his Pure Land to save all beings and make this world a paradise. Against this kind of background the Kūkai cult, according to which Kūkai remains in meditation on Kōya-san continuing to act for the benefit of the people of this world, spread along with mountain worship.

One important pilgrimage route links thirty-three Kannon temples in the Kansai area of western Japan (*saikoku sanjūsanban kannon fudasho*). This originated in the Kannon faith that became widespread during the Heian period. Kannon faith was focused on certain temples, such as Kiyomizu-dera in Kyoto, Hase-dera near Nara, and Ishiyama-dera by Lake Biwa, associated with the bodhisattva of saving compassion. The development of the thirty-three-station pilgrimage is bound up with the *shugendō* movement centered in Kumano. In late Heian this group promoted pilgrimage to Mount Nachi, said to be the earthly paradise of Kannon, and a temple there became the first station on the route known today.

This had an influence on the growth of another important popular practice, the pilgrimage to eighty-eight sacred sites on the mountainous island of Shikoku (*shikoku hachijū-hakkasho reijō*). There were various places in Shikoku closely linked to the historical Kūkai. As Kūkai devotion spread, so did tales of the great master's miraculous accomplishments, giving rise to local legends throughout Japan about the wonders worked by "Odaishi-sama," as he is affectionately called.

The Shikoku pilgrimage was probably centered at first in the Sanuki region, the birthplace of Kūkai, and places such as Cape Muroto and Tairyū Gorge, which are associated with Kūkai's early meditation practice. Other sites on Shikoku were added later to make eighty-eight in all. The customary route includes additional temples not counted in the eighty-eight. There are many legendary accounts of the origin of the Shikoku pilgrimage, such as that En-no-Gyōja founded it, or that Kūkai himself founded it in 815. The pilgrimage probably took regular form during the early Kamakura period, a time when the Kūkai cult was growing rapidly. Many Shinto shrines were also included in the pilgrimage route.

Covering some fourteen hundred kilometers of mountainous terrain, the arduous route as known today is associated with stages of enlightenment. The twenty-three sites in the Awa region (modern-day Tokushima Prefecture) are related to the awakening mind, the sixteen sites in Tosa (Kōchi Prefecture) relate to practice, the twenty-six sites in Iyo (Ehime Prefecture) relate to enlightened wisdom, and the twenty-three sites in Sanuki (Kagawa Prefecture) relate to ultimate enlightenment (*nehan*). These four are differentiated aspects of Dainichi Nyorai's universal enlightened mind, which enfolds all.

The Shikoku pilgrims were not (and still are not) exclusively Shingon followers. As the many literary references to the pilgrimage show, they were embarked upon by anyone who wished to cure illness or gain miraculous benefits. Pilgrims wear a strip of cloth on which is written "two travelling together" (*dōgyō ninin*), signifying that each individual is always accompanied by Kūkai, who may at any time make his presence known through some miraculous event. Other paraphernalia include special white garments, sandals, staff, and bell. Pilgrims proceed reciting mantras of purification and sounding their bells. At each pilgrimage site they receive in a book they carry for the purpose the seal of the temple as a record of the journey. The Shikoku pilgrimage of eighty-eight stations grew within the popular tradition, and the pilgrims today represent all levels of understanding of the Shingon teachings.

THREE

Mikkyo: The Esoteric Teaching

The Mikkyo system of doctrine and practice could well be described by the metaphor of Indra's vast net, which has jewels, like stars, at all intersections, each jewel reflecting all others. These together make up a universal web of which each part contains and influences all other parts. This chapter will introduce several teachings considered characteristic of Mikkyo, most of which will be expanded upon later in different contexts.

It would be difficult to explain precisely and fully how Mikkyo differs from exoteric Buddhism (*kengyō*), since the two are so closely bound together in their historical and doctrinal development. Mikkyo is, however, esoteric in more than just the simple sense that its inmost teachings have been kept secret for initiates alone. The sutras, which are not hidden, contain the essence of the Mikkyo teachings, but the esoteric tradition stresses that these can be fully understood only through experience. This experiential understanding is gained under the guidance of a qualified master in the Dharma lineage, whose instruction is attuned to the needs and capabilities of the student.

Under such supervision, therefore, the Mikkyo practitioner performs meditative rituals that are intended to lead to the proper grasp of the teachings. The distilled experience of Mikkyo's historical masters is conveyed in the form of secret oral instructions (*kuden*) transmitted over the centuries from master to disciple. The traditional Mikkyo understanding is further contained in commentaries on the sutras, in ritual manuals of various kinds, and in written records of oral transmission (*kuketsu*).

Mikkyo doctrines and practices are guarded in this way in order to avoid misunderstanding by non-initiates, to prevent misuse of the ritual techniques, and to keep the teachings from being degraded. Mikkyo is esoteric in another sense as well, which is that the profound understanding pointed to in the teachings cannot be revealed as can ordinary secrets. This is because the greatest mysteries, which are direct manifestations of Buddhahood, are said to be knowable only by the enlightened mind.

THE PRECEPTS

Buddhism early developed a large number of priestly commandments against killing, stealing, adultery, falsehood, drinking intoxicants, and so on, totaling in the hundreds. Many of these rules express a basic morality needed to maintain the priesthood. Some, such as regulations against traveling during monsoon months and rules about eating, are obviously based on the requirements of the time and geographical setting of early Buddhism. Others are more abstract rules concerning spiritual discipline.

Mikkyo values the general Buddhist precepts as providing a necessary basis for correct practice by the priesthood. Thus it was that Kūkai instructed his disciples to receive the precepts at the national ordination center in Nara. Shingon, however, also stresses an additional set of vows. The formal rules of priestly conduct are known in Sanskrit as *vinaya* (Jap., *binaya* or *ritsu*), while the less formalized, more spiritually oriented precepts are called *śīla* (Jap., *shira* or *kai*). The latter, according to the *Commentary on the Dainichi-kyō,* means purity of mind. The esoteric precepts belong to the latter type.

Rather than a code of behavior, these precepts are said to describe the conditions necessary for realization of enlightenment. In written form they are known as the fourfold prohibitions (*shijū kinkai*), given here as in the *Dainichi-kyō:*

> One must never abandon the Dharma, give up the aspiration to enlightenment, be stingy with any of the teachings, or engage in any action that does not benefit living beings.[1]

Expounded in Shingon's two primary sutras, the *Dainichi-kyō* and *Kongōchō-gyō,* these are called the *samaya* precepts (*sanmaya-kai*). *Samaya* means equality, vow, removal of obstructions, and awakening, here referring to the absolute equality of body, speech, and mind in Buddha and all living beings. The esoteric vows therefore embody the fundamental esoteric experience, realization of self as Buddha.

In outer form, the esoteric precepts are admonishments not to act against one's innately enlightened nature, and so they are also called the enlightenment precepts. Their inner meaning is the individual's own harmony with the universe. The enlightenment precepts do not supersede the general Buddhist precepts, but rather affirm a deeper meaning underlying them.

FOUR MAJOR CHARACTERISTICS OF THE ESOTERIC TEACHING

It is difficult to find clear-cut dividing lines between early esoteric and exoteric Buddhism. So far as they can be traced, the beginnings of Mikkyo seem to be inextricably bound up with Mahayana developments, and these two forms of Buddhism continued to influence each other in later history as well. Their teachings were not necessarily mutually exclusive; their differences, though real, were not absolute, though they were sometimes exaggerated for sectarian purposes. As Kūkai wrote in the *Benkenmitsu Nikyō-ron* (Treatise on the Exoteric and Esoteric Teachings):

> The meanings of *exoteric* and *esoteric* are manifold and numberless. Looking from the shallow toward the deep, the deep is esoteric and the shallow is exoteric. Thus the texts of non-Buddhist teachings may also be called secret repositories. Even in the teachings of the Buddhas there are the exoteric and esoteric. . . .[2]

With the development of Mikkyo teachings and practices, the terms *exoteric* and *esoteric* came naturally into use to distinguish Mikkyo from Theravada and general Mahayana Buddhism. Similar terms (*esoteric, secret, hidden*) were also used in certain later Mahayana texts to describe, for example, Hua-yen teachings, but Chen-yen in China and Shingon in Japan represent the teachings to which the term *esoteric* most consistently applies.

In the esoteric understanding, Mikkyo fulfills all preceding exoteric teachings, not merely by superimposing a further layer of doctrine over them, but by placing them in a different frame of reference. In trying to explain the esoteric viewpoint, the Indian masters who first brought the teachings to China understandably tended to stress differences in specific exoteric and esoteric doctrines. In later refinements of the exoteric-esoteric contrast, Kūkai made a broader statement of the primary difference, which was that the Shingon teaching was the direct teaching of the ultimate Buddha of the Dharma Body, while the exoteric schools represented conditioned teachings adapted to particular circumstances. The former was eternal and absolute, while the latter was based on the teaching of the long-departed Shakyamuni Buddha. The above quote from the *Treatise on the Exoteric and Esoteric Teachings* continues as follows:

> The teaching of the Dharma Body is deep and profound, while the teachings adapted to circumstance are shallow and limited. Thus the name *esoteric* is used.[3]

Elaborating on this primary difference in the above text, Kūkai stressed the following four points as characteristic of Mikkyo in contrast to exoteric teachings alone:

1. Mikkyo is the direct teaching of the highest Buddha, the Dharma Body, the all-pervading body of universal enlightenment.
2. Enlightenment can be manifested in this world, and can be communicated.
3. Mikkyo teachings stress immediate attainment of Buddhahood in this life.

4. The esoteric tradition contains a great wealth of teachings for many purposes, and includes methods of practice suited to all predilections and abilities.

Kakuban further examined these distinctions in the light of later Buddhist developments, summarizing the gist of Kūkai's first point as follows in the *Kenmitsu Fudō-sho* (Text on the Differences of Exoteric and Esoteric Buddhism):

> The exoteric is the teaching of the *ōjin* [the Buddha who manifests itself in response to particular historical circumstances]. The esoteric is the speech of the Buddha of the Dharma Body. The exoteric is superficial and incomplete. The esoteric is hidden and profound. . . .[4]

The *ōjin* Buddha referred to here was Shakyamuni, born with human body, who communicated the truth in terms appropriate to his time. This historical Shakyamuni Buddha was considered the source of the exoteric teachings, according to which direct human knowledge of universal Buddha-nature was impossible. Universal Buddha-nature was the Dharma Body (*hosshin*), the eternally self-existing being of Truth, the embodiment of universal enlightenment. According to the general exoteric view, the Dharma Body was perfect Truth itself, and for that reason without manifestation; it was abstract, cold, distant; it had no color, form, or activity. The concept of bodies of the Buddha (*busshin*) was elaborated by Mahayana, resulting in the differentiation of various orders of Buddha-being between the human Shakyamuni and the essential Dharma Body, which in the exoteric view remained remote, silent, and unknowable.

The Buddhist schools in Japan before the introduction of Mikkyo thus considered themselves to be founded in the historical teaching of Shakyamuni. In the esoteric view, however, Shakyamuni was a manifestation of Dainichi Nyorai. Although equal to the teachings of the universal Buddha in essence, the teachings of the historical Shakyamuni and other intermediate Buddhas were considered limited in that they were conditioned by their historical time, place, and audience.

Where the exoteric teachings held that the Dharma Body was not an actual "being" capable of communicating any teaching, Mikkyo affirmed that the Dharma Body was an actually existing entity. While the historical Shakyamuni had long since passed into nirvana, the Buddha of the Dharma Body, according to Mikkyo, exists eternally, continually informing all things. Mikkyo considers itself the secret teaching of the Dharma Body.

The esoteric teaching sees the pure realm of Dharma-nature not as fixed and static, but as dynamic, continually acting and evolving. It is an all-illuminating, all-penetrating, all-embracing life-energy. It may be perceived as a holy principle or as a universal being, but, deeper still, it is an absolute, infinite Dharma-entity transcending any duality between individual beings, things, and principles. Far from being a silent abstraction, therefore, the ultimate Dharma Body is the activity of life itself, present in all that exists, and its teaching (*hosshin seppō*) never ceases.

The quality of the Dharma Body that enfolds all things is also called compassion, and the scope of its activity includes phenomenal things, the senses, and the activities of body, speech, and mind. It extends throughout the all-pervading Dharma Realm, is eternal, and is omnipresent in all levels of being (which Buddhism terms *jikkai,* the ten realms). The teaching of the Dharma Body is perceptible through the symbolic elements of earth, water, fire, wind, space, and consciousness—in other words, all things.

The second of Kūkai's points follows from the nature of the Dharma Body. The exoteric Buddhist view is that enlightenment transcends all language and understanding. No words, thoughts, or means of expression can communicate it—"words are cut off and the mind perishes," "words die and thought is eradicated." In this view, enlightenment is described as void (*kū*) of permanent self-nature and as egoless (*muga*). The exoteric teachings therefore treat enlightenment indirectly by analyzing the delusion that blocks enlightenment, or by discussing it in terms of what it is not.

Mikkyo also says that ordinary language, dualistic by nature, cannot describe enlightenment. It is a central esoteric teaching, however, that enlightenment communicates itself. The language of enlightenment, which includes artistic forms, can manifest that mysterious realm. Mikkyo therefore finds truth embodied in special mantric language, gestures, Sanskrit syllables, mandalas, images of deities, and other phenomenal means. This approach offers a foundation for esoteric practice.

During the centuries when Mikkyo was taking form, the Buddha was considered either as the historical Shakyamuni, or as an idealized body of perfection existing impossibly far from human beings. The possibility of Buddhahood thus receded ever farther into the past or into the philosophical distance. Mikkyo evolved in this context, centered on the search for real expressions of Buddhahood and the means to attain enlightenment within the practitioner's lifetime. The *Kongōchō Gohimitsu-kyō* classified the older forms of Buddhism as exoteric, the mantric teaching as esoteric, on this basis:

> Those who practice the exoteric way undergo three great infinite kalpas, after which they attain the highest realization. During that time, for ten steps forward they take nine steps backward.[5]

The belief that a human being can, in his own lifetime, become a Buddha (*sokushin jōbutsu*) thus can be said to distinguish Mikkyo from exoteric Buddhism in general, in which human beings must undergo aeons of striving for perfection. When Shubhakarasimha and Vajrabodhi arrived in China with the esoteric teachings the Hua-yen and T'ien-t'ai schools had flourished there for some time already. The Indian masters, in seeking to explain the nature of the esoteric teachings by contrasting them with preexisting exoteric teachings, grouped Hua-yen and T'ien-t'ai with the rest of exoteric Buddhism, apparently without realizing the further developments these schools had undergone in China.

Hua-yen and T'ien-t'ai teachings, for example, state the possibility of becoming a Buddha in one's present body. Although in comparison with Mikkyo they had relatively few ritual techniques for fulfilling this aim, these schools could be seen to represent a transition between exoteric and esoteric Buddhism. Mikkyo, however, specializes in such ritual techniques. Ch'an (Jap., Zen) Buddhism, already established in China at the time, was also primarily concerned with immediate enlightenment, and later sects of exoteric Mahayana, too, teach the doctrine of enlightenment in this body, but the issues are too complex to discuss further here.

Enlightenment is called "becoming the Buddha" (*jōbutsu*). According to Kūkai, to become a Buddha means to understand the nature of the three minds (*sanshin*) of self, other (including all things and beings), and Buddha (the macrocosmic enlightened being). As everything in the universe is endowed with Buddha-nature, these three are aspects of an inseparable unity, and Buddhahood is realization of the equality of the three minds.

Generally speaking, exoteric teachings stress that human beings are intrinsically unenlightened and so must seek to gain enlightenment by erasing the defiled self. Mikkyo, however, based itself on the Mahayana teaching of original enlightenment (*hongaku*) of all beings as they are. Since it considers each individual to have inherent Buddha-nature, the purpose of esoteric practice is to realize the Buddha-self.

Mikkyo meditative techniques utilize all the faculties and energies of the human body-mind, focusing them on Buddhahood. The capacities to think, feel, perceive, know, and act are summed up in the three secrets (*sanmitsu*), the basis of esoteric practice, which are the all-pervading, enlightened activities of the Buddha's body, speech, and mind reflected in the individual. Quite simply, when one's three activities of body, speech, and mind unite with those of the Buddha, one becomes Buddha.

Mikkyo is based on the universality of the Dharma Body, the activity of which permeates all things. Its teaching is thus considered equally suitable for all people in all situations at all times. Based on the related concept that all phenomena are themselves manifestations of universal Buddhahood, Mikkyo uses any possible means to transform the "deluded" individual into a Buddha.

For the body, there are prescribed hand gestures called mudras (*ingei*), movements of the entire body, the smell of burning incense, and the taste of certain herbs. There are ritual implements to manipulate, and sculpted and painted forms of art to contemplate. Such ritual art is an important element of practice. For speech, the practitioner recites prescribed invocations called mantras (*shin-*

gon), as well as related verse prayers and chants. For the mind, there are visualizations (*kansō* or *kannen*) of deities and symbolic forms, involving colors, movements, thoughts, imagination, and feelings.

Mikkyo ritual is enriched by the presence of many such elements in a great number of combinations, from simple to complex, from those performed by the solitary meditator to those done by many priests together, from those taking only minutes to those taking months to complete. To mention only a few (which will be presented in more detail later), there are: the Preparatory Fourfold Enlightenment Practice, which includes a basic eighteen-part practice, the Tai-zō and Kongō-kai Mandala practices, and the *goma* fire ritual; various kinds of initiation ceremonies; and practices focusing on a single deity. The Morning Star meditation, one of the latter, and the A-syllable visualization (*ajikan*) concentrate the essence of full-scale esoteric ritual into compressed formats.

The Mikkyo teaching of *shōji jissō* expresses the esoteric approach in condensed form. *Shōji* means literally "voice letter," referring not only to human speech and writing but to the meanings expressed in the elements, the senses, the various realms of being (of humans, gods, bodhisattvas, Buddhas, etc.)—in fact all that can be seen, heard, sensed, and known. The "letter" points to the symbolic quality of the "voice" of all phenomena. This voice is the fundamental energy that takes form in all things that exist, which at the most profound level is understood to be the activity of Dainichi Nyorai's three secrets.

The mandalas, ritual objects, visualized forms, and Sanskrit seed syllables used in esoteric practice are so employed as to concentrate in themselves this universal energy. They are perceived as the direct communication of enlightenment, which is not separate from the self. *Jissō* means "actual aspect," the truth of all that is. Thus Mikkyo says *shōji soku jissō:* this universal energy is itself Truth.

DAINICHI NYORAI: THE CENTRAL DEITY

In the course of its development Mikkyo incorporated many Hindu deities into its system of Buddhas and bodhisattvas. When, sometime during the seventh century, Mikkyo had reached the point of being a relatively distinct system, those gods and Buddhas adopted from outside, together with new ones developed within the esoteric tradition, had considerably increased in number. The Tai-zō and Kongō-kai mandalas made their first appearances sometime during this period as cosmic systems unifying all the esoteric deities. Just as the sun is the center of the solar system (as much as to say the universe, for the ancients), so Dainichi Nyorai was placed at the center of both esoteric mandala systems.

Although Buddhism had no creator god among its hundreds and thousands

Portrait sculpture of Kūkai. Muro-machi period (15th century), Sanbō in Kōyasan.

Mahāvairocana (Dainichi Nyorai). Ka-makura period (1192–1392), Kōyasan.

of deities, Hinduism did have the concept of an original universal creator, embodied in the god Brahmā (Jap., Bon-ten). The Hindu view of a central, cosmic deity no doubt influenced the esoteric view of Dainichi Nyorai as the symbolic all-embracing being of the mandala and of the universe itself. Inseparable from all that exists, this central Mikkyo deity came to represent the originally unborn life-energy of the universe. The originally unborn (*honpushō*) is that which was never created and which exists in all things.

Dainichi Nyorai, as a personification of the Dharma Body, was further seen to unite the wisdoms and qualities represented separately in the many deities of esoteric Buddhism. To personify the entire universe and all manifestations of Buddha-nature in a single all-embracing being was a characteristic esoteric development and an important step in the systematization of Mikkyo.

Among the Sanskrit names meaning sun are Sūrya (Jap., Soriya), Aditya (Jap., Nitten), and Vairocana (Jap., Birushana). Mahāvairocana means Great Sun. This is translated into Japanese as Dainichi, sometimes transliterated as Makabirushana. As the name of a deity, it is now considered more or less interchangeable with Birushana. The *Dainichi-kyō Sho* (Commentary on the

Dainichi-kyō) says that (Mahā)Vairocana is another name for the sun, using the sun as a metaphor to explain the deity that brings light and cuts through darkness.

While the sun does not shine in shadow or at night, however, the symbolic radiance of Dainichi Nyorai is unlimited by time and space. The sun bestows life-energy on all living things, but the illumination of Dainichi Nyorai is the unborn and undying light of supramundane realization. The sun is at times revealed, at times hidden by clouds and storms, but the radiance of Dainichi Nyorai is seen as shining forth eternally.

This central deity was established on the basis of such parallels with the sun. To indicate that its all-permeating powers far surpass the sun's, however, its name was prefixed with "great." The Hindu deity Vairocana, for which the sun's power was a metaphor, was thus taken into Mikkyo and given a more far-reaching significance as Dainichi Nyorai. The deity Nitten, also meaning sun, was included in the Mikkyo pantheon as well, but was given a place among the twelve peripheral deities who are guardians of the earth. For Mikkyo, Nitten personifies the sun, while Dainichi Nyorai symbolically embodies the essential energy of life.

Many deities from the Hindu pantheon—such as Agni (Jap., Ka-ten), Vaiśravaṇa (Jap., Bishamon-ten), and Indra (Jap., Taishaku-ten), to name only a few—were also included among Mikkyo's outer guardians. These and all other esoteric deities are seen as having individual attributes and functions, but at a deeper level each is equal in nature to the Dharma Body, and all are recognized as manifestations of Dainichi Nyorai.

THE UNIVERSAL BODY OF THE SIX GREAT ELEMENTS

According to exoteric doctrine, the essential body of the universe—referred to by such terms as Dharma Body, Suchness, Dharma-nature, Buddha-nature, Truth—cannot be conceived of by the limited human mind. It is discussed as an abstraction, not in terms of what it is, but of what it is not. This kind of approach was not concerned with describing the nature of truth as it relates to the phenomenal world. Two main streams of thought dealing with this central problem developed within Mahayana, the schools of Consciousness-Only and of the Void. The esoteric extensions of these philosophies were expressed in the two fundamental esoteric sutras. Mikkyo united these complementary approaches within a symbolic framework that affirms the active presence of Buddha-nature in the world, relating the Dharma Body to individual things and beings.

Mikkyo's symbolic framework evolved from early concepts of physical matter. Ancient philosophies often postulated fundamental elements, such as earth or fire, as the constituents of all creation. Such elements were thought to exist objectively, independent of the perceiving consciousness, and pre-Buddhist Indian philosophy appears to have considered the elements of earth, water, fire, and wind as the permanent material components of physical things.

Early Buddhism borrowed this concept of elements as the basis of all physical matter. They were variously counted as the four elements, as above, or, with the inclusion of space, five elements, called the five great elements (*godai*) because they were present in all material forms, which existed as combinations of the elements. Where the five elements were originally considered to be the constituents of the physical world, Buddhism sometimes treated consciousness in a similar way, as the basis of mind and spirit. Some early texts therefore refer to "six great elements" (*rokudai*). (For convenience, however, they were ordinarily referred to as the four elements or the five elements.) In the esoteric view this kind of approach was too literal, as the following passage from the *Commentary on the Dainichi-kyō* indicates:

> What the sutras call the "transformations of earth" refers to earth, water, fire, wind, and space. There are those who attach themselves to some one of these and proclaim it to be the truth. Some say that earth is the root cause of all things because all living beings and matter are born from earth. However, they have failed to see that earth exists only because of the union of many interdependent causes. Furthermore, those who bear such views believe that by performing rituals to the earth they will attain true liberation. Others think that water gives birth to all things, or fire, or wind likewise. . . .[6]

The various schools of Buddhism gave the elements increasingly philosophical interpretations, using them to refer to phenomenal qualities as well as substances. Earth, for instance, came to represent firmness, water dampness, fire heat, wind motion. Earth then came to represent the nature of holding to things, water absorbing, fire maturing, wind growing. Such phenomenal attributes were further related to the senses, the objects of sense perception, and the nature of human perception.

In the Buddhist philosophy of Consciousness-Only, the elements in their concrete sense came to signify the sense experience of consciousness—hardness, coldness, warmth, and so forth. Physical forms were no longer objective "things," but transformations of the perceiving consciousness, and attention was focused on the nature of consciousness itself. Mind was considered essential, therefore, while matter, transitory and imperfect, was considered no more than an illusion to be seen through.

The teaching of the Void (*kū*) school held that all things are empty of permanent self-nature. Existing solely due to ever-changing complexes of interdependent causes, all forms were ephemeral, continually coming into existence and passing away. The nature of the void penetrated all things, and so was related to universal Truth. This philosophy was effective in exposing mistaken views of reality, but also tended to the extreme position of denying any phenomenal reality whatsoever.

A development that influenced Mikkyo was a further Void teaching, appearing around the time of Nagarjuna, which said that the universal void actually concealed within itself a mysterious absolute reality. Associated with the Wisdom sutras, this teaching dealt with all-penetrating void-reality in terms of universal Buddha-wisdom.

In the general exoteric view, the elements referred to the transient, imperfect phenomenal realm. By employing the elements in new ways as descriptions of consciousness or of void-wisdom, however, Mahayana opened the way to a positive view of universal Truth. Where Consciousness-Only and Void teachings treated enlightened mind and wisdom in terms of the elements, the evolving esoteric teaching equated Buddha-mind and Buddha-wisdom with the elements. The same elements in Mikkyo represented the mysterious Dharma Body that transcends both phenomenal matter and individual mind while being present in both.

Generally speaking, the esoteric teaching tradition that culminated in the *Dainichi-kyō* grew out of the Void school, while the *Kongōchō-gyō* was based on Consciousness-Only. The former tends to speak in terms of the all-penetrating reality of wisdom, where the latter deals with all-penetrating enlightened consciousness. The two represent complementary approaches to a single subject, the nature of macrocosmic and microcosmic reality. The later union of the two traditions was an important development for Mikkyo.

Founded on the Consciousness-Only perception that everything is actually mind, the esoteric teaching found consciousness always present also in material forms, which are not inferior to mind. Each of the five esoteric elements was seen to be endowed with the dimension of consciousness. Forms of matter were not simply "things," therefore, but partook of the highest reality of mind, or Buddha-nature. Matter and mind were explained as two indissoluble aspects of total reality, and every activity of the universe could thus embody the secret of enlightened mind. Kūkai wrote in the *Sokushin Jōbutsu-gi* (The Meaning of Becoming a Buddha in This Body):

> In the various exoteric teachings, the elements are considered to be non-sentient, but the esoteric teaching explains that they are the Buddha's secret all-pervading body. These . . . elements are not apart from consciousness, and though mind and form may be said to differ, their nature is the same. Form is mind and mind is form without obstruction or limitation.[7]

Incorporating various views of the elements developed in Mahayana, Mikkyo gave the elements an added dimension of meaning. They became embodiments of the mysterious, absolute Dharma Body, the perfect Truth that is something more than either real or unreal, mind or matter, universal or particular alone. For Mikkyo, the totality of the elements form the body of the Buddha—and the very same elements form the body of every living being and object. All the manifestations of Truth could, therefore, be described by the six esoteric elements, and Kūkai explained that the material components of reality, manifested as symbolic language, express the true nature of the Dharma Body. They are the "language" of the Dharma Body's teaching.

Mikkyo uses the all-pervading essence represented in the consciousness element to describe the nature of individual enlightenment. Consciousness itself is enlightened mind, and since all the elements are imbued with consciousness, all things participate in enlightenment. In the *Kongōchō-gyō,* for example, universal Buddha-mind, personified in the deity Dainichi Nyorai, also manifests as Kongōsatta. This bodhisattva, who represents the enlightened individual, is associated with the consciousness element. The mantra associated with Kongōsatta is the syllable UN, and this same syllable is also used, therefore, to symbolize the sixth element, consciousness.

The mysterious universal reality Mikkyo describes by the symbolic elements is the enlightened self. In the *Dainichi-kyō* this Dharma Body-self is described from five perspectives, and this fivefold description is further embodied in mantric syllables based on their Sanskrit names (given below in the romanized Japanese form) as follows:

Originally unborn: A-syllable
Apart from all explanations: BA-syllable
Absolutely undefiled: RA-syllable
Apart from dependent causation: KA-syllable
Absolute unobstructed void: KYA-syllable

These attributes of absolute Truth were then identified with the five esoteric elements, so that both the earth element and the syllable A (pronounced "ah" in Japanese) equally symbolized the originally unborn and undying nature of the Dharma Body; both the space element and the syllable KYA symbolized its perfectly unobstructed and interpenetrating nature; and so on. The *Dainichi-kyō* calls this universal Buddha-nature the Wisdom of All-Wisdom (*issai chichi*), and explains it using the elements as a metaphor:

O Shakyamuni . . . just as the realm of space is apart from all discrimination, having neither discrimination nor nondiscrimination, thus the Wisdom of All-Wisdom also is apart from all discrimination, being without discrimination and nondiscrimination.

O Shakyamuni . . . just as all living beings depend on the great earth, thus gods, humans, and demons depend on the Wisdom of All-Wisdom.

O Shakyamuni . . . just as the realm of fire burns all fuel without ceasing, thus the Wisdom of All-Wisdom burns all the fuel of ignorance without being exhausted or satiated.

O Shakyamuni . . . just as the realm of wind removes all dust, thus the Wisdom of All-Wisdom effaces the dust of all delusions.

O Shakyamuni . . . just as the realm of water allows all living beings joy and pleasure, thus the Wisdom of All-Wisdom gives benefit and joy. . . .[8]

The universe as Buddha-wisdom is an eternal totality that, transcending all dualities, yet includes all particular manifestations of mind and matter in its originally unborn being. Having in this way united everything in oneness, therefore, this teaching proceeds to discover the many within oneness. The all-embracing wisdom is differentiated into five, each of which is also symbolized in a mantric syllable (just as consciousness was symbolized in the syllable of Kongōsatta).

The esoteric elements thus took on a different level of meaning as symbols not bound to any phenomenal interpretation. They refer to one essential reality, and their contents are not limited in any way. They are numbered as four or five or six elements in order to show how the single universal reality is composed of multiplicity. In the *Shōji Jissō-gi* (The True Meaning of the Voiced Syllable), Kūkai wrote:

The exoteric five elements are as commonly explained. The esoteric five symbolic elements are the five syllables, the five Buddhas, and the entire oceanic assembly of deities.[9]

Exoteric Buddhism had long used certain colors and shapes, in much the same way as the physical elements, to describe the basic manifestations of form. In the Mikkyo development, too, colors and shapes were related to the elements and syllables. The associations of elements, syllables, colors, and shapes were further expanded, in a way characteristic of the esoteric approach, to form an interrelated framework of symbolic functions, deities, sections of mandalas, and so on.

Employing the symbolic framework of the elements, the Mikkyo system affirms that what in words may be called "Suchness" or "Truth" is, in actuality, none other than the universe. Thus as part of the webwork of meaning referred to by the elements, they also came to represent concrete aspects of the world and the human body. The element earth, for example, could be seen in mountains and land masses, in bones and muscles. The element water was in oceans and rivers, as well as in body fluids, while fire was found in sunshine and lightning, and in body heat. In this way the universal essence pointed to by the elements could be more easily contemplated as actually existing in the self and its immediate surroundings. The macrocosmic dimension directly informs the microcosmic, and vice versa.

The two major Mikkyo sutras represent philosophies dealing with the same central theme in different terms. The *Dainichi-kyō* for example, describes truth by the five elements and five syllables, without mentioning the consciousness element, whereas the *Kongōchō-gyō* stresses enlightened consciousness in the form of the bodhisattva Kongōsatta. The two streams of thought came together in a single doctrine; consciousness was combined with earth, water, fire, wind, and space as an element pervading them all; these together comprised the Universal Body of the Six Great Elements (*rokudai taidai*), embodying "Suchness" in concrete forms. The symbolic elements are called the universal body because they describe the essential body-nature of all things, and this nature is present throughout the entire universe. It is present in the absolute and in transient form, but its essential nature is not diminished in any of its infinite manifestations.

In a departure from the exoteric approach, the various aspects of the universe—body and mind, physical and metaphysical—were integrated in the six elements as aspects of Buddha-nature itself. The exoteric six elements encompassed transient forms of matter and individual consciousness. The esoteric six elements, however, went further to encompass the mysterious reality that transcends both matter and mind—seeing it in every possible form of matter and mind. Where the exoteric abstraction of "Suchness" lies far from transient forms, the universal body refers to an absolute Buddha-reality formed from the very same constituents as all the myriads of beings and phenomena. Its symbolic personification as Dainichi Nyorai also has existence in the same six elements. The form and activity of Buddhahood, therefore, are the infinite forms and activities of the universe—themselves Suchness—and vice versa.

In the esoteric teaching the universe is described as a continuously active, compassionate being that contains all beings as indivisible aspects of itself. To describe that which is immanent in all dimensions of reality (material and spiritual, microcosmic and macrocosmic, etc.), without at the same time being limited in any way by the objects and beings in which it is made manifest, Mikkyo adapted the Mahayana term *void*. From the Mikkyo perspective, the void is cosmic potentiality, perfect in its freedom and not obstructed in any way, while from yet another viewpoint it is all-penetrating wisdom, or enlightenment. Mikkyo considers that the universal self is constantly evolving toward complete self-knowledge in all its parts. This is the activity of awakening all beings to realization of their own true nature, which Mikkyo terms the activity of self-receiving Dharma pleasure (*jiju hōraku*).

The symbolic system of the universal body provided a doctrinal basis for the essential Mikkyo teaching of the possibility of becoming a Buddha within one's lifetime. As Kūkai wrote in *The Meaning of Becoming a Buddha in This Body*:

> The six symbolic elements interpenetrate without obstruction and are in eternal union.

They are not apart from any of the Four Mandalas [forms of existence].
Through practice of three-secrets empowerment, they are made manifest immediately:
The universal web is what we call this body.[10]

The doctrine of the Universal Body of the Six Great Elements represents a flowering of early esoteric Buddhist thought, particularly that expressed in two texts attributed to Nagarjuna. These texts, of great importance to Shingon, are the *Shakumakaen-ron* (Treatise on Mahayana), which is a commentary on the *Daijō Kishin-ron* (Treatise on Awakening of Mahayana Faith), and the *Bodaishin-ron* (Treatise on Enlightened Mind). The first written statement of this doctrine in Japan was Kūkai's, but his formulation was apparently made on the basis of these important early texts, the fundamental Mikkyo sutras, and the oral teachings of the two esoteric lineages.

Kūkai elaborated the doctrine of the Universal Body of the Six Great Elements in *The Meaning of Becoming a Buddha in This Body,* further describing it in symbolic terms of: universal function (*yūdai*), the activity of the universe; universal aspect (*sōdai*), or form, the expression of the universe; and universal body (*taidai*), the essence of the universe. By ritual practice using symbolic representations of the inseparable aspects of the enlightened universe, the Shingon practitioner aims to experience universal reality in himself and so realize Buddhahood. Thus every element of esoteric ritual practice—mantras, mudras, images, implements, mandalas—is meant to be used as an embodiment of universal reality.

Universal function means all workings and movements. These are encompassed in the Universal Three Secrets (*sanmitsu yūdai*). When the three secrets (body, speech, and mind) of the esoteric practitioner unite with the Universal Three Secrets, both are said to be energized in a process, called mutual empowerment (*kaji*), that makes their union real. Through mutual empowerment the microcosmic self and the macrocosmic Self can reveal their mutual identity.

Universal form refers to the differentiated aspects of totality, all its phenomena. These are explained in terms of the Four Universal Mandalas (*shiman sōdai*). All phenomena in the universe, arising from the six elements, take their forms in the Great Mandala, the Samaya Mandala, the Dharma Mandala, and the Karma Mandala. The Great Mandala symbolizes the existence of all beings and objects in the universe, the Samaya Mandala their essential form, the Dharma Mandala their expression, and the Karma Mandala their activity.

Universal body refers to the all-pervading body of the six esoteric elements which comprise the common substance of all things and beings, which are further penetrated by the same universal life-energy. Shingon therefore views individual physical entities as inseparable from the entire universe. Where exoteric teachings may suggest that the human body is intrinsically impure, defiled by its material substance, in the esoteric view the human body-mind being is equal to Dainichi Nyorai, the personification of the enlightened universe. Dainichi Nyorai does not exist without human beings; there is no truth apart from matter and things.

In the Mikkyo system the syllable A symbolizes the element earth and, by extension, form. The Indian patriarch Shubhakarasimha explained the *Dainichi-kyō* in terms of the Universal A-syllable Body (*aji taidai*), which symbolizes Dainichi Nyorai and embodies the condensed significance of all the teachings in that single syllable. This microcosmic mantric form expresses the macrocosmic universal body, unfolding into the five transformations of the A-syllable (*aji goten*). The resulting five syllables represent transformations of the innately enlightened mind, present in all beings, as it goes through various stages that culminate in the highest wisdom. This is the wisdom of "skillful means," the ability to act compassionately in changing circumstances to benefit both self and others. At this level, the individual mind interpenetrates freely with Buddha-reality, illuminated from within by the same perfect freedom and potentiality that characterize the universal body.

The doctrine of the Universal A-syllable Body alone was comparatively abstract. When it was combined with the six elements, however, the result was that the body of the universe could be symbolically concentrated in a single point, the syllable A, which, expanded to its utmost extent, would reveal itself as the totality of the universe, comprised in the six elements. Signifying much more than such physical substances as earth, water, or fire, therefore, the six elements embody entire ranges of symbolic meanings.

The elements can be differentiated into the two aspects of matter and mind. (To do so is also to be reminded of their origins in Mahayana philosophies as developed in the two esoteric sutras.) This framework is no more than a tool, however, the real purpose of which is to convey the essence of the esoteric experience. The underlying assumption is that matter and mind interpenetrate without obstruction, neither existing without the other. Thus the Buddha and the unenlightened individual, composed of the same substance, are as inseparable as the moon and moonlight.

Early Buddhism saw mind as being outside such physical things as mountains and trees, and Consciousness-Only teachings found only the perceiving mind, thus denying the independent reality of mountains and trees. Mikkyo, however, found life and consciousness in all things. Each of the six elements symbolizes the perfection of any single aspect of the total universe in itself, but no element exists apart from its relationship to everything else. The six elements interpenetrate freely, without any hindrance either in matter or mind, to form the body of life. On the largest scale, this body is the totality of the universe, which Mikkyo names Dainichi Nyorai.

THE MIKKYO AFFIRMATION OF THE SELF
AND HUMAN DESIRE

The Mikkyo concept of Great Bliss (*tairaku*) was the esoteric development of Mahayana teachings identifying birth-and-death with nirvana and delusion with enlightenment. In the esoteric expression, all human desires were affirmed as bodhisattva activities, and sexual desire in particular was used as a metaphor for the practitioner's desire to unite with the deity, Great Bliss referring to the accomplishment of esoteric union with the universe, symbolized in the deity.

Popular movements, often combining Hindi and Buddhist elements, also arose involving actual sexual activity, but these are not to be confused with the symbolic sexuality found in much of esoteric Buddhism as it later developed in India. The Shiva sect of Hinduism absorbed a folk cult centered on Kālī, a goddess associated with sexual energy. The god Shiva, who as the ultimate Hindu deity was considered not to be active, was thought to be energized through the motive force of the goddess Kālī. Worship of Kālī was thus thought to bring great blessings, and certain yogic teachings stressed sexual energy in conjunction with physical exercises, breathing techniques, and meditation as a means to attain liberation. In the later period of esoteric Buddhism's development, after Mikkyo had already arrived in Japan, the so-called left-handed Tantric Buddhism employing ritual sex appeared in India, apparently influenced by Hinduism.

Orthodox Shingon does not employ sexual energy ritually in this way, but sexual and other desires are considered vital sources of energy for Mikkyo practice. The *Wisdom-Truth Sutra*, an important text recited daily by Shingon priests, represents the esoteric culmination of Mahayana teachings expressed in the earlier Wisdom sutras. Based on the all-penetrating wisdom of the void, those exoteric teachings showed that the self-nature of all things and beings is intrinsically pure.

The *Wisdom-Truth Sutra* takes this insight further, comparing human desire to the lotus, which though rooted in mud is not defiled. It explains Great Bliss in "seventeen phrases of purity" that list specific aspects of sexual desire as being on the level of the bodhisattva. Explicitly stating the essential purity of human desire, this sutra expresses the Mikkyo affirmation of human life and the phenomenal world. In it is written:

> The purity of the arrow of desire, this is the level of the bodhisattva. . . .
> The purity of love, this is the level of the bodhisattva. . . .[11]

Buddhism has many terms for desire, all conveying a sense that desire is an impure attachment, an impediment to realization. Indeed, much of Buddhism stresses desire as something negative that should be rooted out and destroyed once and for all in order that the self may be extinguished. General Buddhism lists as obstacles to practice the five desires (*goyoku*) for possessions, fame, sex, food, and sleep. These, however, represent basic human needs for security, recognition, love, food, and sleep, and to deny these could be to frustrate the energy of life.

In the esoteric tradition desire is recognized to be an essentially pure energy, a vital aspect of the self. Desires do cause human attachment, since satisfaction of one simply gives rise to another. Desire, however, is one of the basic energies of human existence. In the Mikkyo view the individual's desires are among the energies of the Buddha, and all can be summed up in the desire for enlightenment, attainment of which represents the Great Bliss of true satisfaction.

This view of the individual is illustrated in the Mikkyo mandalas, which portray hundreds of different deities, some static and some dynamic, some smiling and some wrathful. These are individual embodiments of the various energies of passion, desire, emotion, sensation, wisdom, discrimination, and so on, in their enlightened dimensions, and all are different manifestations of the all-embracing activity of Dainichi Nyorai.

The *Gohimitsu Giki* (Ritual Manual of the Five Secrets) details the process by which the energies of deluded beings reveal themselves as pure bodhicitta (*bodaishin,* the mind of highest enlightenment), explaining that the seed of wisdom is to be found in delusion. This text describes Kōngōsatta, the bodhisattva embodying enlightenment, as being accompanied by four attendant bodhisattvas representing desire, sensation, love, and satisfaction. These are not different from the deluded energies present in all beings, yet at the same time they represent aspects of Kōngōsatta's enlightenment. (A similar arrangement of deities is also portrayed in the Kōngō-kai Mandala's True Meaning Assembly, discussed in Chapter 6 under "The Nine Assemblies of the Kōngō-kai Mandala.")

Together known as the Five Secrets (*gohimitsu*), these figures embody deluded human desires revealing their true nature as enlightened wisdom. The first attendant deity, Desire Vajrabodhisattva (Jap., Yoku Kongōbosatsu), represents all human desires and appetites. In terms of esoteric practice this is the desire for enlightenment that results in the awakening of inherent enlightened mind. The second attendant, Sensual Vajrabodhisattva (Jap., Soku Kongōbosatsu), represents all the phenomenal senses, which are the means by which the practitioner can approach enlightenment. Love Vajrabodhisattva (Jap., Ai Kongōbosatsu), symbolizing all lust and desire, represents the unfolding of compassion, which is inseparable from wisdom. Satisfaction Vajrabodhisattva (Jap., Man Kongōbosatsu), also symbolizing pride and arrogance, represents the joy of perfect enlightenment.

Human desires are seen in their suprapersonal aspect as energies directed toward the benefit of all beings: sorrowing over others' suffering and determining to bring them to liberation is desire; approaching them is sensation; having compassion for them is love; and experiencing the joy of their enlightenment is satisfaction. Mikkyo stresses that "delusion is itself enlightenment" (*bonnō soku bodai*), and, in fact, Kongōsatta and his four attendant bodhisattvas together represent the five perfect wisdoms of Buddhahood.

This view of desire is also evident in the esoteric fire ritual. Since ancient times the making of offerings to the gods in order to avert disaster, bring prosperity, and pray for rebirth in heaven has been a vital part of Indian religion. Of such offerings, special reverence was accorded the fire ritual (*goma*), in which offerings were placed on a special hearth to be burned in the sacred fire. The offerings, in the form of flame and smoke, were then carried to the gods in heaven by Agni, the god of fire. This practice reached a level of considerable sophistication, and was thought to bring vast merit and supernatural power.

Mikkyo adopted the *goma* ritual bodily into its system of practice. It retains the earlier, magical aspect of ritual to avert disaster and bring material prosperity, but its central purpose is as explained in the *Commentary on the Dainichi-kyō*:

> The meaning of *goma* is to burn the firewood of delusion with the wisdom flame, consuming it completely.[12]

Special wooden sticks are arranged ritually in an altar hearth and burned in a complex process during which various substances are offered to deities invoked by the practitioner. The sticks and offerings are visualized as the practitioner's own attachments and delusions, which become the fuel that feeds the flame of wisdom. Just as fire cannot exist apart from its fuel, so delusions are not separate from the wisdom of enlightenment and are not to be abhorred. The practitioner enters the relationship of mutual empowerment (*kaji*) with the deities of the ritual, thus energizing his own efforts by the added suprapersonal power of the deities. Through mutual empowerment resulting from the esoteric union of the practitioner with the deities, the energy of delusion is transformed into the all-consuming flame of wisdom.

Viewing Buddha-nature as all-inclusive, Mikkyo expanded the idea of original enlightenment to embrace the whole of human nature, revealing human drives and energies to be aspects of wisdom and compassion. Human sexuality can be a beautiful expression of human nature, and Mikkyo does not value this facet of human existence less than any other. Misunderstanding and misuse of human potentialities, however, is thought to result in suffering. Kūkai wrote in the *Hannya Shingyō Hiken* (Secret Key to the Heart Sutra):

> How pitiful, the children long asleep, how miserable, how painful, the mad, intoxicated people. The suffering mad ones laugh at those who are not drunk. The cruel sleepers mock the awakened. Never asking the King of Medicine for his cure, when will they see Dainichi Nyorai's light?[13]

In the Mikkyo view the "ordinary" person is intrinsically enlightened. The deluded individual, however, fabricates suffering where none really exists. Release from suffering can come by examining the unconscious fabrications of delusion, analyzing them, and going to the source of the self. Kūkai also wrote, in the same text:

> How can endless life and death be transcended? Only by correct meditative mind.[14]

Building on the Hindu concept of the individual self known as the *ātman* (Jap., *jiga*), early Buddhism taught that as long as there is a self, no matter how subtle or fine, it is impossible to escape from the wheel of death and rebirth. Thus, in the doctrine of no-self (*muga*), liberation meant elimination of the ego, which, bound by delusions, creates its own suffering. Mikkyo, however, affirms the individual personality and the desires that motivate it as highly evolved expressions of Buddha-nature—not denying the self but dissolving its limitations to reveal the great self (*daiga*).

Shingon explains that, from the perspective of enlightenment, there is one perfectly realized body of self and universe continuous together, without obstruction. This great self is also called the Buddha-nature ego. In the *Unji-gi* (Meaning of the UN-Syllable), Kūkai wrote: "In no-self gain the great self," and, "The self is the Dharma Realm, the self is the Dharma Body, the self is Dainichi Nyorai, the self is Kongōsatta, the self is all Buddhas."[15]

The exoteric ideal of no-desire (*muyoku*) is brought about by extinguishing the self. Mikkyo sees all desires as manifestations of a root desire for enlightenment, called the great desire (*daiyoku*), which it cultivates by raising egocentric desires into the dimension of enlightenment. Desire used for the benefit of self and others is not egocentric or negative; it is what Buddhism terms the vow of the bodhisattva.

THE MAGIC OF MANTRA

The name Shingon, as we have seen, means "true word," referring to the mantric words and syllables that convey the essence of the Buddha-teaching. Esoteric Buddhism is sometimes called Mantrayana, the Mantra Vehicle, because these "true words" are its foundation. The Sanskrit word *mantra* (*shingon*) originally meant a vessel heaped up with sacred thoughts. Another word for incantation was *vidyā* (Jap., *myō;* hereafter simply vidya), meaning knowledge or learning. Vidya came to refer to occult knowledge, and a compound word meaning knowledge-holder referred to a sorcerer or magician. Early Theravada texts in Pali refer to mantra as *paritta,* meaning protection, that being the first Buddhist use of mantra. The term *dharani,* literally meaning all-holding, derives from an ancient word used for the practice of controlling the senses and concentrating the mind. The word first used in Buddhism for this kind of incantation was *mantra,* and the term *dharani* was not employed until the appearance of Mahayana. Shingon uses the general term *mantra* to refer to all types of esoteric incantation.

Use of mantras flourished in all schools of Buddhism, and even in the austere Theravada, priests gathered before stupas, bodhi trees, or Buddha-images to perform offerings and recite mantras in unison for such purposes as bringing rain. The early *Matōga-kyō,* translated into Chinese in the third century, tells the story of how a young woman, having fallen in love with Shakyamuni's disciple Ānanda, had her mother recite vidyas in a magical ritual to draw Ānanda to their house, where she intended to bind him in the coils of love. Ānanda's plight, however, was known to the Buddha, who in turn recited vidyas to rescue his disciple from this worldly attachment.

Mahayana incorporated the vidyas which early Buddhism had taken from preexisting practices primarily concerned with protection from misfortune. These it used together with the dominant Mahayana form of mantra, the dharani, employed as an aid to concentrate the mind in contemplation. With the development of many new Buddhas and bodhisattvas in Mahayana, the belief grew that invoking the name of a particular deity could bring its aid. The *Lotus Sutra,* for example, teaches the practice of calling on Kannon as a way to avert disaster, and Wisdom sutras give corresponding practices. The *Kanmuryōju-kyō,* translated into Chinese in the fifth century, teaches invocation of Amida as a way to attain rebirth in the Pure Land.

Exoteric dharani invocation was meant to lead to contemplative states of mind by concentrating the meditator's mind—through long, continuous recitation—on the deity being invoked. Some esoteric recitation also consists of calling on particular deities by name, and functions similarly to concentrate the mind without necessarily involving any contemplation of the mantric syllables' meaning. The literal sense of many mantras and dharanis has in any case been long forgotten (or in some cases had never existed), repeated recitation alone being considered to have the desired effect.

In a development of this type of practice, Mahayana meditators began to use dharanis as abbreviated expressions of certain teachings, or as core symbols for regulating the mind in meditation. Recitation of symbolic dharanis in this way was intended both to increase concentration and to clarify understanding of the teachings (as well as improve retention in memory). Then, in an important transition toward esoteric practice, dharanis became not just a means to concentrate the mind but objects of internal visualization symbolizing Buddha-truth. Originating in this kind of Mahayana dharani recitation, esoteric mantra practice had the aims of uniting the self and the deity, experiencing wisdom, and manifesting the universal self in the particular practitioner. In *The True Meaning of the Voiced Syllable,* Kūkai wrote:

By performing empowerment with the Buddha, the way will be pointed out for [living beings'] return. If the way to return is not founded on this teaching, it will not be established. If the vitality of this teaching is not in the voiced syllable, it will not be accomplished. By reciting the voiced syllables with clear understanding, one manifests the truth.[16]

In the general exoteric understanding, mantras and dharanis remained simply tools useful in attaining meditative states of mind. Although they had long been an integral part of Buddhism, they were not seen as a full embodiment of Buddha-truth. The esoteric tradition, however, stressed that mantras were the living, concentrated essence of the Buddhist teachings. Mikkyo treats mantras as embodiments of Truth, affirming that mantras themselves are the universal Buddha. The *Commentary on the Dainichi-kyō* says:

> The voiced syllables themselves are the empowerment bodies of the Buddhas, and these empowerment bodies become all bodies in all places, so that there is no place they are not.[17]

Esoteric mantra practice, therefore, more than simple voiced recitation, focuses rather on contemplation within the mind. Characteristic of this practice is contemplation of the written form, the sound, and the inner meaning of a mantra, by which the mantra reveals the image, the voice, and the mind of the deity. Although their form often resembles that of earlier magical incantations, in Mikkyo their content and use differ in that esoteric mantras are considered to embody the actuality of enlightenment. In the *Commentary on the Dainichi-kyō* is written:

> The fire ritual, offering rituals, and so on are all held in common from the Vedas. The reason that only the Mantra Gate fulfills the secret is that [ritual is performed] by empowerment with the truth. If mantras are recited only in one's mouth, without contemplation of their meaning, then only their worldly effect can be accomplished—but the adamantine body-nature cannot.[18]

As embodiments of enlightenment, mantras represent all-pervading Truth, present in all things. It should not be surprising to find, therefore, that Mikkyo mantra practice can have a twofold purpose. On the one hand, esoteric mantras are directed toward supramundane realization, but on the other hand, reflecting their origin in magical practice, they can also be directed toward immediate material benefit. The esoteric practitioner employs mantras to unite with the universe, and so to function as the great self, which, however, is not separate from the phenomenal world. Esoteric ritual, therefore, may also concern itself with the fulfillment of proper worldly needs.

Since some Mikkyo practices are directed to the fulfillment of material needs, the mantras and dharanis employed in them may be misunderstood as mere magical incantations. Although esoteric practice may also result in apparently occult phenomena, Mikkyo practices should not be equated with occultism. In explaining the nature of Shingon, Kūkai stated that it was the central teaching of all Buddhism; that the teachings were for protecting the nation and the world; that the practices were for real benefit in this life by averting misfortune and inviting happiness and good fortune; and, as the ultimate extension of this, that the teachings could result in becoming a Buddha in the present body (*sokushin jōbutsu*).

As this suggests, Mikkyo, like most religious systems, does perform rituals of prayer for immediate secular benefit—to cure illness, to bring good fortune, to drive away misfortune, and so on. A term often used for this kind of Mikkyo ritual is *kaji kitō*. *Kitō* means prayer, and *kaji* refers to mutual empowerment with the deity, without which Mikkyo prayer is not thought to be effective. One risk observed in such ritual is that the practitioner may become attached to worldly things or even power for its own sake. Efforts to gain this type of benefit are, therefore, considered with great care.

Exoteric Buddhist—and pre-Buddhist—magical ritual by which the adept would take on a deity's power through mantric techniques was adapted by Mikkyo. Most esoteric rituals are classified even today as being for the purpose of averting disaster, or inviting blessings, or vanquishing a foe; but this is the superficial format of ritual as it was adopted into esoteric Buddhism, and these are but symbolic names for what is actually of spiritual, not secular, meaning. By employing well-established, traditional three-secrets techniques, the Mikkyo practitioner "becomes" the deity, and the power thus "gained" is the power of realization. Mantras are employed by the solitary practitioner as an essential part of three-secrets practice for attaining immediate Buddhahood, therefore, but they are also used in large-scale Mikkyo rituals involving dozens of priests on behalf of the nation and the entire world.

In the esoteric view, mantras are "true words" that convey the experience of mystical union. Since that experience transcends all dualities, ordinary language, based on dualism, cannot express it, any more than purely material elements of earth, water, fire, wind, and air alone could express the reality of the Dharma Body. Mikkyo raised mantric language to a symbolic level, in the same way that it placed the six exoteric elements in a different dimension of meaning, and set it within the systematic framework of three-secrets practice.

Where the early, Vedic type of mantra had, like ordinary prayer, communicated the worshiper's thoughts and wishes to a deity, esoteric mantras are rather a means of internal revelation. In one kind of esoteric mantric practice, for example, the practitioner visualizes the energy of the Buddha entering him in the form of a mantra. Taking this energy into his entire body-mind and making it his own, the practitioner then returns it to the Buddha, and so on in a cyclic process. The esoteric practitioner seeks to join his individual activity with the deity's suprapersonal activity, and so realize essential oneness with the deity.

The mantra operates by its symbolic content, so that its esoteric function is not defined by its length or etymology. It is likely, in fact, that the original, literal meaning of many mantras was lost because they were transcriptions into Sanskrit from earlier languages. In the mantric dimension, a single syllable can represent the totality of meanings that exists as the background to any single meaning. As described earlier, the symbolic elements, shapes, and colors in the esoteric tradition came to signify aspects of the universal Dharma Body. This process began with the esoteric development of the mantric syllable.

Most if not all mantras were probably first used in their original, literal meaning, but long use within the Buddhist tradition showed their effectiveness as symbols on the mystical level. Through meditative experience, certain words and letters were made into mantras symbolizing all Buddhist teachings. Syllables were said to take on transcendent meaning and become mantras by being "empowered," so that they could communicate the esoteric experience. The *Dainichi-kyō* says:

> Why is this the way of mantra? It is said that the written words and letters are empowered. . . .[19]

Buddhism most often uses Sanskrit for this purpose because that was the language of the land where Shakyamuni Buddha taught. Mantras are not, however, understood as deriving their value from being written in Sanskrit (or in Chinese characters as phonetic transcriptions of Sanskrit). In Mikkyo, mantras are the speech of the Dharma Body, and, from this viewpoint, all things are mantras. Thus, in *The True Meaning of the Voiced Syllable,* Kūkai wrote:

> The teaching of the Buddha is always by syllables. The syllables exist in the six objects of sense perception which are their body. The root of the six objects of sense perception is the three secrets of the Dharma Buddha. The three secrets of equality [of nondiscriminating union] fill the Dharma Realm and are eternal. The five wisdoms [of enlightened discrimination] . . . exist without imperfection in all things.[20]

THE ORIGINALLY UNBORN

As shown earlier, Mikkyo embodies the macrocosmic universe in the single universal A-syllable. This same syllable is the first syllable of the Sanskrit words *ādi* (origin) and *anutpāda* (unborn), which combine to form the word *ādyanutpāda,* meaning "originally unborn" (*honpushō*). Mikkyo thus employs the A-syllable to symbolize the originally unborn nature of the universe. In explaining the A-syllable of the originally unborn, Kakuban analyzed it as having both negative aspects (*shajō*) that deny phenomenal nature, and affirmative aspects (*hyōtoku*) that manifest the power of the phenomenal. About the negative expression, he wrote in the *Aji Mondō* (Questions and Answers on the A-Syllable):

> The dark, stained things that are created and deluded [*ui uro*] are originally like this. Their self-nature void and nothing, they are ultimately unborn.[21]

In contrast, Kakuban assigned to the affirmative expression such meanings as: knowing one's mind as it truly is, the originally enlightened nature of all beings, the realm of the single truth, the Middle Way, the meditative mind, the essential purity of self-nature. In the same context, Kakuban also analyzed the phrase "originally unborn," pointing out various meanings of *originally* (*hon*), *un* (*fu*), and *born* (*shō*). These three elements of the phrase "originally unborn" are assigned, respectively, the meanings of: Dharma Body, the Buddha's historical body, and the Buddha's many transformations; the secrets of body, speech, and mind; and form, essence, and function.

The universe is the full development of the meanings condensed in the A-syllable, which, as the essential "voice" of all things, also embodies the original life-energy penetrating all things. In the *Dainichi-kyō* is written, "The A-syllable is the first life."[22] Explaining this passage, the *Commentary on the Dainichi-kyō* says:

> This means that the A-syllable is the first life-root. Since it gives life to all syllables, it is called life. If there were no A-syllable, no other syllables could be born. Therefore it is the first life. This phrase well embraces these meanings. By contemplating this syllable, one encompasses all things, internal and external.[23]

The early esoteric *Shugokokkai-shu Darani-kyō* (Nation-Protecting Lord Dharani Sutra) explains the "not coming, not leaving, not going, not dwelling, no original nature, no root origin, no teaching, no end, no birth, no going out, no searching, no obstruction . . ." etc., of the universe and all things in terms of the hundred significances of the A-syllable. It also says, "The A-syllable gate is infinite and all-pervading and cannot be exhausted."[24] Since the mysterious realm of the originally unborn is ungraspable, Mikkyo speaks of the ungraspable A-syllable of the originally unborn. Its true import is in direct experience of the macrocosmic reality pervading all things.

This doctrine of the originally unborn indicates that the individual body-mind is one with the very basis of all existence. The A-syllable in Mikkyo thus embodies an affirmative truth limited neither to phenomenal form nor to philosophical abstraction, joining the absolute and the relative. As Kūkai explains in the *Unji-gi* (The Meaning of the UN-Syllable):

> The meaning of unborn is that it is the realm of the one reality, in other words it is the Middle Way.[25]

THE SUPRAHISTORICAL NATURE OF
THE ESOTERIC SUTRAS

The primary textual sources for the teachings of Shingon Buddhism are the *Dainichi-kyō* and *Kongōchō-gyō*. These sutras, with their companion bodies of written and oral commentary, represent two traditional lineages of esoteric doctrine and ritual practice. The long evolution of these Mikkyo lineages can be traced to some extent, and with difficulty, in the many miscellaneous category esoteric sutras written up to the middle period of esoteric Buddhism in India. Such earlier texts are also valued parts of the Shingon canon. The two fundamental sutras, however, were the first systematic presentation of esoteric ritual and doctrine combined with Mahayana philosophy.

The *Dainichi-kyō* and *Kongōchō-gyō* contain what Shingon knows as the pure category Mikkyo teachings. Developing separately under the influence of the two major streams of Mahayana thought, the Void and Consciousness-Only schools, the two sutras present different approaches to the all-embracing wisdom and enlightenment personified in Dainichi Nyorai. These approaches are depicted in symbolic form in the two major mandalas, the Tai-zō and Kongō-kai, which are based on the teachings of the two Mikkyo lineages. Shingon considers these approaches to be independent yet nondual, and the practitioner seeks to unite these two syntheses of Buddhist wisdom in a further synthesis within the self.

Buddhist sutras ordinarily have an introductory section (*jobun*), an argument (*shōjūbun*), and an ending (*rutsūbun*). Since a sutra reveals its central theme from beginning to end, there is no formal conclusion, the *rutsūbun* conveying instead a prayer that the merit and power of the sutra will benefit all beings. The introductory section has two parts. The first contains the five fulfillments (*go-jōju*), common to all sutras, while the second relates to the particular sutra.

The five fulfillments signify that the sutra meets the five requirements of verity, time, master, place, and audience. Sutras ordinarily begin with the phrase "thus have I heard" (in Shingon pronounced *nyoze gamon*), signifying that the words to follow are not the personal opinion of the writer but the teaching of the Buddha. This fulfills the first requirement, verity.

The next of the fulfillments states that the sutra was preached "at one time." Although the specific date is not given, this is meant to indicate that the teaching took place on a certain day during the life of the Buddha. The third fulfillment names the master of the particular teaching, which in early Buddhism is always Shakyamuni Buddha. The fourth, fulfillment of place, states where the teaching was given, naming the geographical location in India. The fifth fulfillment names the Buddha's audience at that place and time—for instance, Ānanda, Mahākāśyapa, or Maudgalyāyana, who were among the Buddha's known disciples.

The first Buddhist council was held not long after Shakyamuni Buddha's death. Some five hundred of his disciples, including Ānanda and Mahākāśyapa, in order to preserve and transmit his teachings, are said to have collated their recollections of the Buddha's words. The result was the first sutras. Several such councils took place over the succeeding centuries, up to the early centuries C.E. Sutra writers continued using the phrase "thus have I heard" hundreds of years after Shakyamuni's death to show that their texts represent authentic teachings.

It was apparent when such later exoteric sutras were being compiled that what had at first been intended as literal records of Shakyamuni's words had taken on a suprahistorical character. In the course of centuries, persons and places named in the sutras naturally came to lose their association with historical individuals and locations. No longer confined within the historical chronology of past, present, and future (the "three times" spoken of in Buddhism), the sutras took on a mythical cast. With the esoteric sutras, in which the central Buddha becomes the universal Dainichi Nyorai rather than the historical Shakyamuni, the suprahistorical aspect predominates. This is clear in the five fulfillments in the *Dainichi-kyō:*

> Thus have I heard: At one time, the Buddha was dwelling in compassion in the great and vast Palace of the Vajra-Dharma Realm, with all the Vajra Wielders, every one, assembled together around him. Born out of the Buddha's playful transformations of faith and understanding, the precious lord of the great towering pavilion rose boundlessly high in their center, and the various precious lords of great mystery arrayed themselves gorgeously, seating their bodhisattva bodies in the lion posture. Their Vajra-names were . . . [here are named nineteen Vajra Wielders and four bodhisattvas].
>
> On a day of the Buddha transcending the three times, arising out of compassion, expressed equally in body, speech, and mind, this Dharma Gate [was given] . . . Dainichi Nyorai is not born out of body, or speech, or mind, and his arising and extinguishing is not in any place or time.[26]

What this passage describes is not any historical person or place, but rather an extraordinary mythical realm. The symbolic focus of Mikkyo is a universal being transcending the limits of time and space. Thus the *Dainichi-kyō* states that its teaching was expounded "on a day of the Buddha transcending the three times"—in other words, not limited to any conceivable phenomenal time.

Regarding the location of this teaching, the *Commentary on the Dainichi-kyō* says:

> It is called the great and vast Palace of the Vajra-Dharma Realm. It is called great because it is without limit, and called vast because it is immeasurable. Vajra means true wisdom. It is beyond all language and thought. Truly, it

does not depend on place. Wherever the Buddha is, he cannot but be in this palace. It is beyond the three worlds and yet not outside them.[27]

THE DAINICHI-KYŌ

The full title of this sutra is *Dai Birushana Jōbutsu Jinpen Kaji-kyō,* but it is ordinarily called simply the *Dainichi-kyō.* Although the time and place of its composition have not been definitely identified, it was probably written in the mid-seventh century in western or central India. The original Sanskrit text did not survive (although a fragment of a *Dainichi-kyō* in Sanskrit was found in Java), so the sutra exists today only in Chinese and Tibetan translations. The Chinese version was translated ca. 724–725 by Shubhakarasimha in collaboration with I-hsing. The Tibetan version, translated in the early ninth century by Śīlendrabodhi and dPal-brtegs, seems to have been based on a later, revised Sanskrit text.

Numerous commentaries on the *Dainichi-kyō* have been written. The most important of these for Shingon is the twenty-volume *Commentary on the Dainichi-kyō,* written by I-hsing based on explanations made by Shubhakarasimha. The fourteen-volume *Dainichi-kyō Gishaku* (Explanation of the Meaning of the Dainichi-kyō) is an edited version of the *Commentary* begun by I-hsing but finished by others. This text, very close in content to the *Commentary,* is particularly valued by Tendai Mikkyo. There are also, among others, Tibetan versions of a commentary by the eighth-century Indian master Buddhaguhya (Jap., Kakumitsu), and the *Dainichi-kyō Kaidai* (Interpretation of the Dainichi-kyō) by Kūkai. Study of this sutra in Shingon has tended to focus more on such commentaries than on the sutra itself.

The *Dainichi-kyō* is said to exist in various forms. Kūkai said that one of these was the eternal natural Dharma, the "sutra" comprising the universe and all phenomena. Another form, known as the "vast text," was traditionally held to have had 100,000 verses in 300 volumes. The abridged text, which condensed this vast work into 3,000 verses in 7 volumes, has traditionally been considered to be the basis for the present Chinese version.

The Chinese *Dainichi-kyō* has six volumes in thirty-one sections (*hon*) comprising the main substance of the sutra, and a seventh volume in five sections explaining details of ritual practice. A priest named Wu-hsing (Jap., Mugyō, 630–?), who travelled from China to India in search of Buddhist learning, studied at Nalanda. Gathering together a number of sutras, he began the journey back to China, but died en route in northern India. Wu-hsing's collection of Sanskrit sutras was sent on to Ch'ang-an, and in it were the first six volumes of the *Dainichi-kyō.* These Shubhakarasimha later translated into Chinese together with the seventh volume which he had himself brought from India.

The sutra's first section, known as the *Jūshin-bon,* is in the format of the Buddha Dainichi replying to the questions of the Vajra-Wielding Lord of Secrets (another name for Kongōsatta) as to how the Wisdom of All-Wisdom (*issai chichi*) can be attained. The comprehensive and many-faceted answers are summarized in an important formula known as the Dharma Gate of the Three Phrases (*sanku no hōmon*): "Enlightened mind is the cause, great compassion is the root, and skillful means are the ultimate."[28]

Enlightenment, all-penetrating in nature, is not separate from the individual mind, and Buddha-wisdom is to be gained within one's own mind. The Wisdom of All-Wisdom, therefore, is succinctly propounded in the core phrase "knowing one's mind as it truly is" (*nyojitsu chijishin*). Not only the *Dainichi-kyō*, but all Buddhist sutras could be said to deal, in effect, with this single point. The *Commentary on the Dainichi-kyō* describes the state of the ordinary person who, not knowing himself for what he is, binds himself with a rope of his own creation:

> Because they do not truly know themselves, they are ignorant. Fallen into ignorance, they grasp at form . . . and thus experience various sufferings and pleasures. With as little reason as the silkworm spinning its cocoon, they themselves spin out the threads with which they bind themselves. They then experience the same agony of being boiled [as the silkworm when it is boiled in its cocoon in order to extract the thread].[29]

The sutra also enumerates various levels of mind in evolution toward this self-knowledge. Concerning errors easily fallen into on the way to knowing the self, the *Commentary* says:

> One type of serious mistake is to speak without understanding one's own mind and say, "I, when I look at my true self, see that its color is blue, although other people cannot see this." Or say, "It is truly yellow" or "truly red" . . . Or say, "I, when I look at my true self, see that it is extremely long," or "extremely short" . . . saying that only the one thing is true while all the others are delusions. All these truths, however, arise from causation, and have no self-existence.[30]

In succeeding sections the sutra gives detailed instructions on ritual practice. The second section, the *Guen-bon,* for example, describes the complicated procedure for constructing a mandala platform, where the Mikkyō master initiates his disciple. The qualifications of master and disciple are also described. Later sections relate other forms of the mandala, and describe basic Mikkyo practices such as the initiation ritual, the fire ritual (*goma*), and the uses of mudras and mantras. Among other essential visualization and recitation practices found in this sutra are the Five-Syllable Sublime-Body Visualization (*goji gonshinkan*), in which the five syllables of the five elements are visualized within the practitioner. The four esoteric precepts are given in the sutra's eighteenth section, the *Juhōben Gakusho-bon.* The *Dainichi-kyō* is the original textual source for the Tai-zō Mandala, and this mandala, in its evolved form today, is seen as a concrete expression of the sutra's full teaching.

The Kongōchō-gyō

The second fundamental sutra of Shingon, after the *Dainichi-kyō,* is the *Kongōchō-gyō. Kongō* (vajra), meaning adamantine and imperishable, describes the power and virtue of Dainichi Nyorai. *Chō,* meaning peak, summit, or crown of the head, refers to Dainichi Nyorai's unsurpassed wisdom. The complicated history of this sutra is still not entirely clear, but the first in the group of related texts ordinarily referred to under this title by Shingon was probably written in the latter half of the seventh century in South India. Further texts in this lineage continued to be written during the later period of Indian esoteric Buddhism.

Shingon traditionally considered the *Kongōchō-gyō* to have consisted of eighteen parts (*jūhatte,* "eighteen assemblies") in 100,000 verses, compiled from teachings given at eighteen different places. The eighteen parts were thus considered to comprise the complete sutra, and Amoghavajra wrote a text called the *Kongōchō-gyō Yuga Jūhatte Shiiki* (Indication of the Basis of the Eighteen Assemblies of the Kongōchō-gyō), which is said to be an outline of the complete sutra he received in Ceylon.

This outline, however, does not describe more than the first part of the complete sutra in detail, nor does that complete sutra exist in the Shingon canon, though there are shorter, related sutras. The earlier of these were translated by Vajrabodhi and Amoghavajra. According to early accounts, the entire text was not translated, either because portions of it were lost in a storm during Vajrabodhi's sea journey to China, or because neither he nor Amoghavajra lived long enough to complete the translation.

Among the actual texts Shingon knows under the title of the *Kongōchō-gyō* is the sutra that Amoghavajra did translate. This, in the traditional view, is a portion of the first part of the full eighteen-part sutra. The Chinese translation done by Amoghavajra in 753 is, however, a complete sutra in itself, in three volumes, called the *Kongō-chō Issai-nyorai Shinjitsu-shō Daijō Genshō Dai Kyō-ō-kyō.* Closely related to this is the *Kongō-chō Yuga Chū Ryaku-shutsu Nenju-kyō,* in four volumes, translated by Vajrabodhi in 723. It covers much the same material as the above, though in somewhat less organized form.

Some texts of the later period of Indian esoteric Buddhism were translated in China by Shih-hu in the early eleventh century. One of these was the thirty-volume *Issai Nyorai Shinjitsu-shō Daijō Genshō Sammai Dai Kyō-ō-kyō,* which, according to the traditional explanation, is the full text of the first part of the complete eighteen-part sutra. Two other sutras translated around this time are similarly considered to be the sixth and fifteenth parts of the complete *Kongōchō-gyō.* Sanskrit and Tibetan versions of these later texts also exist, but there is doubt as to whether they could have been written as early as the mid-eighth century, when Amoghavajra described the *Kongōchō-gyō* in eighteen parts. Many questions concerning this group of sutras remain to be resolved.

Shingon refers to these various sutras and their many related ritual texts in general as belonging to the *Kongōchō-gyō,* a title that also refers specifically to Amoghavajra's three-volume *Kongō-chō Issai-nyorai Shinjitsu-shō Daijō Genshō Dai Kyō-ō-kyō.* Several commentaries on this assembly of sutras have been written, but they do not bear the same relation to the originals as the *Commentary on the Dainichi-kyō* does to that sutra. In general, Shingon has emphasized textual study of the *Dainichi-kyō* more than of the *Kongōchō-gyō.*

The *Kongōchō-gyō* presents Dainichi Nyorai in the midst of an assembly of eight vajra-wielding deities, headed by Kongōsatta. In this setting, he answers Shakyamuni's questions as to how to realize enlightenment and become a Buddha. The meditation practice given for doing so is the Five-Aspect Attainment-Body Visualization (*gosō jōshinkan*). Embodying the enlightenment attained by this practice is the Kongō-kai Mandala. The *Kongōchō-gyō* explains various forms of this mandala, as well as other important elements of Mikkyo ritual practice.

THE DHARMA LINEAGE AND THE LEGEND OF THE IRON TOWER

As described above, early exoteric sutras place the Buddha in an actual geographical location and name his audience. The *Dainichi-kyō,* according to Mikkyo, originated through the Buddha's compassionate empowerment (*kaji*) in a dimension transcending time and space. Nevertheless, this sutra begins with the usual formula "thus have I heard."

In his *Interpretation of the Dainichi-kyō,* Kūkai writes that the "I" in this formula has four meanings: Ānanda, Kongōsatta, Dainichi Nyorai, and the enlightened universe. Ānanda, who heard more of Shakyamuni's teachings than anyone else, is most often the "I" of the exoteric sutras. Where Ānanda was a historical individual, the last three are the "I" of the esoteric sutras and are suprahistorical.

The relationship between human beings and Dainichi Nyorai is personified in the bodhisattva Kongōsatta. Considered to be a particular manifestation of Dainichi Nyorai, Kongōsatta represents the innate enlightenment in all beings, an enlightenment as adamantine and imperishable as the vajra. Representing both enlightened individuals as well as beings on the way to enlightenment, Kongōsatta is an important deity in both the Tai-zō and Kongō-kai Mandalas, where he is depicted in several places in varying forms as the personification of enlightenment in this body.

Where Dainichi Nyorai symbolizes the totality of universal enlightenment,

Kongōsatta, as a particular aspect of that enlightenment, on the one hand represents all unenlightened beings, and on the other hand is the enlightener of unenlightened beings. In other words, Kongōsatta represents both the individual practitioner and the true self which the practitioner is to realize. In esoteric practice, the meditator's mutual empowerment with Kongōsatta, occurring by the compassionate response of the deity, makes enlightenment possible.

Mikkyo sutras often name Kongōsatta as the direct recipient of Dainichi Nyorai's secret teachings. This bodhisattva is, therefore, placed second in the Shingon line of Dharma transmission. The eight great patriarchs Shingon considers to have transmitted the esoteric teachings are: Dainichi Nyorai, Kongōsatta Bodhisattva, Nagarjuna, Nagabodhi, Vajrabodhi, Amoghavajra, Huikuo, and Kūkai.

As the eternal enlightened Mikkyo practitioner, Kongōsatta is not meant to be any particular historical individual, but rather a suprahistorical being embodying all Buddhas and Mikkyo masters who lived before the esoteric Dharma succession became historical. Although Shakyamuni is not specifically named in the Shingon lineage, he is, of course, recognized as a historical Buddha. Shakyamuni and all the recipients of Shakyamuni's esoteric teachings are represented in Kongōsatta.

Of the eight patriarchs, the first historical figure is Nagarjuna. Although accounts of his life conflict, there was undoubtedly an important Buddhist teacher sometime around the second century known by that name. The historical link between Nagarjuna and Nagabodhi is problematical, since either Nagarjuna or Nagabodhi would have had to live several hundred years in order to have direct personal contact with each other. No doubt many individuals were given these same names at different times, and Mikkyo uses the names of Nagarjuna and Nagabodhi with the understanding that they include others whose historical identities are no longer known.

More important for Shingon, however, is not the precise dates and people involved, but rather the continuity of the teachings. The Dharma lineage is carefully maintained, and detailed records of such Dharma transmissions have been kept. Priests receiving initiation as masters in the Shingon line today may, for example, count back through some fifty generations of teachers to the suprahistorical origin in Dainichi Nyorai. For Shingon, this involves no contradiction, since the timeless experience of realization is itself considered to be Dainichi Nyorai's Dharma transmission. In the higher esoteric initiations the master ritually enacts the role of Dainichi and the disciple that of Kongōsatta.

The ancient legend of the Iron Tower of South India (*nanten tettō*) describes the first transmission to Nagarjuna of the esoteric teachings recorded in the *Dainichi-kyō* and *Kongōchō-gyō*. The *Kongōchō-gyō Giketsu* (Analysis of the Kongōchō-gyō), Vajrabodhi's oral commentary recorded by Amoghavajra, tells the story as follows:

For several hundreds of years after the Buddha's death, there was an iron tower in southern India that had never been opened. When Buddhism was dying out in central India, a great master came to the tower. Grieving, he walked around the tower scattering white poppy seeds and praying. He continued in this way for seven days, and at last the door opened. When he entered, bright lights were shining, the air was filled with the fragrance of incense, flowers filled the tower, and he could hear voices singing in praise of the Buddha. Then the secret Buddha appeared before him and entrusted him with the ultimate esoteric teaching. This was the *Kongōchō-gyō*.[31]

The teaching Nagarjuna received in the legendary Iron Tower and disseminated to his successors is the core experience of the esoteric tradition. The various Mikkyo sutras represent the subsequent attempts to communicate what Nagarjuna realized through union with Kongōsatta. Thus, in the *Kyō-ō-kyō Kaidai* (Interpretation of the King-of-Teachings Sutra), a commentary on the *Kongōchō-gyō*, Kūkai wrote:

> This sutra [the *Kongōchō-gyō*] and the *Dainichi-kyō* are together the essence of the Tathagata's Secret Repository which Nagarjuna Bodhisattva discovered in the Iron Tower of South India.[32]

The place where Nagarjuna first received this teaching is the enlightened universe, in which nothing exists that is not Buddha. Thus the Iron Tower represents realization of the Buddha-self. Kūkai designed a great pagoda, modelled after the Iron Tower, later constructed on Kōya-san as a physical representation of the essential Mikkyo experience.

Accounts of Nagarjuna's life indicate that he held all the secular arts and sciences in high esteem as necessary complements to the Buddhist teachings. It appears, too, that he may have erected an actual tower where rituals were performed before Buddha-images; if so, this tower may have been a historical basis for the legendary Iron Tower. The visualization and mantric practices attributed to him represent, for Mikkyo, the earliest identifiable esoteric Buddhist practices, and for this work Nagarjuna is named as the first historical individual in the Shingon lineage. In the *Gyokuin-shō* (Summary of the Precious Mudra), a text explaining the esoteric Dharma lineage, the priest Gōhō (1306–1362) wrote:

> The Iron Tower of South India expresses the firm innate enlightenment of Nagarjuna Bodhisattva. It is not a material tower such as would arise from external causes. Thus the great Commentary explains that it is the Buddha Tower arising from Mind, and the great patriarch [Kūkai] explains that it was erected not by human power but by the divine power of the Buddha. . . .
>
> With this, the enlightened mind that unfolds through practice is awakened, the three delusions are suddenly cut through, and innate enlightenment is revealed, manifesting the Dharma Body of Truth and Wisdom

with which one's mind is inherently endowed. This is called revealing the Iron Tower.

Striking the gate with seven white poppy seeds means that the enlightened mind [*bodaishin*] of practice is first awakened. The white poppy seeds are the Wish-fulfilling Jewel [*nyoi hōshu*], just as the enlightened mind of practice that awakens in the self is the Wish-fulfilling Jewel. The seven seeds are the seven esoteric attainments. They unite just as seven minute particles combine to form a single subtle particle. The Iron Tower is the innate enlightened mind with which the self is endowed. Thus the enlightened mind of practice is used to break open the innate enlightened mind.

The door of the tower is the three levels of delusion. To open the door means to realize that the three delusions are themselves the three Buddha-realms.

The two great sutras within the tower are the two heart-minds, the mind [*shin*] and the corporeal heart [*karita shin*]. These are the form and mind, the Truth and Wisdom, with which the self is endowed.[33]

Shingon symbolizes the totality of the universe in the form of the *tō* (also *sotoba, tōba,* translated here as pagoda or tower). One of the root meanings of this word in Sanskrit is assemblage or accumulation, and the symbolic tower represents the totality of all things, beings, and activities of past, present, and future. The five-storied tower (the five stories related to the elements, syllables, and so on) therefore symbolizes the universal form of Dainichi Nyorai. The thirty-volume version of the *Kongōchō-gyō* translated by Shih-hu explains the symbolic importance of the Iron Tower of South India in the Mikkyo tradition:

Looking again at the symbol of the tower with the eye of the mind, strive to realize that it is the real form of the self, an adamantine, imperishable world.[34]

FOUR

The Ten Levels of Mind

THE EIGHT LEVELS OF CONSCIOUSNESS

The development of the exoteric Buddhist teaching of Consciousness-Only (*yuishiki*), which minutely analyzed certain levels of the human mind, culminated in the work of the Indian philosophers Asaṅga (Jap., Mujaku) and Vasubandhu (Jap., Seshin) in the fourth and fifth centuries. These Mahayana philosophers treated the inner workings of the human unconscious in terms of a "storehouse consciousness." This was the eighth level of consciousness described by Buddhism.

The first five levels of consciousness were the senses of sight, hearing, smell, taste, and touch. The sixth level was simply consciousness (*shiki*), or awareness. These were described in terms of the six "roots," or faculties, of eyes, ears, nose, tongue, body, and thought, each faculty associated with its "realm," or object, of form, sound, scent, taste, sensation, and things, respectively. The functions that apprehended these objects were seeing, hearing, smelling, tasting, touching, and knowing, while what governed these functions were the consciousnesses of eye, ear, nose, tongue, body, and consciousness itself. The sixth consciousness, which perceives objects by means of the first five, included in itself the preceding five senses.

The developing Mahayana philosophy found beyond these a seventh level, called the *mana-shiki,* awareness of the individual self. Deeper still was the eighth level, the storehouse consciousness (*araya-shiki*), which lay submerged beneath ordinary consciousness. The doctrine of this eighth level is included among the important developments of Mahayana Buddhism.

Araya-shiki, often translated as storehouse consciousness, refers to the underlying substratum of all mind. Beneath individual awareness, this level of mind records the past and gives the individual a foundation for existing in the present and into the future. Here, also, are held the seeds that develop into all things. The repository of the reaction of the mind to all phenomena, the storehouse consciousness came to be seen as the source of all phenomena as well.

According to the Consciousness-Only teaching, the seventh level of consciousness holding the concept of the self comes into being through the accumulation (in the storehouse consciousness) of unenlightened experience gathered on the sixth level of consciousness. One's body feels cold on a winter day, for example, by operation on the first five levels of the senses. The sixth level is that which is aware that it is cold. The seventh level makes a judgment on the coldness, saying, for example, that it cannot stand the cold and must get warm. In this view, the seventh level of consciousness is attached to limiting conceptions and prejudices. It is only on the eighth level, out of which all the preceding arise, that the essential unreality of the judgment-making consciousness of the self can be understood.

From this eighth level, everything that exists (or seems to exist)—both matter and mind—is seen as none other than a temporary manifestation of the activity of consciousness. Without consciousness, nothing can exist. What may be seen as material phenomena existing outside the self are simply the transformations of mind, which tend to be misunderstood as separating self and other. These transformations are rooted in the storehouse consciousness, which stores the seeds of all potential manifestations as well as individual reactions to phenomena, which create in turn the seeds of new potentialities.

The Sanskrit term for consciousness is the compound word *vijñāna*, made of the prefix *vi*, usually translated as divide or analyze, and the element *jñāna*, which means to know. The Consciousness-Only teachings often employ a causative form of this word meaning to inform or to manifest, because the mind at one level creates what the mind at another level perceives. The self at this level of consciousness is self-involved, bound to itself. Buddhist teachings compare the person who suffers in a world of his own fabrication to "an ignorant artist who is terrified by the picture of a demon he himself drew."[1]

The complex philosophy of Consciousness-Only ultimately reached the conclusion that only consciousness exists—no individual self or matter is real. Nothing remains unchanging, nothing exists that did not come into being because of something else. Everything, therefore, is void of permanent self-existence. The false idea of a real self arises out of the eternal transformations of the storehouse consciousness, and, according to Consciousness-Only teaching, enlightenment is attained by realizing this truth.

The teaching of *kū,* usually translated as void or emptiness, reached a similar conclusion. The Mahayana philosophers of the Void school employed this concept to analyze delusion, listing Four Voids, Seven Voids, Eleven Voids, Eighteen Voids, and so on, in ever more minute detail approaching an endless negation of the independent reality of all things. This school of thought denies any formulation, delimitation, or definition of enlightenment—thereby tending, however, to the extreme position of denying all reality and all existence.

The Buddhist doctrine of the three kinds of existence (*sanshō*) offers a basis for understanding the void nature of the individual consciousness. The following metaphor is often used to clarify this doctrine: First, a fool thinks he sees a snake in the dark of the night and is frightened. Second, on the advice of a sen-

91

sible person, the fool looks at the snake and sees that it is only a rope. Third, further examination reveals that even the rope is no more than a temporary condition of hempen fibers.

In the first stage illusory images that arise from various karmic (cause and effect) relationships are thought to be real objects. In the second stage all things that exist are seen as arising from cause and effect. The third stage is perception of reality. The above simple metaphor employs snake, rope, and hemp, all of which can be grasped by the sixth level of consciousness. This teaching shows that although external circumstances, by inducing desires and attachments on a subconscious level, are an indirect cause of suffering, the direct cause lies in the way circumstances are perceived. Buddhism minutely analyzes the ways in which the mind creates illusory images based on deluded attachments. When the true nature of delusion is exposed, layer by layer, then at the same time the wisdom of the void is said to unfold within the mind, making apparent the infinite network of living beings and phenomena of which each individual forms an integral part. This is called contemplating the whole body-mind of the self.

THE NINTH, TENTH, AND INNUMERABLE LEVELS OF CONSCIOUSNESS

Mahayana philosophy continued to refine and evolve its teachings through subjective analysis of the mind at ever deeper levels. Where the storehouse consciousness had at first been considered the deepest, indivisible level of the self, it was even further analyzed into two different aspects: a deluded aspect that clings to its own constructions, and an undeluded aspect of pure consciousness. Although some thinkers kept this pure consciousness within the eighth level, others assigned it to a separate level, the ninth.

The doctrine of the ninth level of consciousness was first elaborated in Hua-yen and T'ien-t'ai teachings. A profound region of mind intrinsically free of attachments and delusions, the ninth level, the *amara-shiki* (also *anmara-shiki*), is sometimes called the unstained consciousness, suchness consciousness, or true consciousness. From the pure ninth level the eighth level is seen as deluded to the extent that it contains a mixture of true and deluded consciousness.

This teaching, however, did not overcome the tendency to treat the "real" world as of secondary importance. The individual mind and body were considered to exist entirely within the eternal storehouse consciousness, only raised to the ninth level. The myriad objects and beings were seen as no more than evanescent transformations of a single mind, the many revealing themselves as an all-inclusive one. Thus the phenomenal universe and individuals born into it were no more than abstractions apart from true reality.

Building on this profound but self-limiting insight, the esoteric teaching penetrated deeper into the mind to find a tenth level of consciousness. This realm of mind is expressed pictorially in works of art, such as mandalas, as a meditative medium for experience of the deepest regions of the self. Seen from this tenth level, each of the nine consciousnesses has its own realm of enlightened reality. Cold is cold, whether enlightened or deluded. Rather than reject the senses, the tenth level focuses instead on their essential purity. The limited individuality of the seventh level is transformed into true self-autonomy, and the desire (*yoku*) of the small, egocentric self reveals itself as the compassionate energy (often called the "vow," *gan*) of the great self. That which benefits the self (*jiri*) is transformed—because the self itself is transformed and enlarged—to become of benefit to others (*rita*). In describing this tenth level of consciousness, Mikkyo made an important step beyond the abstraction of the ninth level to affirm the concrete, living reality of the universe.

This "most secret and profound" consciousness is not a linear extension of the nine levels, as if another step up a ladder, nor does it exist apart from them. Expressing the characteristic Mikkyo synthesis, this view of consciousness raises what is known and experienced in the world into an all-inclusive dimension. It does not reject human experience but rather stresses its validity. In the *Hizō-ki* (Record of the Secret Treasury), Kūkai differentiates between exoteric and esoteric views of mind in these terms:

> Question. Exoteric Buddhism sets forth eight levels of consciousness, but how many does Mikkyo set forth?
> Answer. One, or eight, or nine, or ten, or innumerable levels of consciousness.[2]

Beyond the simple consciousness of self, Mahayana found the deeper storehouse consciousness, which, further analyzed in terms of purity and impurity, resulted in the ninth level. This was so perfectly profound, according to Consciousness-Only teaching, that it could not be deepened further. Beyond it, however, the esoteric teaching postulated a tenth level encompassing all forms and states of consciousness. In *The Meaning of Becoming a Buddha in This Body,* Kūkai wrote:

> In its aspect as the cause [*in,* which leads to enlightenment] it is called consciousness, while in its aspect as the effect [*ka,* the fruit of enlightenment] it is called wisdom.[3]

The innumerable consciousnesses are associated with the deities of the esoteric pantheon, particular consciousnesses being linked to certain aspects of wisdom symbolized by the major deities. Buddhism speaks of transforming the consciousnesses to attain corresponding enlightened wisdom (*tenjiki tokuchi*). In the exoteric view the eight consciousnesses were transformed into four

Buddha-wisdoms. Mikkyo doctrine sees the nine consciousnesses transforming into the five wisdoms (*gochi*) of the tenth level.

The Wisdom of Accomplishing Metamorphosis (*jōsosatchi*) expresses realization of the enlightened nature of the first five levels of consciousness, the senses. This wisdom symbolizes the universal activity that encompasses the activity of all individual things and beings, the numberless manifestations of undivided reality.

The Wisdom of Magical Perception (*myōkanzatchi*) expresses realization of the enlightened nature of the sixth level, consciousness. Penetrating all delusion, this wisdom represents the subtle, enlightened perception that realizes the essential purity of all things and beings as integral parts of the whole.

The Wisdom of Equality (*byōdōshōchi*) expresses realization of the enlightened aspect of the seventh, ego-consciousness. This enlightened wisdom, apart from all discrimination, realizes the equality of the essential nature of all things and beings.

The Great, Perfect Mirror Wisdom (*daienkyōchi*) expresses realization of the enlightened aspect of the storehouse consciousness. Like a mirror, this enlightened wisdom reflects the universal life-energy that informs all things and beings.

The above four wisdoms (*shichi*), based on general Mahayana doctrine, point to the essential unity of all things in the light of single, all-enfolding Dharma-nature. In the *Treatise on the Exoteric and Esoteric Teachings,* Kūkai wrote:

> As to stages of mind, there are ten. These are, first, eye-awareness. Second, ear-awareness. Third, nose-awareness. Fourth, tongue-awareness. Fifth, body-awareness. Sixth, consciousness. Seventh, self-consciousness. Eighth, storehouse consciousness. Ninth, consciousness of the many as one. Tenth, consciousness of the one as one.[4]

The esoteric teachings viewed the above four wisdoms from the perspective of the tenth level, in which the unique, individual reality of every differentiated phenomenon is revealed through the fifth wisdom, the Wisdom of the Nature of the Dharma Realm Body (*hokkai taishōchi*). Expressing the enlightened aspect of the pure ninth consciousness, this fifth wisdom explained the true nature of the all-pervading Dharma body, which exists in and gives existence to all things and beings. The fifth wisdom involves perception of the whole of reality as mysteriously fulfilled in every individual.

Dainichi Nyorai personifies the Wisdom of the Nature of the Dharma Realm Body. The four preceding wisdoms, which describe various aspects of this central reality, are symbolized in the four Buddhas (depicted around Dainichi Nyorai in the mandala) that manifest the central deity's major aspects. The wisdoms represent transformations of consciousness attained by the individual in the process of realizing his true nature. At the same time, however, they also represent the true nature realized by the individual—in other words, the enlightenment of Dainichi Nyorai. The five wisdoms (*gochi*) together symbolize the enlightened perception of reality discriminated in all its separate aspects, but also symbolize (since mind and matter, microcosm and macrocosm, are inseparable) reality as itself comprising enlightenment.

The five wisdoms, therefore, take their place in the symbolic Mikkyo framework together with the elements, the mantric syllables, the major deities, the consciousnesses, and so on. Encompassing all these is the tenth level of consciousness, itself the Wisdom of All-Wisdom. In Mikkyo this is also called knowing one's mind as it truly is.

THE TEN LEVELS OF MIND

Kūkai's Ten Levels of Mind (*jūjūshin*) present a view of enlightened mind in ten aspects or stages (not to be confused with the ten consciousnesses). Although the Ten Levels have been interpreted in many ways, essentially they represent stages through which the esoteric practitioner passes as delusions are penetrated and ever deeper realms of mind revealed. The levels can also be viewed as descriptions of various Buddhist teachings as they were in Kūkai's time. The Ten Levels of Mind are as follows:

1. The Unstable, Goatish Mind (*ishō teiyō-shin*). The unenlightened mind that understands neither good nor evil, cause nor effect. Like a goat filled with lust for sex and food, a person of this mind is driven by instincts.

2. The Foolish, Abstinent Mind (*gudō jisai-shin*). Here, some karmic cause has stirred the individual's inherent Buddha-nature so that he begins to restrain himself. This is the mind that strives to be ethical and moral.

3. The Childlike, Fearless Mind (*yōdō mui-shin*). Wearied with human suffering, the person at this level seeks the peace of dwelling in heaven. This is the mind first awakening to religion. Like a child seeking the comfort of its mother's embrace, unaware that its mother, too, is subject to sickness, old age, and death, the person at this level seeks to believe in an eternally unchanging god or spiritual doctrine.

4. The Mind of Aggregates-Only Without Self (*yuiun muga-shin*). The mind at this level sees the self as impermanent, but still thinks that the five aggregates (form, perception, mental activity, will, and consciousness) have real existence. (The early stage of Buddhism known as the *shōmon-jō*, the "vehicle of one who hears the voice" of Shakyamuni teaching, by which the individual seeks salvation for himself alone, belongs to this level.)

5. The Mind Free of the Seeds of Karmic Causation (*batsu gōinju-shin*). By understanding the process of karmic causation, the person on this level has destroyed the ignorance that is the seed of bad karma. This mind, however, like that of the fourth level, lacks compassion for other beings. (To this

level belongs the teaching of the *engaku,* the self-enlightened person who achieves liberation by understanding causation.)

6. The Compassionate Mahayana Mind (*taen daijō-shin*). At this level of mind, compassion for all living beings wells forth. Although realizing that objects are void, this mind still considers the self-nature of the storehouse consciousness (which recognizes the objects) to be real. (The doctrine of Consciousness-Only belongs here. This and the following levels describe Mahayana Buddhism.)

7. The Mind Awakened to the Unborn (*kakushin fushō-shin*). At this level the individual realizes the void nature of both the objects within the mind and the mind itself (the storehouse consciousness). Such realization alone, however, does not reach beyond negation.

8. The Mind of the Single Way of Truth (*nyojitsu ichidō-shin*). This level of mind understands that the worlds of delusion and enlightenment, the worlds of matter and mind, the human world, and all possible worlds, are contained in a single thought within the individual mind. This is the level of realization that consciousness and its objects form one body, but it does not know that yet other realms transcend it.

9. The Mind of Ultimate No-Self-Nature (*goku mujishō-shin*). In this, the ultimate realm of exoteric understanding, the mind sees that all things interpenetrate, and that all things contain eternal truth. Still, limited by void and nothingness, this mind does not progress beyond negation. It must yet go beyond the cause to the result, enlightenment.

10. The Secret, Sublime Mind (*himitsu shōgon-shin*). The mind on this level breaks through its attachment to void and fully realizes its true nature. In this realm of affirmation, the individual experiences the externally self-existing enlightenment of the universal Buddha. This is the creative mind at the source of all things. It is called sublime because it rises to ultimate Buddha-enlightenment—is "made sublime"—by means of the three macrocosmic activities of body, speech, and mind. It is called "secret" because the three activities (the three secrets) manifest the profound mystery of Buddha-mind. In his *Treatise on the Exoteric and Esoteric Teachings,* Kūkai wrote:

> The names of the secret are manifold and innumerable. What is here called the secret is that which lies in the secret repository within the realm of the ultimate Dharma Body.[5]

The ten levels are not all of the same magnitude, as if a rising staircase of ten equal steps. It may be but a slight step from some levels to the next, as from the sixth to the seventh; but others, like the first and the second, are separated by a vast chasm. Depicted in graph form, the ten levels would not make a straight line climbing upward, a sawtoothed line, or anything, in fact, that can be shown in just two dimensions and one or two directions. A better image may be a solid sphere composed of ten layers in constant motion in all dimensions, changing shape and size but always bound together as a whole.

The ten levels have often been misunderstood as sectarian criticism rather than as descriptions of the various teachings that provided the foundation for Mikkyo's development. All are necessary and valid in their own spheres. Although each stage must be passed through in order to reach the next, the "higher" does not exclude the "lower." A profounder understanding, in fact, shows that the tenth level does not reject but fulfills all the preceding levels, and that each level embodies the potential fulfillment of all others.

In the *Jūjūshin-ron* (Treatise on the Ten Levels of Mind), Kūkai wrote as follows about the relationship of Buddhist teachings and levels of consciousness:

> The two vehicles of the *shōmon* [on the fourth of the ten levels] and the *engaku* [fifth level] know only the sixth consciousness. The two teachings of compassion for other beings [sixth] and of awakening mind [seventh] point only to the eighth consciousness. The single way [eighth level] and the ultimate negation [ninth level] know only the ninth consciousness.
>
> The *Commentary on the Dainichi-kyō* gives innumerable levels of consciousness and innumerable manifestations. To know the truth of this body-mind is to realize the dwelling-place of the secret, sublime mind.[6]

The *Treatise on Mahayana,* an important source for esoteric doctrine, contains many discussions of the tenth level of consciousness. This text adds to the eight consciousnesses two more, making ten in all. The first of these additional two is the Many-in-One Mind Consciousness (*ta-ichi shinshiki*), which sees the essential unity of discriminated (divided) phenomena. The tenth is the One-in-One Mind Consciousness (*ichi-ichi shinshiki*), the fundamental consciousness which sees the uniqueness of individual beings in the light of the undiscriminating (undivided) truth of equality. Innyū (1435–1519), in his *Shakuron Myōmoku,* a commentary on the above treatise, examines the exoteric and esoteric views of consciousness as follows:

> In these [levels of consciousness] are the two meanings of negation and affirmation. Negation is the exoteric teaching. The One-in-One Mind Consciousness is . . . a single consciousness which is both the gate and those who enter therein. The equality of the single essence of all things itself arises from causation, and is thus an affirmation in the esoteric teaching. Here, with the One-in-One Mind Consciousness, the "one" is . . . not one alone, while the all is made one. This is of the profoundest significance. . . .[7]

However the exoteric philosophy of consciousness developed, it continued an objectifying process of finding everything at ever deeper levels within the storehouse consciousness. The esoteric teaching exhausted this storehouse, finding, in a dimension beyond it, the tenth consciousness. The tenth consciousness, however, is not to be realized by penetrating ever deeper in the same direction as the first nine. It does not exist apart from the first nine conscious-nesses, but is seen as bringing them to new life. It is at this level, according to Mikkyo, that the true nature of the self reveals itself.

Buddhism often uses the term equality (*byōdō*) to mean the single, undifferen-tiated universal totality, in which all things are equal. Discrimination (*shabetsu*), on the other hand, allows the uniqueness of every individual being or phe-nomenon as different from all others. The "one" of the One-in-One Mind Consciousness consists not of a one in contrast with many, but of the one which, as the wellspring of the many, embraces all and manifests as the many. This level of consciousness thus unites the truths of equality and of discrimina-tion. It is endowed with and luminously embodied in all things. From the very existence of the Dharma Body, itself its own teaching, the realm of enlighten-ment is seen to unfold.

THE THREE LAYERS OF DELUSION

Esoteric texts often employ the full moon as a metaphor for the pure and per-fect Buddha-nature that is in all beings, while delusions are clouds that hide the moon. The full moon that is revealed when obscuring clouds clear away shines with a marvellously white and soothing light. The *Dainichi-kyō* explains that these clouds (delusions) are in three layers, made up of three types of delusion known in Sanskrit as *kalpa*s (*kō*).

Buddhism ordinarily used this word to mean an extremely long period of time. The boulder *kalpa,* for instance, was explained as the time it would take to wear away to nothing a huge rock, the length of each side being the distance an ox cart can drive in one day, if a heavenly maiden, descending once every hundred years to dance, brushed her garment lightly against the rock. The poppy seed *kalpa* was the length of time it would take to empty completely a great steel enclosure the same size as the above rock, filled with poppy seeds, if a single seed were removed every hundred years. This unit was commonly used to indicate the immense lengths of time involved in attaining Buddhahood. In Mikkyo, however, the penetration of delusion is not linked with time, as the *Commentary on the Dainichi-kyō* explains:

> The Sanskrit word *kalpa* has two meanings. One is a unit of time. The other is delusion. According to the ordinary explanation, it is possible to attain true awakening by going through three *kalpa*s of practice.
>
> In the esoteric explanation, the yogic practice that transcends the first such *kalpa* is the removal of the coarse layer of delusion . . . and this is called one *kalpa*.
>
> The yogic practice that transcends the first two *kalpa*s is the removal of

the fine layer of delusion . . . and this is called two *kalpa*s.

Practitioners of mantra, transcending yet another *kalpa,* can remove the subtle layer . . . and attain the first Buddha-mind of wisdom.

Thus it is called becoming the Buddha in three *kalpa*s. If these three delusions are removed in one lifetime, the practitioner becomes a Buddha in one lifetime. It is not a question of time.[8]

In Mikkyo, the three *kalpas* signify coarse, fine, and subtle layers of delusion; to transcend these three is to become a Buddha. The coarse level of delusion is attachment to the self—the belief that there exists in the individual body-mind a permanent, unchanging self. The shallowest and crudest of the three delusions, it is said to be rooted deep in consciousness. According to early Buddhism, the body-mind comprises no more than the temporary coming together of five sense-aggregates (*goun*). These are form (*shiki*), perception (*ju*), mental activity (*sō*), will (*gyō*), and consciousness (*shiki*). According to this teaching of no-self (*muga*), when the causation of the sense-aggregates ceases, the self is annihilated and the source of suffering eliminated.

The "fine" delusion represents attachment to things—the belief that, although the self results from the temporary union of the five aggregates, the aggregates themselves have real existence. "Subtle" delusion is the fundamental, deep-seated ignorance, rooted in the depths of the storehouse consciousness, from which all delusion is thought to arise. Beyond this, Mikkyo finds the core of reality, where the Wisdom of All-Wisdom is experienced. In *The Meaning of the UN-Syllable,* Kūkai wrote:

The truth of the mind is the Wisdom of All-Wisdom. In other words, it is the Dharma Realm [universe]. The Dharma Realm is the body of all things.[9]

THE STAGES OF SAMADHI

Samadhi (Jap., *sammai,* also *sanmaji*) is a meditative state in which body and mind are focused on intuitive perception. Indian religious tradition presents this as a way to grasp the reality of the true self. Although Kūkai often termed Mikkyo the *samadhi gate* and *samadhi dharma gate* as if samadhi were uniquely characteristic of the esoteric teaching, techniques for achieving samadhi had long existed in Indian religion. Indian meditators minutely analyzed the various stages and aspects of samadhi, naming them variously in Sanskrit as *samāhita* (*sanmakita*), *samāpatti* (*sanmahachi*), *śamatha* (*shi*), *dhāraṇī* (*darani*), and *dhyāna* (*zen* or *zenna*). These terms came with Buddhism to China, where they were both transliterated and translated before being brought to Japan. Shingon ordinarily uses these terms more or less interchangeably, though subtle distinctions may be observed.

In deep samadhi, body and mind are said to progress beyond the state of concentration on a single object so that the gulf between the self and its object of concentration disappears. As samadhi involves body and mind together, methods for entering this state coordinate internal meditation with techniques of sitting and breathing. Indian yoga texts describe graded levels that lead systematically to the samadhi state. These internal processes appear to be similar in yoga and Mikkyo, but differ in their doctrinal frameworks. In general, the practitioner begins by controlling the body, the breath, the emotions, and the senses, then concentrating the scattered mind. The practitioner deepens concentration until the same clarity of mind can be maintained. The further stage in which the observing self fades away, leaving only awareness of the object of contemplation, is called samadhi.

At this depth of contemplation, the self unites with the object, so that the object no longer remains an object to the self. Samadhi, therefore, unites the subject and object of practice; in the esoteric tradition, it is said to result in the union of self and Buddha. Mikkyo often uses the Sanskrit word *yoga,* meaning union, interchangeably with samadhi. This samadhi state is not supposed to impair consciousness in the least, nor distort it with visions of some other, unearthly realm. The awareness of a samadhi adept, however intensely concentrated, should remain balanced and steady.

The *Mui Sanzō Zenyō* (Shubhakarasimha's Essentials of Meditation) and the *Shugokokkai-shu Darani-kyō* (Nation-Protecting Lord Dharani Sutra) classify the deepening of the samadhi state in five stages as follows:

Essentials of Meditation	*Nation-Protecting Sutra*
Momentary Mind	Ephemeral Samadhi
Drifting but Concentrated Mind	Partial Samadhi
Sweet, Beautiful Mind	Gradually Manifesting Samadhi
Breaking, Dispersing Mind	Rising and Falling Samadhi
Bright Mirror Mind	Peacefully Dwelling Samadhi

These two texts describe the stages of samadhi somewhat differently, but both texts agree on essential points, providing the Mikkyo practitioner with a rough gauge for his own samadhi. The moon disk is used below as an example of the object of meditation in describing Shubhakarasimha's five steps:

"Momentary Mind": The meditator can visualize the moon disk clearly, but the image is ephemeral, disappearing in a moment like a light snuffed out.

"Drifting but Concentrated Mind": The moon disk may disappear suddenly, but by diligently continuing meditation, a faint image of it will reappear.

"Sweet, Beautiful Mind": With further practice, the moon disk image becomes bright and clear, and the meditator's body and mind become light and stable.

"Breaking, Dispersing Mind": The meditator is able to maintain a clear image of the moon disk, but despite a determination to continue practice, he suddenly becomes lethargic or experiences extremes of emotion. This is a condition as unstable as a pair of swinging scales. The meditator may feel that all efforts have become useless, as though he faced an impenetrable barrier. To experience full samadhi, this stage must be transcended.

"Bright Mirror Mind": The bright mirror reflects beauty and ugliness without like or dislike. When the object it reflects is gone, the reflected image also disappears without a trace. In this samadhi, the meditator is said to see things and events clearly, without bias or attachment.

Meditation of this kind can at times induce ecstasy, euphoria, and other intensely pleasurable emotions and sensations. Samadhi, however, is not a state of temporary ecstasy or euphoria. Since the pleasure of samadhi can be almost addictive, the Mikkyo meditator is taught that blissful sensations are not the goal of esoteric practice. Meditation may also bring sudden, mysterious insights, visions, or other extraordinary experiences, all differing from person to person. In Mikkyo such experiences are not sought after, since, as the *Commentary on the Dainichi-kyō* makes clear, they have no lasting validity:

> Within the realm of esoteric union, everything is like an image in a mirror or the moon reflected in water, without nature, without birth.[10]

As this text explains, sensations of spiritual experience may arise when the energies of self and Buddha unite in the process of mutual empowerment (*kaji*). Such sensations are regarded as passing phenomena, by-products of samadhi states. If an experience of this kind intrudes, the experienced meditator simply ignores it as a diversion. Kakuban's *Musō-kan* (Formless Meditation) contains this advice: "Even if you see Buddhas, do away with such conceptions."[11] The absence of unusual experiences does not indicate any lack of progress in meditation. Kakuban wrote the following advice for the meditator in his *Matsudai Shingon Gyōja Yōjin* (Cautions for Future Shingon Practitioners):

> All those who awaken Mind inevitably attain enlightenment. It is said that those of profound faith will obtain enlightenment, but what is profound faith? It is not to permit doubt or turn one's mind away, even if long-continued practice brings no Dharma experience. It is inevitable that such people will attain enlightenment.
>
> It may appear, due to karmic obstruction, that enlightenment is not attained, whereas it is already attained but the enlightenment is hidden so that the practitioner himself does not recognize it. . . . There can be various reasons for this, but one should not doubt or neglect one's practice because of them.[12]

The meditator often experiences a flow of memories, thoughts, and subconscious stirrings that can disturb concentration. Mikkyo teaches that such distractions should not be suppressed, since the effort of suppressing them tends only to give rise to more thoughts. In the *Bodaishin-ron* (Treatise on Enlightened Mind) is written:

> If deluded thoughts arise in the mind, be aware of them but do not follow them. When delusions are forcefully suppressed, the source of the mind becomes powerless and empty. All power is present here, and its mysterious phenomena are eternal.[13]

Since distracting thoughts arise from the ceaseless activity of the mind, Mikkyo does not set the meditator to the vain task of suppressing thought entirely. Instead, the energy that gives rise to thought is rechannelled toward perception of the true self. The esoteric practitioner is meant to achieve samadhi naturally and spontaneously by systematically reciting mantras with a calm mind, forming mudras with the hands, and visualizing prescribed internal images. These samadhi methods are said not to depend on the meditator's conscious will and imagination alone, but rather to activate the energy of a profounder level of mind. In the Mikkyo view, visualized images that appear only by an effort of will are limited creations of a superficial level of mind. The master Rikan (1635–1693) wrote as follows in his *Ajikan* (A-Syllable Visualization):

> In doing the visualization, first face the painting [the object of meditation] and look at the A-syllable, lotus, and moon. Then, with the eyes neither open nor closed, visualize them within. If at this time they appear as the Dharma reality in samadhi, it is a matter for congratulation. If they appear by your own thought, they are delusions.[14]

At another extreme, meditators may experience a stage in which conscious thought ceases and the mind goes blank. Although in deep samadhi the mind may have no consciously willed thought, the meditative mind is described as holding more than just emptiness. Mikkyo practice uses the mind's creative faculty (itself a major source of distractions) by concentrating the mind on an object for meditation. The esoteric tradition teaches that it is an active, alert body-mind—outwardly calm but inwardly dynamic—that can use the creative energy of the mind to achieve deep samadhi. Shubhakarasimha's *Essentials of Meditation* points to the dynamic nature of esoteric meditation:

> O beginners, many of you fear that thoughts arising in your mind will tempt you, and so you follow your breath and maintain a state of no-thought, thinking that this is the ultimate. You seek to improve in this way, but cannot.
>
> Thought is of two kinds. One is negative and the other positive. Negative, deluded thoughts should be removed completely. Correct thoughts of the good Dharma should not be extinguished.

Practitioners with the correct attitude should not concern themselves about temptation, but strive first to maintain and increase correct thoughts. After this, they will attain the purity of the ultimate. When people learn archery, do they not practice for a long time before achieving excellence? Furthermore, if you do not think at all, how can your practice have any stability?

Do not be afraid of your mind's workings. Consider it a disturbance of your practice only if you slacken in moving forward. . . .[15]

Exoteric samadhi methods emphasize regulation of the senses and concentration on a passive state of "no-mind no-thought" (*munen musō*), while esoteric methods cultivate positive activity within the mind. In the sense that they result in the cessation of negative thought, these methods can be said to pass through a "no-mind no-thought" state. Esoteric samadhi might better be described, however, as "holding firm in the single-mind experience" (*ichinen kenji*) of esoteric union. The *Commentary on the Dainichi-kyō* describes this union as "the mind itself proving the mind, the mind becoming aware of itself."[16]

WISDOM AND SKILLFUL MEANS

Buddhist practice can be summarized in the three types of learning (*sangaku*): precepts, meditation, and wisdom. Cultivation of the self makes the meditative state of samadhi possible, while samadhi creates the condition for the birth of wisdom. The *Dainichi-kyō* contains the following question and answer:

Master of secrets, how to attain wisdom?
Know one's mind as it truly is.[17]

As the *Commentary* on this sutra explains:

This passage expounds the unified meaning of the sutra. What is called the self-mind of living beings is all-embracing wisdom. One who knows it as it truly is is named the all-wise.[18]

Enlightenment is said to bring about perfection in an eternal now. This supra-historical, "perfect bright day" also encompasses phenomenal time, which contains the potential for evolution toward further perfection. The universal self, by its nature, never ceases creation and evolution, expressing the infinite possibilities of the individual.

Terms that Buddhism uses to mean wisdom include *bodai* ("awakened") and *hannya*. The latter is also known as the "Buddha-mother" because to realize this wisdom is to attain enlightenment and become a Buddha. Another word for wisdom, *chi,* is related in meaning to the Sanskrit word for consciousness, (*jñāna*), whereas the term *myō* refers to the light or radiance that cuts through the darkness of ignorance. Wisdom is not defined as an abstraction, a thing, a relationship, or an activity. Rather, wisdom consists in the individual manifesting the Buddha-self through union with the Dharma Body. Wisdom is therefore described as the self-existing enlightenment of the Dharma Body.

Mikkyo refers to the individual who has realized enlightenment as a Buddha, one who has awakened. Bodhisattva (*bosatsu*), referring to both the being in search of enlightenment and the already enlightened being, has the same meaning. The Sanskrit *bodhi* means wisdom or enlightenment (exactly as in the word *Buddha*), while *sattva* means having emotion and mind, existent. *Bodhisattva* means "wisdom-being," referring to one who uses wisdom for the benefit of other beings. Thus when Mikkyo speaks of becoming a Buddha in this body, it could as well say becoming a bodhisattva in this body. The esoteric teachings place importance not on any differences between Buddhas and bodhisattvas, enlightened and unenlightened, but rather on how wisdom functions in the person.

Although expressing the timeless fulfillment of the individual, wisdom also involves endless transformation. These transformations are portrayed in mandalas, in which every deity embodies a particular aspect of compassionate activity. Shingon mandalas represent the actualization of the Five Wisdoms in the phenomenal world. Each of the Five Wisdoms represents perfection; each contains all others in itself; yet each is unique, representing the single essence of wisdom changing according to circumstances.

Mikkyo's symbolic framework of deities, wisdoms, mantras, elements, consciousnesses, and other doctrines may seem difficult to comprehend in its separate parts and as a whole. Taking the metaphor of a river, if one stands on a bridge looking down at the water, the river flows past so continuously and unceasingly that no part of it can be grasped. If one becomes the river itself, however, then nothing within it moves out of grasp. The "river-consciousness" permeates equally throughout. The esoteric teachings are meant to be known in this way, from within.

For Mikkyo, the unmoving center that realizes the ever-moving whole is the true self. That which moves and changes, however, is also the true self. Whether seen as enlightened or deluded, the individual undergoes the constant changes that manifest the dynamic nature of the true self. The major Shingon mandalas, for example, have Dainichi Nyorai at the center surrounded by many subsidiary deities, but other mandalas exist centered on different deities with Dainichi Nyorai on the periphery. Although represented in different form, the central deity still embodies the unmoving center of the true self, which, despite its differing names or attributes, is inseparable from Dainichi Nyorai, the universe. The mandala system, with its hundreds of deities, appears extremely complicated. From within the mandala, however, all aspects of complexity express the infinite individual manifestations of the enlightened self.

Mikkyo describes wisdom as a dynamic force that does not exist apart from compassion (*jihi,* or *hi*). The *Treatise on Enlightened Mind* lists three interrelated requirements for realization: to unfold wisdom, to practice compassion, and to deepen samadhi. Wisdom, the esoteric teachings emphasize, becomes real through the activity of compassion. This is the practice of "skillful means" (*hōben*), meaning techniques used to attain a goal.

Mikkyo values skillful means as the dynamic activity of enlightenment in this world. From the point of view of the person striving toward enlightenment, skillful means represent realization of this goal. From the point of view of compassion, skillful means is the spontaneous activity of the cosmos evolving to complete awareness in every part and in every dimension. In traditional Mahayana terms, it is called "saving all beings." The *Dainichi-kyō* relates universal enlightenment to the awakening enlightenment of all beings in the Dharma Gate of the Three Phrases, described earlier:

> Enlightened mind is the cause,
> Great compassion is the root,
> Skillful means are the ultimate.

Kūkai interpreted the last phrase in two ways. One stresses the imperative sense that skillful means should lead to ultimate enlightenment. The other emphasizes the declarative sense that skillful means themselves are the ultimate. The former expresses the view of self-benefit in seeking enlightenment, and the latter, the view of enlightenment fulfilled in compassion toward others. From the perspective of the Dharma Body, the two cannot be separated, just as the energy of mutual empowerment (*kaji*) flows simultaneously from Buddha to practitioner and from practitioner to Buddha. The compassionate activity of wisdom happens because it happens, just as wisdom exists because it exists. Mikkyo sees these as the highest play and the deepest enjoyment of the universe.

FIVE

The Secret Activities of Body, Speech, and Mind

The esoteric tradition unites the Buddha and all beings in a single entity, personified in Dainichi Nyorai, whose aspects are symbolized in elements, syllables, wisdoms, and so on. The Universal Body of the Six Great Elements describes the substance of this ever-evolving whole, the Four Mandalas describe its manifestations in form, and the Universal Activities of the Three Secrets (*sanmitsu yūdai*) describe its functions. The three secrets thus symbolize the macrocosmic functions and processes constantly at work in all things and beings. In *The Meaning of Becoming a Buddha in This Body,* Kūkai relates these to the central experience of enlightenment:

> The six symbolic elements interpenetrate without obstruction and are in eternal union.
> They are not apart from any of the Four Mandalas.
> Through practice of three-secrets empowerment, they manifest immediately.
> The universal web is what we call this body.
> All things are naturally endowed with bodhisattva wisdom transcending the essential mind, the subsidiary minds [limited aspects of mind], and the objects of the senses.
> Each of the Five Wisdoms is endowed with unlimited wisdom.
> Since it is the power of the perfect mirror, this is true enlightened wisdom.[1]

By concentrated activity of body, speech, and mind, the esoteric practitioner activates the suprapersonal energy of empowerment (*kaji*). Mikkyo calls this process *nyūga ga'nyū* (literally, "entering-self and self-entering"), in which the power of the Buddha flows into the practitioner, and the practitioner's power flows into the Buddha. Esoteric practice thus unites the three human activities (*sangō*) of body, speech, and mind with the three secrets (*sanmitsu*) of the universe. Mikkyo often uses these two terms interchangeably. Since this union symbolizes enlightenment, esoteric meditation is called *sanmitsu yuga,* union of

106

Half lotus meditation.

Full lotus meditation using the dharmakāya mudrā.

the three secrets, and *sanmitsu kaji,* empowerment of the three secrets. Kūkai's *Meaning of Becoming a Buddha in This Body* says:

> If a Shingon practitioner carefully observes the meaning of this, forming mudras with the hands, reciting mantras with the mouth, dwelling in samadhi with the mind, then the three secrets bring about the response of empowerment and he quickly attains great enlightenment.[2]

In terms of ritual practice, the hand gestures known as mudras represent the secret of body, mantra represents speech, and the samadhi of visualization represents mind. The meditation techniques of mudra, mantra, and visualization employ phenomenal symbols based on sensation, motion, form, color, smell, speech, thought, and imagination, giving the practitioner concrete means to know the true self. Mikkyo uses the three secrets to experience universal enlightened activity.

Although mudras correspond to the activity of body, mantric recitation to speech, and visualization to mind, the three secrets symbolize a reality that cannot be confined within human body, speech, and mind. Esoteric teaching and practice treat the three secrets as mutually inseparable and equal in essence. The *Commentary on the Dainichi-kyō* says:

> The various activities of the Buddha's three [secrets] all attain to the realm of the primary mysterious ultimate reality. Body is equal to speech, speech is equal to mind, just as all parts of a great sea are filled with the same salt taste.[3]

Three-secrets practice has the two aspects of "with form" (*usō*) and "without form" (*musō*). Practice with form refers to systematic meditative ritual using mudra, mantra, and visualization. Practice without form, however, is an individual's every action, whether in a ritual format or not, as a reflection of universal enlightened wisdom. This is the ultimate esoteric practice, in which every word is a mantra, every bodily movement a mudra, and every thought a meditation. At the same time, with form and without form are inseparable aspects of a single unity.

ESOTERIC PRACTICE BASED ON FORM

As already described, early exoteric Buddhism viewed the Dharma Body as an abstract universal Truth apart from the world. With the evolution of Buddhism, this term gradually came to mean an actually existing eternal "body," which then came to be associated with the phenomenal universe. Later teachings eventually regarded phenomenal things themselves as embodiments of Truth, and saw the phenomenal world as the pure Dharma realm. Mikkyo therefore came to affirm the transient world of birth and death as indivisibly one with the eternal Dharma Body. In the *Secret Key to the Heart Sutra* Kūkai wrote:

It is not far removed from the Buddha Dharma. It is in the mind, nearby. It is not apart from things as they are. Throwing away the body, who can seek it?[4]

The esoteric tradition developed methods of meditation based on form, considering these a means to direct contemplation of the Dharma Body. Mikkyo uses tangible, material objects and activities to express the experience of mystical union. When Kūkai first presented the esoteric teachings to the court in his memorial, the *List of Items Brought from China,* he stressed the importance of form in realizing truth:

The various meditative rituals, the various mudras, come out of Great Compassion. One glance at them results in Buddhahood. What is condensed in the sutras and commentaries in secret form is set forth pictorially. The essence of the repository of secrets is truly bound up with compassion.[5]

The use of form as a meditative aid in attaining samadhi dates very far back in Indian religion. Early Buddhism, for example, had a "ten-fold all-pervading visualization" (*jippensho-kan*), in which the practitioner visualized the six elements and four colors as a means to see the principles of causation in tangible things. Mantric incantations, too, are of early date, used to attain magical ends, and, in Mahayana, to concentrate the mind. Visualization also underwent a great change in content and meaning when incorporated by esoteric Buddhism. Mikkyo places emphasis on the use of form precisely to overcome the false duality of the phenomenal world and ideal truth, of that with and without form. The *Commentary on the Dainichi-kyō* says:

> If practitioners discard their various practices and seek to dwell only in that without form, they will not succeed. On the other hand, neither will they succeed if they cling to their practices, seeking to dwell in that which has form.[6]

Mikkyo employs visualization as a means to experience the inseparability of phenomena and truth, of mind and matter. It considers the objects of visualization and the words of recitation themselves as "beings" imbued with energy, as embodiments of the enlightened universe, and as varying forms of the true self. In the esoteric view, the means to realization is inseparable from realization itself. As the *Dainichi-kyō* says, "All things, just as they are, dwell in Truth."[7] This sutra names enlightened mind—with which all beings are originally endowed—"the great and vast Palace of the Vajra-Dharma Realm."[8] The *Commentary on the Dainichi-kyō* explains:

> Wherever the Buddha appears cannot be elsewhere than in this palace. He is alone, yet is not apart from the three realms [of past, present, and future].[9]

All objects and phenomena are, therefore, potential symbols of the Dharma Body. The priest Raihō (1279–1330) wrote in the *Shingon Myōmoku* (Shingon Glossary):

> With-form and without-form are of manifold varieties. The shallow meaning of with-form is that it is the material things apprehensible to ordinary people who know mind and matter. That which the mind apprehends, which is easily known and comprehended, is called with-form. Without-form means that the body-nature of things is unreal and transient, like a phantasm, void of self-nature, having neither color nor form. Since no aspect of it can be known, it is called without-form.
>
> The profound, secret meaning of with-form is that it dwells clearly and distinctly in the forms and aspects of all things. Without-form means that each form and aspect is endowed with all. There is no ending in a single aspect. Because it is endowed with all aspects and has no single aspect, it is called without-form.
>
> The first meaning is the ordinary . . . teaching. The latter is the Shingon affirmation.[10]

This mysterious "without-form," according to another text, is "not unendowed with form." Thus truth is symbolized by means of form in Mikkyo images which, at the same time, are understood as transcending form. Each of the deities, mantras, syllables, and other symbols used in meditation functions as a single focal point of enlightenment which is equal to all other focal points. The *Dainichi-kyō,* for example, describing how all transient things and beings are informed by eternal Buddha-nature, says, "In its originating and its extinguishing, in the universal and the particular, it is ungraspable."[11] Similarly, the *Commentary on the Dainichi-kyō* explains that "self, other, their combination, as well as that without causation" are all originally unborn.[12] Kūkai in *The Meaning of Becoming a Buddha in This Body* says, "The fruits of mantra are all removed from cause and effect."[13] These passages refer to the void—the indescribable, ungraspable, universal reality present in all things.

The *Dainichi-kyō* gives a meditation called the "ten similies" (*jūyu*) in which the practitioner meditates on such things as illusions created by a magician, mirages, dream images, reflections, and the wheel of fire made by the burning end of a rope whirled in the dark. Illustrating the attachments and delusions that one must overcome, this meditation reminds the practitioner that all things are empty of permanent reality, and that, ultimately, everything is a mystery.

Esoteric practice, based on the identity of the absolute (which is formless and ungraspable) with the phenomenal (which has form and is perceptible), reveals how the individual is at once an integral, functioning part of the universe and also void—that is, without permanent self-existence. Mikkyo seeks a spontaneous understanding of universal truth by using concrete phenomena to unlock the mind's creative powers.

THE MYSTERY OF EMPOWERMENT

The esoteric tradition assimilated great numbers of mudras, mantras, and symbolic objects directly from other religious systems, making them effective as symbols of the Dharma Body by empowering them. This was, as the *Commentary on the Dainichi-kyō* says, "Using symbols commonly known in the world and making them into secret symbols of the transcendent world."[14] The union of the three secrets of practitioner and Buddha operates by mutual empowerment (*kaji*) and its response, the mysterious process of central importance to Mikkyo practice.

The term *kudoku,* often translated as virtue or merit, refers to the beneficial result of good action, implying a spiritual power accumulated through pious activity. Mikkyo finds no such merit in one's own actions alone, but only from the conjunction of one's own power, the Buddha's responsive power, and the power of the Dharma Realm. Buddhism often uses the terms *self power* (*jiriki*) and *other power* (*tariki,* meaning from outside the self) in discussing whether an individual attains enlightenment by his own effort and merit or through a compassionate external power coming from the Buddha. Mikkyo approaches this question from a different viewpoint, saying that the power of self and other are

110

"not-two" (*jita muniriki*). Rather, the energy of enlightenment is seen as the Three Powers (*sanriki*):

1. The Power of Self-Merit (*ga kudoku-riki*). This is the energy generated by the individual in three-secrets practice.
2. The Power of Buddha-Empowerment (*nyorai kaji-riki*). The protective, responsive, enfolding power of Buddha-mind.
3. The Power of the Dharma Realm (*hokkai riki*). The universally interpenetrating self-nature, symbolized in the six elements, that makes self and Buddha essentially equal.

When the Three Powers unite in the individual body-mind, innate Buddha-nature is said to reveal itself so that the individual becomes an embodiment of wisdom and compassion. Mutual empowerment is not a simple process of adding self to other, or power to power, but rather a subtle process involving the self, the deity, and the universe. The *Record of the Secret Treasury* states:

> The meaning of empowerment. *Ka* is the protective, supporting mind of the Buddha. *Ji* is one's own conduct.[15]

Or, according to the *Dainichi-kyō Kaidai* (Interpretation of the Dainichi-kyō):

> In other words, this is the Buddha entering the self and the self entering the Buddha.[16]

Mikkyo therefore describes the mutual empowerment of Buddha and practitioner as transformations of a single, all-penetrating universal energy, beyond cause and effect, which take place in several different dimensions at once. In striving "upward," the individual perceives an energy flowing "downward" as if to aid his striving. Further experience reveals the apparent "upward" and "downward" movements of energy as dual aspects of the single movement of enlightened wisdom. According to the *Interpretation of the Dainichi-kyō*:

> The not-upward-and-not-downward universal transformation extends to the essential reality of the one mind that is neither made nor not-made. The indivisibility of the essential Dharma . . . is the root of that which is beyond thought, the source of transformation.[17]

The Meaning of Becoming a Buddha in This Body makes clear the mutual nature of the *kaji* process:

> Empowerment manifests the great compassion of the Buddha and the faith of living beings. The sun of the Buddha reflected in the water of the mind of all beings is called *ka* [adding or increasing]. The water of the practitioner's mind experiencing the sun of the Buddha is called *ji* [holding or grasping]. If the practitioner meditates concentratedly on the import of this

principle, then, through the response of the three secrets, the inherently existent three bodies immediately manifest enlightenment in his body.[18]

Knowledge of the self as it truly is, therefore, results from the mutual empowerment of the practitioner's microcosmic and macrocosmic activities. This is said to require the proper use of body, speech, and mind, with faith. Faith here means a willingness to set aside doubts, a state of mind open to participation in something beyond the grasp of logic and reason. Given this inner willingness of mind, the practitioner's three-secrets practice brings about a response that raises the activities of body, speech, and mind to a universal dimension. It is when the practitioner is no longer attached to limited views of the self, and when the deity is no longer seen as an external object of worship, that inherent Buddha-nature reveals itself.

THE SECRET OF BODY: THE ESOTERIC MUDRA

The secret activity of body takes the form of hand gestures called mudras, which symbolically identify the individual with the universe. In this way the human body functions as a living symbol of the macrocosm. Kūkai wrote in the *Nenji Shingon Rikan Keihaku-mon* (Discourse on Visualization of Truth by Mindful Recitation of Mantra):

> If the Buddhas are the Dharma Realm, they exist within my body. If I myself am also the Dharma Realm, then I exist within the Buddhas.[19]

The Sanskrit word *mudra* (Jap., *in*, "seal," or *ingei*) has a wide range of meanings but in esoteric practice refers specifically to prescribed gestures of the hands and fingers (*shuin*, "hand seal") performed in coordination with mantras and visualizations. The word's etymology is unclear, but it may derive from an Avestan (ancient Persian) name for Egypt, Mudraya. Since the Egyptians were noted for their use of seals, the Persians called seals mudras, and this word then entered the Sanskrit vocabulary. Buddhism first used *mudra* to mean seal, and early sutras tell how such seals (mudras) were impressed on documents as proof of their authenticity. This word later took on a broader meaning as seal (or sign) of truth.

The Buddhist use of ritual hand gestures can be traced back at least to the Gandharan Buddha-images made sometime around the first century. These images depict the Buddha with hands in gestures of fearlessness, teaching the Dharma, earth-touching (to subdue demons), and so on, associated with specific incidents in Shakyamuni's life. As Buddhist meditation practices developed, meditators came to visualize Buddha-images internally, and then to visualize associated symbolic images as well. The Buddha's hand gestures then also became part of such visualization practice.

(*Left*) Vajra prayer mudrā. (*Center*) Lotus mudrā. (*Right*) Armor protection mudrā.

The *Muri Mandara Shu-kyō,* an early esoteric sutra probably predating the sixth century, instructs the practitioner to imitate the Buddha by forming the same gestures, here for the first time called mudras because they were signs of the Buddha's enlightenment. Mudra thus came to mean symbol of Buddha-activity, and thereafter also came to include attributes, such as the swords or lotuses they held in their hands, signifying their particular nature or function.

The above sutra contains the first recorded instance of esoteric mudra practice, listing some sixteen mudras. The *Darani Jikkyō,* written only about a century later, lists more than three hundred such symbols, including attributes as well as hand gestures, to be used as objects of meditation. The esoteric tradition, assimilating large numbers of these symbolic gestures and objects, developed systems to classify them according to their varying uses and meanings.

The *Kongōchō-gyō* (that translated by Amoghavajra) uses the word *mudra* in its broadest sense, applying it to mantras, all Buddhist images, the body of the Buddha, and hand gestures. The sutra classifies mudras in the following four types: The Great Mudra is the body of the deity with which the practitioner unites, symbolized by its image, attribute, or mantric syllable. The Samaya Mudra is the hand gesture representing the deity's symbolic attribute (such as vajra, sword, etc.), while the Karma Mudra is the hand gesture symbolizing the deity's activity. The Dharma Mudra is the deity's mantra. In the esoteric understanding, therefore, mudras include all symbols of the enlightened universe. The *Commentary on the Dainichi-kyō* says:

Mudra is none other than a symbol of the Dharma Realm [universe]. Using mudra, one points to the body of the Dharma Realm.[20]

The use of mudras as ritual hand gestures thus draws significance from their wider meaning as symbols of enlightenment. The thousands of Mikkyo mudras employ virtually all possible movements of the fingers, some being a single gesture and others involving complicated sequences composed of several changing mudras. The practitioner's entire body posture may also be employed as a symbol of essential oneness with the deity.

As part of the symbolic framework of esoteric Buddhism, the hands and fingers were assigned various meanings. For example, Mikkyo generally considers the right hand to symbolize the Buddha, the left hand to symbolize ordinary beings (no doubt influenced by the traditional Indian view of the right hand as pure and the left as unclean). The right also came to represent wisdom and active visualization, the left meditation and passive contemplation. By joining the two hands in various ways, therefore, the practitioner enacts different aspects of esoteric union, as follows:

Left Hand	Right Hand
Samadhi	Compassion
Passive Absorption	Active Visualization
Truth	Wisdom
Tai-zō Mandala	Kongō-kai Mandala
Finite Phenomenal Realm	Buddha-Realm
Moon	Sun

A fundamental Mikkyo mudra is the *gasshō,* originating in the Indian gesture of respect and reverence in which the hands are placed together palm to palm at the breast. The *Dainichi-kyō* accords this mudra great value, counting it (together with material offerings, compassionate activity, and internal symbolic offerings) one of the four principal ways of paying homage to the Buddha. Held together in *gasshō,* the hands symbolize the unity of the eternal Buddha Realm (right) and the transient world of phenomena (left).

The sutra names twelve varieties of *gasshō,* two of these that commonly appear in practice being the vajra (*kongō*) and the lotus (*renge*). In the vajra *gasshō,* both hands are held together lightly at chest level, palm to palm and fingertip to fingertip. Fingers more or less extended, the fingertips interlace slightly, the right thumb overlapping the left. Joining the hands in this way symbolizes the single truth described in terms of self and Buddha, static and dynamic, truth and wisdom.

In the lotus *gasshō,* the hands are held as above but with the fingers curved, fingertips lightly touching, and palms held slightly apart so that the hands form a shape like a lotus bud, symbolizing the innate purity of both Buddha and self. In successive mudra variations, this lotus bud unfolds stage by stage, finally becoming an open lotus flower symbolizing full realization of purity in body, speech, and mind.

Mikkyo finds several levels of esoteric meaning in mudras. The fingers, for example, represent the symbolic elements (counting from the little finger) of earth, water, fire, wind, and space. (The consciousness element is understood as penetrating all the other elements.) The same fingers are associated with the corresponding mantric syllables. The five fingers on each hand also represent the sense-aggregates (*go-un*)—form, perception, thought, will, and consciousness—that in Buddhism are considered to make up all phenomenal beings. To join the two hands, therefore, signifies in many different ways the inseparability of microcosm and macrocosm.

The Wisdom Fist Mudra (*chiken-in*), formed by Dainichi Nyorai in the Kongō-kai Mandala, embodies teachings considered among the most secret in Mikkyo. Each hand first forms a Vajra Fist (*kongō-ken*), in which the thumb is folded across the palm and the fingers curled over the thumb. The left index finger is then extended and gripped inside the right hand's Vajra Fist, held above it, so that the tip of that finger is touched by the right thumb.

The wind element (the index finger) on the left hand symbolizes the breath of life, while the element space (the right thumb) represents the great void, which in terms of consciousness is the wisdom of the Buddha. By joining the breath of life with the all-pervading void, the practitioner enacts the activity of wisdom in living beings. This mudra represents the enlightened activity of the universe as dynamic wisdom. Composed of two interlocking Vajra Fists, the Wisdom Fist also symbolizes the practitioner's adamantine grasp of truth through the Buddha-wisdom inseparable from all things and beings.

As formed by Dainichi Nyorai, the Wisdom Fist symbolizes the all-pervading activity of enlightenment throughout the universe. By further extension, the left hand represents the innate truth of all things as they are (as symbolized in the Tai-zō Mandala), and the right the wisdom of evolving enlightenment (as symbolized in the Kongō-kai Mandala). Together, these represent the essential unity of truth and wisdom, of all beings and the Buddha, of delusion and enlightenment.

Another mudra of fundamental importance in esoteric practice is the Dharma Realm Samadhi Mudra (*hokkai jō-in*), the "mudra of dwelling in the enlightened mind of the universal Dharma Realm and the self as one body." Dainichi Nyorai in the Tai-zō Mandala forms this mudra. The hands, turned palms up, are held in front of the abdomen, the right hand above the left, the tips of the thumbs (space element) barely touching one another. The space between the thumbtips encompasses the universe where Buddha and self interpenetrate without obstruction. This minute space between the thumbtips, therefore, represents the intersection of the world of finite phenomena and the world of infinite mind. The practitioner enters union with the Dharma Realm (the universe) by forming this mudra, contemplating its significance, and reciting the appropriate mantra. The *Commentary on the Dainichi-kyō* says:

All Buddhas are born, every one, from enlightened mind, the seed of Buddha-nature. Know this well. All mudras also are born from enlightened mind.[21]

The Secret of Speech: Esoteric Mantra Practice

Mikkyo three-secrets practice employs the secret activity of speech in the form of mantric symbols of universal truth. *The True Meaning of the Voiced Syllable* says:

> By reciting the voiced syllables with clear understanding, one manifests the truth. What is called "the truth of the voiced syllable" is the three secrets in which all things and the Buddha are equal. This is the original essence of all beings. For this reason, Dainichi Nyorai's teaching of the true meaning of the voiced syllable will startle into awakening those long sleeping.[22]

The esoteric tradition, as described earlier, gives formulas of invocation using the various names of vidya (*myō* or *myōju*), dharani (*darani*), and mantra (*shingon*). *Vidyā* means shining wisdom, in contrast to which *avidyā* means ignorance and delusion. The longer invocations called dharani were first used in Mahayana as a means to concentrate the mind. Mantra itself, deriving from ancient Vedic hymns of praise, means a vessel heaped with sacred thoughts, and is the general Mikkyo term for all kinds of incantation.

Mikkyo describes mantras in terms of voice (the sound), letter (the written Sanskrit syllable), and truth (the symbolic meaning). The voice and letter of a mantra express its truth—in fact, as the symbolic essence of the universe, they embody truth. In *The True Meaning of the Voiced Syllable,* Kūkai describes how these aspects of mantra represent the enlightened universe:

> The five elements have sounds,
> The ten realms possess language,
> The six senses are embodied in syllables.
> The Dharma Body [universe] is their true reality.[23]

Mantric practice, therefore, involving more than the simple physical activity of vocalizing certain prescribed sounds, uses the concentrated mind and body in *nenju,* "mindful recitation." Concentrated recitation of a mantric syllable employs the sound, the image, and the meaning of the syllable. These correspond to the mantra's "voice," the written syllable, and the mantra's "truth." According to the Indian yogic tradition, silent recitation has a thousand-times greater effect than voiced. In advanced meditation using the voiced syllable, the Mikkyo practitioner voices the sound within the mind. Other practices do involve voiced chanting, however, and novices often start meditation by reciting a mantra aloud.

Kūkai's *Record of the Secret Treasury* explains the following five methods of mantra recitation:

> Voice-Bearing Recitation. The practitioner visualizes a conch shell above a lotus within his mind, and recites so that his voice issues as though from the conch.

Lotus Recitation. He recites so that his voice can be heard only in his own ears.

Vajra Recitation. The lips and teeth are held together and only the tip of the tongue moves slightly in recitation.

Samadhi Recitation. Without moving even the tongue, the practitioner recites only within the mind.

Light Recitation. While the practitioner recites, whether silently or out loud, he constantly visualizes light streaming from his mouth.[24]

Mantras provide a fundamental means for the esoteric union of the practitioner and the deity of practice. The Buddhist deity as an object of reverence and worship is called the "deity image as an essential body" (*honzon*), ordinarily understood to be a painted or sculpted image separate from the worshiper. In Mikkyo, however, as the *Commentary on the Dainichi-kyō* states, the deity is "also called the self-*honzon*, for it is . . . the *honzon* contained in the self."[25] Esoteric Buddhist practice is meant to operate at a level of mind where deity and practitioner exist in inseparable unity.

Mikkyo deities are represented in a wide variety of forms, not only as paintings and sculptures but as voiced mantras and visualized mantric syllables and symbolic objects. Depicted anthropomorphically, with the prescribed posture, dress, mudra, and associated objects, the deity is said to be in the iconographic form (*son-gyō*). Depicted as a deity's particular attribute, such as a lotus, vajra, or sword, the deity is in the samaya form (*sanmaya-gyō*). (The pagoda, for example, is a samaya form of Dainichi Nyorai.) In the form of a mantric syllable, the deity is the seed syllable (*shuji*), which symbolizes the essence of a deity in a single Sanskrit syllable.

A seed syllable may be taken from a deity's mantra, its name, or one of its attributes. While some deities may have more than one seed syllable, some may share the same syllable. The mantra of Dainichi Nyorai in the Taizō Mandala is A BIRA UN KEN, and in this case the seed syllable is the first letter of the mantra, A. This syllable in Sanskrit is a negative prefix, but as the first letter in Sanskrit and the seed syllable of Dainichi Nyorai, it can be given incalculable meaning. Mikkyo considers the A-syllable (*aji*) the root of all syllables and mantras. The *Commentary on the Dainichi-kyō* says:

The A-syllable is the basis of all words, and the mother of all syllables. It is the wellspring of all teachings.[26]

It further states:

All words are bound in the A-syllable, therefore each and every syllable gate [mantric practice] is endowed with all the syllable gates.[27]

In the Sanskrit written in the *siddham* (*shittan*) style used in Buddhism, the first stroke of every syllable is, in fact, a form of the A-syllable. Literally present in all syllables, therefore, the A-syllable provides a metaphor for all-

117

pervading enlightenment. It was also considered the primal human sound, as the *Commentary on the Dainichi-kyō* indicates:

> In the sound made when the mouth first opens, there is always the sound A. To be apart from the sound A is to have no words. Therefore it is the mother of human speech.
>
> The languages of the three realms all depend on names. Names depend on syllables. Therefore the *siddham* syllable A is the mother of all syllables.
>
> This you should know. The true meaning of the A-syllable penetrates all Dharma meanings.[28]

The A-syllable, as the first syllable of the Sanskrit word *ādyanutpāda*, "originally unborn," symbolizes the source of birth, becoming, and transformation. The A-syllable also represents earth, first of the six elements, and thus symbolizes the place where life originates and where it ultimately returns. Mikkyo uses this and other seed syllables in three-secrets practice as a means to realize the total body-mind of the universe. The seed syllable represents the most condensed symbol of enlightenment. The first image used in esoteric visualization is often a seed syllable, which the practitioner then visualizes as changing into other symbolic forms.

The *Dainichi-kyō* gives a typical Mikkyo mantra practice called the "mind-conceiving concentrated recitation" (*shinsō nenju*), which integrates mantra recitation with Dharma Body visualization as a way to experience universal body-mind activity. It involves expressing doctrinal truth in the mantra, visualizing this truth in the mind, and soundlessly reciting it with the mouth. This practice has two varieties, one using an image with which the practitioner unites, and the other making the practitioner himself the deity. The first is "worldly" (*seken*), and the latter "supramundane" (*shusseken*).

In the "worldly practice" the meditator contemplates a Buddha-image placed before him, and visualizes a lotus within the deity on which appears a moon disk. Within this disk appear the syllables of the mantra, emitting light. The practitioner visualizes the syllables individually, seeing their radiance grow stronger, and then visualizes them entering through the crown of the head to circulate throughout his own body, removing all impurities and obstructions. The sutra calls this stage "syllable recitation."

The practitioner next visualizes each syllable emitting a sound like bells in the wind. This sound circulates through the practitioner's body, further purifying and illuminating him. This stage is called "voice recitation."

Next, the syllables and their sounds unite to form words and phrases expressing the true meaning of the mantra. The practitioner visualizes this as the mantra itself, which is also, at the same time, Dainichi Nyorai, the body of wisdom that makes up the entire universe. The sutra calls this stage "phrase recitation."

After the form, sound, and meaning of the mantra have thus been achieved, the practitioner visualizes mantric phrases moving with his own breath in and out of his body. Leaving from his mouth, they enter the deity's abdomen, circulate through the moon disk in the deity's breast, leave by the deity's mouth, and enter the practitioner through the crown of the head. After circulating through a moon disk he visualizes in his own breast, they leave by his mouth and enter the deity's abdomen again in an unbroken flow. This stage is called "life-breath recitation."

By continuing this practice over thousands of recitations, the sutra says, the practitioner can gain certain phenomenal powers to bring good fortune and avert disaster. Used for this purpose, this meditation is of the magical type that esoteric Buddhism employs to benefit others. In Mikkyo, however, the primary purpose of ritual practice is to cultivate wisdom. The sutra calls this supramundane practice "absolute recitation," which leads not to secular powers but to the experience of Buddhahood. In *The Secret Key to the Heart Sutra,* Kūkai wrote:

> Mantras are mysterious. By visualizing and reciting them, we remove ignorance. One syllable embraces a thousand truths, manifesting universal reality in this very body.[29]

The Secret of Mind: Internal Visualization

Inextricably linking body and speech, the secret activity of mind is expressed in internal visualization of deities, mantric syllables, and other symbolic forms. In its universal aspect, the activity of mind extends throughout all beings and phenomena. Kūkai explained this in *The Meaning of the UN-Syllable* as follows:

> The three secrets of the Dharma Body are not limited even in the finest particles, and are not dissipated even by filling all of space. They enter stones, plants, and trees without discrimination. They enter humans, gods, demons, and animals without choosing. They extend to all places. There is nothing through which they do not act.[30]

The goal of exoteric meditation was the state of "no mind, no thought" (*munen musō*), known also in Sanskrit as *āsphānaka samādhi* (Jap., *asahanaka sanmaji*). This is a void state in which body and mind are absorbed in non-activity and no-thought. This has also been called "no-consciousness no-body samadhi" (*mushikishin sanmai*) and "unmoving samadhi" (*mudō sanmai*). Mikkyo considers this to be no more than a necessary preliminary stage that the practitioner passes through on his way to an awareness that affirms the self and all that exists. In the *Analysis of the Kongōchō-gyō,* Amoghavajra wrote:

> In the esoteric mantra teaching, which teaches sudden . . . enlightenment, this [*āsphānaka*] samadhi is not dwelt in. This is because this samadhi is a void samadhi that denies all forms and phenomena, whereas from the

standpoint of the esoteric mantra teaching, all forms and phenomena are, just as they are, truth. In illuminating them and making them come to life, the . . . mantra teaching has its special character. . . .

The attitude that shuns forms and phenomena and delights in empty samadhi is a deluded attitude that does not realize the use of true wisdom.[31]

The *Kanbutsu Sanmai-kai-kyō* describes practices using Buddha-images by which the Buddhas could be made to appear before the meditator. Through total concentration on the image, the meditator could eventually see it with eyes open or closed. After this, he would visualize further Buddhas, who would rise up from their seats and move, filling all of space and emitting a miraculous radiance liberating all beings from suffering. Symbols of Buddha-activities were also used in such practice. Translated into Chinese during the early fifth century, this sutra may have had some influence on the *Kongōchō-gyō*. Similarities between the two, however, relate to the superficial format of visualization. The older, exoteric visualizations derived from the practice of remembering Shakyamuni, and then contemplating increasingly idealized forms of other Buddhas—a type of visualization that tends to reinforce the conception of Buddhas as supernatural beings separate from the self.

Another pre-esoteric text, the *Shiui Yōryaku-hō* (Essentials of Concentrated Thought Techniques), gives several similar visualization practices, but instructs the meditator to go on, after visualizing the Buddha-body, to visualize the Buddha's body of truth (i.e., its powers, compassion, good activities, etc.), just as, "after visualizing a golden container, one visualizes the precious jewel within it."[32]

Similarly, in the *Jūjū Bibasha-ron* (a commentary on the *Kegon-kyō,* or Flower Garland Sutra), Nagarjuna wrote that Buddhas should be visualized not only in their corporeal form but in their perfect Dharma-nature. Not becoming attached to perfect Dharma-nature either, however, the meditator also visualizes the true aspect of all things. Nagarjuna therefore advises Buddha-visualization in three stages: contemplating the Buddha's anthropomorphic body, the Dharma Body, and the truth in phenomena. Mahayana thus developed various practices of meditation on the virtues and powers as well as the appearance of the Buddha.

An early esoteric sutra dealing with the mantra practice of the bodhisattva Kannon (the *Kanjizai Bosatsu Tabatari Zuishin Darani-kyō*) gives the first systematized three-secrets deity visualization. In it, the practitioner forms hand mudras and visualizes the deity first as a mantric seed syllable, then as a symbolic object, and finally in human form. Beginning with the abstract syllable form, the object of visualization becomes progressively concrete, finally assuming a form relating directly to the practitioner himself—a standard pattern in esoteric visualization.

The *Dainichi-kyō* states that visualization may employ images of the Buddha, saints, bodhisattvas, other deities, human beings, or nonhumans. All are manifestations of Buddha-nature; nothing is to be looked down upon as unworthy or unenlightened. Esoteric symbols therefore represent more than convenient, limited vehicles for conveying a reality greater than themselves. Mikkyo considers them as actual embodiments of the universal self. Finding the universe in all things, Mikkyo also uses the individual self as an image of the universal Buddha, and visualization of Buddha or Dharma Body represents in itself the cultivation of the meditator's mind.

According to the *Kongōchō-gyō,* the meditation practice by which Shakyamuni attained Buddhahood was the Five-Aspect Attainment-Body Visualization (*gosō jōshin-kan*). In this meditation the practitioner visualizes the Buddha-body perfected in his own body in five stages equivalent to the Five Wisdoms.

The practitioner begins by visualizing his innately enlightened mind within his own breast as a moon disk covered by a light mist. In order to increase the radiant wisdom of his mind the practitioner contemplates the moon disk as a symbol of awakening mind, visualizing the mist disappearing to reveal the moon shining bright and clear. The practitioner visualizes a vajra within the moon disk, and thus symbolically attains the adamantine mind. Contemplating within the moon disk the immovable firmness of the five-pronged vajra (symbol of enlightened wisdom), the practitioner realizes his own innate vajra-nature. Seeing the moon disk and vajra as symbols of his true self, he then gradually expands them in size until they become one body with the Dharma Realm, thus attaining oneness of his body with the universal Buddha-body. They are then contracted back to their original size before the meditation ends.

The *Dainichi-kyō* gives a corresponding practice, based on the symbolic elements, called the Five-Syllable Sublime-Body Visualization (*goji gonshin-kan*). This meditation complements the Five-Aspect Attainment-Body Visualization given in the *Kongōchō-gyō,* just as the Taizō and Kongō-kai mandalas, and the teachings of the two main sutras, complement each other. Like the earlier "tenfold all-pervading visualization" using the elements, the Five-Syllable practice also had an exoteric, magical aspect, being performed, for example, to cure illness or summon someone from a distance. In Mikkyo, however, this aspect was subordinated to the esoteric aim of using phenomenal symbols to experience truth.

This practice employs the mantric syllables of the five symbolic elements of earth (A), water (BA), fire (RA), wind (KA), and space (KYA), which form the body of Dainichi Nyorai in the Tai-zō Mandala. Visualized within the practitioner, these represent five aspects of inseparable mind and matter, the five wisdoms of enlightenment. While forming mudras the practitioner visualizes the areas of his body in the shapes associated with the elements, and within those shapes visualizes their respective mantric syllables.

This pattern, recurring in most Mikkyo practices, represents the combined use of body (in the mudras), speech (in the mantric syllables), and mind (in the visualization as well as in concentration on mudras and mantras). The syllables and elements form a five-storied pagoda, the samaya form of Dainichi Nyorai, superimposed on the practitioner's body, symbolizing identity with the universe.

Although the elements are not meant to be taken in a sense as components of physical substance, their symbolic meaning can extend into very concrete terms within the practitioner's own body. The feet and legs, for example, being made of bone and muscle, can be associated with the earth element. The abdomen, where there is the greatest proportion of liquid, similarly relates to the element water. The heart, which pulsates with fiery red blood, is like the element fire, and the throat, through which the breath passes, is related to the element wind. The crown of the head (or sometimes the whole body) can be visualized as the element space. In this way the practitioner employs his entire body as a symbol of the all-pervading unity of the substance of the universe.

In the *Gorin Kujimyō Himitsu-shaku* (Secret Explanation of the Five Elements and Nine-Syllable Mantra), Kakuban explained that the deity of this practice is Dainichi Nyorai in the ultimate universal aspect as the deity of both Tai-zō and Kongō-kai mandalas in one. This view represents a further step in the Mikkyo synthesis of the traditions of the two sutras and the two mandalas in a single, all-encompassing teaching that is expressed in a practical meditation technique.

SIX

The Dynamic Mandala

In Mikkyo, the word *mandala* (*mandara*) means the full perfection of Buddhahood, the realm of enlightenment. The source of the Mikkyo mandala is Shakya-muni's experience at Buddha-gayā, where he realized enlighten-ment through meditation under a bodhi tree. Mikkyo seeks to convey this experience of the source of the self by means of painted and sculpted forms, and by meditation and ritual employing these forms. This is the inner meaning of the mandala. As Kūkai wrote in the *List of Items Brought from China:*

> The secret repository is profound and mysterious, and difficult to convey in writing. Thus we borrow pictures to point to what is to be realized.[1]

The word *mandala* is composed of the Sanskrit root *maṇḍa*—meaning essence, center, true meaning, the purest flavor of clarified milk—with the suffix *la,* meaning accomplishment, possession. Mandala originally meant platform, essence, or circle in Sanskrit, and, by extension, that which is endowed with all power and virtue. In other words, mandala means that which has essence. The eighth-century Indian master Buddhaguhya wrote that in this case essence refers to the Buddha's enlightenment, and that the realm of this enlightenment is the mandala.

The word *mandala* was translated into Chinese in various ways, including:

Perfectly endowed: Perfect as a wheel is round, the mandala is endowed with all the myriad powers.

Highest incomparable flavor; unsurpassable highest flavor: Buddhahood is the "flavor" of enlightenment to which nothing can be compared. The *Commentary on the Dainichi-kyō* calls the mandala the "highest incomparable flavor," the "unsurpassable highest flavor," and "nectar."[2]

Assembly: The mandala assembles in one place all the powers of enlightened truth.

Generation: The mandala generates infinite manifestations of Buddha-bodies, mantras, meanings, and the three secrets.

Altar, place of meditation: The mandala represents the place of practice, where enlightenment is attained, and by extension can also mean "temple."

Śākyamitra, a master of eighth-century India, wrote in his commentary on the *Kongōchō-gyō* that the Buddha's attainment of the highest enlightenment is the mandala. The *Commentary on the Dainichi-kyō* calls the very place where Shakyamuni attained realization the Enlightenment (*bodai*) Mandala. The primary meaning of mandala as the essence of the Buddha's enlightenment grew to include all places where wisdom was attained.

In the Shingon view the aspects of enlightenment are embodied in rich detail in the two fundamental mandalas, which symbolize the primary source of all Shingon deities, doctrines, and other mandalas. Kūkai wrote in the *Treatise on Ten Levels of Mind:*

> The secret, sublime mind means realizing the ultimate basis and origin of one's mind and proving the measure of the self as it truly is. In other words, it is the Tai-zō . . . , the Kongō-kai Mandala. . . .[3]

As a representation of enlightenment, the painted mandala, though drawn with line and color, is not an ordinary painting. The deep blue in a mandala's background, for instance, symbolizes the infinite universal realm that pervades (and simultaneously transcends) the phenomenal realm. It represents the infinite void reality that is the original source of mind. The enlightened activities symbolized in the mandala's deities project from this mysterious realm of potentiality into our world. The following passage from Kūkai's *The Meaning of Becoming a Buddha in This Body* describes the universal activity symbolized in the mandala:

> The three secrets of all things and the Buddha are profound and extremely subtle. Since even the bodhisattvas in the ten stages of enlightenment cannot see or hear them, they are therefore called secrets. Each and every one of the innumerable deities alike is endowed with its three secrets. The three secrets of the different deities flow into and augment one another, and are absorbed and held. The three secrets of all beings are also like this.[4]

As described in the *Dainichi-kyō* and other Mikkyo texts, early esoteric mandalas in ancient India were earthen platforms made specially for use in a seven-day platform mandala ritual. The text for this ritual, still extant, relates that when a master initiated his disciple, he created a particular platform mandala according to his own style of teaching and the disciple's individual capacity. The master would then lead the disciple into the mandala to perform the initiation ritual.

This seven-day platform ritual died out in China and was never practiced in Japan, one reason no doubt being that seven days of uninterrupted good weather could not be expected in these countries. Instead, the platform altar (further described in Chapter Seven), a kind of mandala, came into use as the center of ritual. Mandalas themselves became permanent images, and the spaces left open because the practitioner no longer physically entered them were later filled with deities representing the practitioner. Thus where the Shingon sutras (written before the mandalas' full evolution) list only certain deities in the mandala, mandalas later developed to include many more. Mikkyo mandalas in actual use today, though mostly painted, two-dimensional representations, are not meant to be viewed passively from the outside. The practitioner still "enters into" the mandala through techniques of esoteric union with its deities in order to realize the truths embodied therein.

The earthen platform mandala, prototype of the current painted mandala and platform altar, was a symbol of the Wisdom of All-Wisdom (*issai chichi*), further symbolized by the element earth, which also refers to all of nature. Because it equally pervades all things and beings, Mikkyo calls this wisdom the mind-ground, which is identified with the earth as a symbol of all nature. Esoteric mandalas thus represent patterns of the totality of existence. At the same time, the earthen platform represented the pure enlightened mind with which all beings are originally endowed, just as all share in the benefits of the earth and nature.

The earthen platform practice included a preparatory ritual of purification in which objects symbolizing defilements and delusions in the practitioner's mind were removed from the earth. After being purified, precious objects were buried in the earthen platform, a practice paralleled in Shingon by placing treasure vases on the wooden platform altar. Thus mandala practice shows a profound relationship between the earth, the mandala, and the self. In reference to the mandala, the *Dainichi-kyō* says:

> Gaining this Wisdom of All-Wisdom, spread it widely for the sake of the innumerable beings. According to their various ways and temperaments, use various skillful means to teach the Wisdom of All-Wisdom. . . . The ways of this wisdom are of one essence, the essence of the Buddha's enlightenment.[5]

The *Dainichi-kyō Sho* explains this as follows:

> The meaning of this . . . is the awakening of the Great Compassion Tai-zō Mandala. In the undifferentiated mind ground of the Wisdom of All-Wisdom, draw the circular platform of the fourfold universe with all the Buddhas and Bodhisattvas and the eight kinds of protectors . . .
>
> The sutra says, "All is of one essence because it is the essence of the Buddha's enlightenment." This is because the truth of the form and mind of all living beings is, from the beginning, in equality with the wisdom body of Dainichi Nyorai. This does not mean that in attaining wisdom, one realizes the Dharma Realm by forcing all things into emptiness. The Buddha develops the inexhaustible, sublime repository great mandala out

125

of the equality of his mind ground, and with this develops the inexhaustible, sublime repository great mandala out of the equal mind ground of living beings. His subtle responses all issue from the gate of the A-syllable.[6]

In other words, the universal Wisdom of All-Wisdom gives rise to various manifestations in response to the individual characters and capacities of the numberless beings. Because it is of one essence equal in all things and beings, this Wisdom of All-Wisdom is called the mind ground, which is symbolically identified with the earth and nature. Everything manifests the Wisdom of All-Wisdom and thus participates in the intrinsic self-mandala. Phenomena are the Dharma Body's skillful means to bring about this realization. The altar platform and other kinds of mandala are also such skillful means.

TYPES OF MANDALA

Mandalas exist in great variety of form and content. The most familiar mandalas today may be those painted on hanging scrolls, but Borobodur is an architectural mandala, while the mandala in the lecture hall at Tō-ji is composed of three-dimensional sculptured deities. At the temple of Sennyū-ji in Kyoto, a ritual is held annually in which masked and costumed people play the parts of bodhisattvas in a living mandala. Initiation rituals use a *shiki* ("laid out") mandala, made to be spread out on an altar platform, in place of the ancient earthen platform mandala.

The esoteric mandala illustrates enlightenment, and so the true self. As such it also depicts the entire body-mind of the cosmos. In terms of Mikkyo doctrine, the mandala symbolically represents the "universal form" of all things and beings, which Mikkyo describes by the Four Mandalas. The four aspects of phenomena, these are also names for the basic types of ritual mandala:

> Great Mandala (*dai mandara*): Mandalas depicting the deities in perfect human form.
> Samaya Mandala (*sanmaya mandara*): Mandalas depicting the deities in their symbolic samaya forms.
> Dharma Mandala (*hō mandara*): Mandalas depicting particular aspects of the deities in the form of their Sanskrit seed syllables.
> Karma Mandala (*katsuma mandara*): Three-dimensional mandalas depicting the deities in sculptured form. (Karma means activity.)

The many kinds of mandala can generally be classified under three different systems:

> Considered as depictions (graphic or three-dimensional) of deities, mandalas would fall under the four types listed above.

126

Considered as systematic assemblies of deities, they include depictions of all the major deities arrayed around Dainichi Nyorai, of a subgroup of related deities, of a single deity with attendants, etc.

Considered as representations of the relationship between self and Buddha, mandalas have been interpreted various ways. The *Dainichi Kyōsho Gijutsu* (Relation of the Meaning of the Commentary on the Dainichi-kyō) by Yūshō, a Shingon master of the thirteenth–fourteenth century, gives the following three classifications:[7]

Mandala of the Equality of the Great Void (*daikū byōdō mandara*): The great void is that which is beyond void and nonvoid. Its power informs all the myriad phenomena, which are equal in it, and so the entirety of existing things is found in this mandala. This is the mandala of the entire universe, also called the Great Void Dharma Realm (*daikū hōkai*). The mandala of the universe means the self and all of nature, every tree and blade of grass. Everything is seen as filled with cosmic life-energy, in the same way that a drop of seawater is of the same essence as the entire sea, and a dewdrop clinging to a leaf-tip embodies all of heaven and earth.

Mandala of the Self-Mind of All Beings (*shujō jishin mandara*): The enlightenment of Shakyamuni is the unfolding of the Buddha-nature with which all beings are originally endowed. This innate Buddha-nature is also called the mind-lotus of living beings (*shujō shinren*), the mind-lotus being the human heart. In other words, this is the mandala of the self.

Mandala Manifesting Through Causation by Buddha Empowerment (*nyorai kaji shigen engi mandara*): This type includes graphic and three-dimensional mandalas. Limited by delusion, ordinary beings cannot perceive the great void mandala. The pictorial mandala, however, is a visible, phenomenal manifestation of the universe itself. By correct use of the mandala, one realizes the source of one's being and perceives the equality of the individual with the cosmos.

In this view, the individual may realize his original enlightenment by contemplating pictorial or internally visualized mandalas. One practice in which the mandala plays a major part is the initiation ritual called Dharma Transmission (*denpō*). In the sanctified initiation hall, the Tai-zō and Kongō-kai mandalas are hung on the walls to the left and right of the altar platform. The altar platform itself is made into a "great mandala platform" (*dai mandara dan*) by laying out on its upper surface two *shiki* mandalas (in which deities are represented in samaya form) one on top of the other. When the initiation is into the lineage of Kongō-kai practice, the Kongō-kai Mandala is on top, the Tai-zō beneath, and vice-versa—the two mandalas being separate yet inseparable aspects of a single truth.

The master presiding over the initiation uses three-secrets techniques to unite with the two mandalas. In a state of consciousness in which the two mandalas are fully energized in his body-mind, he transmits the Dharma to his disciple.

127

The disciple forms a karmic bond with the deity of the mandala, Dainichi Nyorai, in a relationship of mutual empowerment leading to realization of his innate Buddha-mind. (This ritual, of primary importance for the Shingon priesthood, is further described in Chapter Six.)

It is easy to view mandalas only as symbols of transcendent, universal Buddhahood, which, as symbols of the universe, they indeed are. This universe, however, is not apart from the self. The deities in the mandala are symbols of the self as well as of the universe. Shingon considers mandalas to be both mirrors of the mind and patterns of the manifold, ever-evolving activities of consciousness and of phenomena. The same patterns are equally applicable to all humanly conceivable levels of vision, macrocosmic and microcosmic. The innate Buddha is both the true self and the deity of the mandala, and both are the universe.

Outline of the Tai-zō Mandala

The Tai-zō Mandala represents the enlightened universe from the viewpoint of compassion. Its full name is Daihitaizōsei Mandala, the Great Compassion Womb Repository Birth Mandala. Tai-zō means literally "womb-repository." As a mother enfolds and nurtures a child in her womb, so the energy of compassion nurtures and protects one's innate enlightenment.

The metaphor of the lotus is also employed to explain the nature of the mandala. Since the lotus seed is endowed with the potential for growth, the seed is innate enlightened mind. The sprouting and growth of the lotus is great compassion, and its flowering is skillful means. The compassion nurturing the lotus (the practitioner) is the "womb" out of which he is born. Therefore the full name of this mandala is the Great Compassion Womb Repository Birth Mandala.

The primary textual basis for this mandala is the *Dainichi-kyō* and its *Commentary,* but the mandala as we know it today is not fully described in these texts. Various types of Tai-zō Mandala existed, based on different texts that were successively elaborated on and added to. Oral teachings also played an important part. The Shingon Tai-zō Mandala appears to have been first drawn in China.

Based on the cursory description given in the *Dainichi-kyō,* Shubhakarasimha and Amoghavajra made different versions of the Tai-zō Mandala with, for example, varying numbers of deities and differently named sections. Although it appears that the mandala in Shubhakarasimha's line was more widespread in China, the Tai-zō adopted by Shingon is based on Amoghavajra's version. This is called the "drawn as revealed" (*genzu*) mandala because, according to one legend, it was copied from a supernatural mandala that mysteriously appeared in midair.

The deities of the Tai-zō Mandala represent the many differentiated activities of compassion. The lotus, therefore, is its primary symbol, and all its deities are seated on lotus thrones. In the painted mandala, the essence of compassion is symbolized in a flattened eight-petalled lotus at the center, on which the primary deities are seated. The layers of the mandala extend out from this lotus, with three layers on each side and four to the top and bottom. These layers are composed of sections called "halls" (*in*), each of which portrays constellations of related Buddhas, bodhisattvas, and other deities. In all, 409 deities are depicted in twelve "halls." The mandala's deities together represent the power inherent in Dainichi Nyorai, and all represent the unfolding of different aspects of the central deity.

The central section, the Hall of the Eight-Petalled Central Dais (*chūdai hachiyō-in*), is a square set off by lines of the five elemental colors (white, yellow, black, red, green). The nine primary deities of the mandala are depicted on a red eight-petalled lotus within the square. While a white lotus symbolizes innate Buddha-mind, the red one here is the color of compassion. Red also symbolizes the human heart (*nikudanshin,* "flesh heart"), indicating that Buddha-mind is to be realized within the living human being. As the body of compassion, Dainichi Nyorai is depicted in the center of the Eight-Petalled Central Dais, his hands forming the Dharma Realm Samadhi Mudra.

Four Buddhas, primary manifestations of the central deity, are depicted on the lotus petals at the four cardinal points: (Mandalas are directionally oriented, like maps, with north, south, east, west, and the intermediate directions clearly defined. In the Tai-zō, east is at the top, south to the right, west at the bottom, and north to the left.)

On the east petal (the top petal) sits Hōdō Buddha, who embodies the realization that self and universe are one. He forms the wish-bestowing mudra.

To the south (the right petal) sits Kaifuke-ō Buddha, who represents the unfolding of the lotus from the seed syllable of enlightened wisdom. He forms the mudra of fearlessness.

To the west (the bottom petal) sits Muryōju Buddha, who symbolizes the infinite activity of compassion throughout the universe. He forms the Dharma Realm Samadhi Mudra.

To the north (the left petal) sits Tenkuraion Buddha, who represents the spontaneous activity of skillful means. He forms the earth-touching mudra.

The eight petals also symbolize the first eight levels of consciousness, which after enlightenment reveal themselves as the four wisdoms. This is the meaning of the vajras visible between the lotus petals. The four treasure vases in the corners symbolize the enlightened mind, the wisdom, the compassion, and the skillful means of Dainichi Nyorai. These four powers are the activities of the four bodhisattvas on the intermediate petals. In the center, Dainichi Nyorai is depicted with golden body, crowned, his hair plaited with bodhisattva ornaments. The four Buddhas which are his emanations are shown uncrowned and wearing simple robes, as Buddhas are commonly depicted.

The four bodhisattvas of the intermediate directions are crowned and hold symbolic objects. Each with its own distinct characteristics, the four are objects of popular devotion. Here, they represent activities of Dainichi Nyorai. Their names and directions are as follows:

Fugen is southeast (between top and right).
Monju is southwest (between right and bottom).
Kanjizai is northwest (between bottom and left).
Miroku is northeast (between left and top).

Beneath the central hall is the Wisdom-Holding Hall (*jimyō-in*), in the mandala's first layer. Originally, when the earthen mandala was made to be physically entered by the candidate for initiation, the central place in this section was left open as a place for the candidate to sit. In the hanging mandala, however, this open space came to be occupied by Hannya (meaning wisdom) Bodhisattva, who represents the practitioner. Here the deity has six arms, wears armor as a symbol of overcoming obstructions to enlightenment, and is accompanied by four wrathful deities of like function.

In the first layer above the central hall is the All-Pervading Wisdom Hall (*henchi-in*), also known as the Buddha-Mother Hall or Buddha-Mind Hall. Its central deity is Issai Nyorai Henchi-in (All-Pervading Wisdom Mudra of the Buddhas), the mudra of Buddha-Wisdom, depicted as a triangular wisdom-flame symbolizing the three wisdoms of void, formlessness, and no-desire (*mugan*). The swastika within the triangle symbolizes the power of the enlightened universe. This is the only deity in the mandala not represented in "human" form.

To the immediate right of the central hall, in the first layer, is the Vajra-Wielding Hall (*kongōshu-in*). The primary deity of this section is Kongōsatta. He is surrounded by thirty-two subsidiary bodhisattvas, all wielding various kinds of vajra.

The Kannon Hall (*kannon-in*), also known as the Lotus Division Hall (*rengebu-in*), is in the first layer of the mandala, to the immediate left of the central hall. The meaning of this section is that all beings are, like the lotus, originally pure. The central deity is the esoteric form of Kannon known as Shōkanjizai or Shōkannon, who also appears in three other places in the mandala.

In the second layer of the mandala, above the All-Pervading Wisdom Hall, is the Shakyamuni Hall (*shaka-in*). In its center is a large gate, within which sits a red-robed Shakyamuni (Jap., Shakamuni), the transforming Buddha-body that is bound neither to birth-and-death nor to nirvana. The thirty-eight subsidiary deities also include several historical disciples of Shakyamuni (such as Subhūti, Kāśyapa, Śāriputra, and Ānanda). The presence of human beings indicates that the human body and the pure Dharma Body are not-two. Other deities symbolize Shakyamuni's enlightenment under the bodhi tree, his activities, and the three treasures of Buddha, Dharma, and Sangha.

In the mandala's third layer, immediately above the Shakyamuni Hall, is the Monju Hall (*monju-in*). The central deity is Monju, bodhisattva of wisdom, depicted holding the vajra of wisdom, his body golden in color to show his adamantine thought, seated on a lotus that is blue to show that he is unstained by the myriad phenomena of the universe. To his immediate left and right are Kanjizai (deity of mercy) and Fugen (deity of wisdom and blessings), beneath whom are two gate guardians. The other twenty deities are Monju's attendants and subsidiaries.

In the second layer of the mandala to the right is the Obstacle-Removing Hall (*jogaishō-in*), which removes delusions and obstructions to realization. The central deity is Jogaishō Bodhisattva, also known as Delusion Vajra. There are eight subsidiary bodhisattvas symbolizing various activities of compassion, wisdom, fearlessness, and non-obstruction.

In the corresponding place to the left is the Jizō Hall (*jizō-in*), a complement to the Obstruction-Removing Hall on the right. The central deity is the bodhisattva Jizō, whose name means "earth repository." This section depicts deities who endure suffering—as both earth and nature endure—to find joy. Eight subsidiary bodhisattvas are also present.

In the second layer of the mandala, to the bottom, is the Kokūzō Hall (*kokūzō-in*). Based on the enduring activity of the Jizō Hall, this section embodies the unhampered activity of benefit to self and others. The central deity is Kokūzō Bodhisattva, whose name means "void repository," depicted with twenty-seven subsidiary deities. To the far left is the Thousand-Armed Thousand-Eyed Kanjizai, and to the right is the One-Hundred-and-Eight-Armed Vajra Repository King (Jap., Kongōzō-ō) Bodhisattva, a manifestation of Kongōsatta.

In the mandala's third layer, immediately below the Jizō Hall, is the Unsurpassed Attainment Hall (*soshitsuji-in*), with eight bodhisattvas but no central deity. Originally a part of the Jizō Hall, it was made a separate section in order to balance the mandala

The Outermost Hall (*saige-in*) is also known as the Outer Vajra Hall or the Hall of the Gods. This is the fourth and last layer, completely surrounding the mandala. The deities here are the many gods (*ten*) adopted into Buddhism as guardians. There are 202 deities in all (though versions of the Tai-zō may vary), with 39 on the top, 62 on the right, 48 on the bottom, and 53 on the left. To name only a few:

In the top left corner is Ishana-ten, the wrathful aspect of Daijizai-ten.

In the top right corner is Ka-ten, god of fire.

In the bottom right corner is Rasetsu-ten, ruler of ghouls and destructive demons.

In the bottom left corner is Fū-ten, god of the wind.

In the eastern gate (on the top) are two pairs of gate guardian gods, and on either side of the gate are the great god Taishaku-ten, ruler of the four heavenly kings, and his liege Jikoku-ten.

In the southern gate (to the right) are two serpent-god kings, the king of ashuras (war-like gods), and a representative of the *ashuras*. Enma-ten, the god of death, sits beneath the gate, and Zōjō-ten, ruler of the hungry ghosts and one of the four heavenly kings, sits above it.

In the western gate (to the bottom) are two serpent-god kings, Taimen-ten and Nanpa-ten. To the right of the gate is Sui-ten, god of water, and to the left is Kōmoku-ten, another of the four heavenly kings, ruler of the serpent-gods.

In the northern gate (to the left) are two serpent-god kings with Kubira and his consort. Beneath the gate is the prominent figure of Taishaku-ten (also found in the east), and above it is Bishamon-ten, god of the underworld and god of wealth.

THE CONCENTRIC STRUCTURE OF THE TAI-ZŌ MANDALA

The universal enlightenment symbolized in the center of the mandala is the tenth level of consciousness, the level of "innumerable minds." This central consciousness radiates throughout the mandala. In the Eight-Petalled Central Dais, this outward radiation passes through the Buddhas and bodhisattvas, "descending" through the levels of consciousness and moving outward toward the phenomenal world. Becoming gradually more concrete as it moves outward from the center, it reaches the human world and then descends further into the realms of animals, hell, and hungry ghosts. The outermost section of the mandala does not represent the limit of this movement. Rather, the limited mandala is meant to show that skillful means based on wisdom and compassion well up like a spring in the center and flow out unceasingly in all directions in numberless concentric rings spreading out to infinity.

The *Dainichi-kyō*, commentaries, ritual manuals, and records of oral transmission explain the nature of the mandala by interrelating its major sections and deities in different ways. These explanations are traditionally seen in terms of the Three Divisions (*sanbu*), the Dharma Gate of the Three Phrases (*sanku no hōmon*), and the bodies of the Buddha (*busshin*). Each approach deals with different aspects of doctrine and practice, yet all are equally valid in the context of the mandala, which portrays the entire system of Mikkyo teachings. These various approaches all have in common the view of the mandala center as primary, essential, and of a "higher" order relative to the outer sections. Proceeding away from the center, the outer layers are seen as relatively more subsidiary, phenomenal, concrete, and of a "lower" order in relation to those closer to the center.

The mandala is seen in the three divisions of Buddha, Lotus, and Vajra. The Buddha Division refers to perfect enlightenment, endowed with both truth and wisdom. The Lotus Division refers to the truth of innate enlightenment which is never stained. The Vajra Division refers to the power of wisdom in that truth, which like the vajra is adamantine and destroys delusion. The Buddha

Division is associated with the great samadhi and, of the three secrets, expresses the secret of body. The Lotus is associated with compassion and the secret of speech, and the Vajra with wisdom and the secret of mind. The halls of the Tai-zō Mandala are assigned to the three divisions in various ways. In general, again, that which is closer to the center is considered more essential and primary relative to that which is toward the periphery. For example:

Buddha Division:
    Hall of the Eight-Petaled Central Dais
    All-Pervading Wisdom Hall
    Wisdom-Holding Hall
Lotus Division:
    Kannon Hall
Vajra Division:
    Vajra-Wielding Hall[8]

The Dharma Gate of the Three Phrases, the important *Dainichi-kyō* formula, deals with enlightenment and the way to enlightenment: To the question, "What is the cause of All-Wisdom, what is its root, and in what is its ultimate?" the answer is, "Enlightened mind is the cause, great compassion is the root, and skillful means are the ultimate."[9] The sections of the Taizō Mandala are related to this threefold statement as follows:

Enlightened mind is the cause (first layer of mandala):
    Hall of the Eight-Petaled Central Dais
    All-Pervading Wisdom Hall
    Wisdom-Holding Hall
    Kannon Hall
    Vajra-Wielding Hall
Great compassion is the root (second layer of mandala):
    Shakyamuni Hall
    Monju Hall
    Kokūzō Hall
    Unsurpassed Attainment Hall
    Jizō Hall
    Obstacle-Removing Hall
Skillful means are the ultimate (third layer):
    Outer Vajra Hall

Also related to the Tai-zō Mandala's sections are the teachings of the "bodies of the Buddha" (*busshin*). From the early Buddhist concept of two Buddhas, the historical Shakyamuni and the eternal, absolute Dharma Body, theories of the bodies of the Buddha developed along with Mahayana doctrine. The basic Mahayana teaching referred to three bodies: the Dharma Body (*hosshin*); the Buddha in the Pure Land, often called "the Body of Bliss" (*hōjin*); and the

Buddha as a historical manifestation responding to the needs of living beings (*ōjin*), in other words, Shakyamuni.

The fundamental Mikkyo doctrine of Buddha-bodies includes all Buddhas, bodhisattvas, and other deities as aspects of the Dharma Body itself, which is divided into four manifestations. In the historical process of consolidating all the vast numbers of deities in the single being of Dainichi Nyorai, Mikkyo came to see the "lower" forms of Buddha also as aspects of the Dharma Body:

The first of these is the "Self-Proving Dharma Body" (*jishō hosshin*), the Buddha who teaches the three secrets and is the originally self-existing universal being of Truth and Wisdom. This is the body-nature of the Dharma essence of the universe. Transcending cause and effect, purity and impurity, it is the source Buddha of all existence.

The second is the "Accepting Dharma Body" (*juyū hosshin*), which has the dual aspects of the "Self-Accepting" and "Other-Accepting" bodies:

> The "Self-Accepting Dharma Body" (*jijuyū hosshin*) is the Buddha body that receives and enjoys by itself the perfect spiritual activity of the "Self-Proving Dharma Body." It is the Wisdom Dharma Body.
> The "Other-Accepting Dharma Body" (*tajuyū hosshin*) is the Buddha body that enables bodhisattvas in the ten stages of developing Buddhahood to enjoy the Dharma.

The third is the "Transforming Dharma Body" (*henge hosshin*), which manifests in forms appropriate to communicating with human beings according to their particular capacities.

The fourth is the "Equally-Permeating Dharma Body" (*tōru hosshin*), which takes on the forms of beings of all realms of rebirth in order to bring them to enlightenment.

The deities and sections of the Tai-zō Mandala are associated with these Buddha-manifestations. Dharma Body (*hosshin*), the historical manifestation (*ōjin*), Transformation Body (*keshin*), and Equally-Permeating Body (*tōrushin*) are identified in the mandala as follows:

Dharma Body	Dainichi Nyorai
ōjin	The Four Buddhas
Transformation Body	Shakyamuni
Equally-Permeating Body	Outer Vajra Hall

The four manifestations of the Self-Proving Dharma Body, the Accepting Dharma Body, the Transforming Dharma Body, and the Equally-Permeating Dharma Body are identified in the Tai-zō Mandala as follows:

Self-Proving Dharma Body:
    Hall of the Eight-Petaled Central Dais
    All-Pervading Wisdom Hall

> Wisdom-Holding Hall
> Kannon Hall
> Vajra-Wielding Hall
Accepting Dharma Body:
> Shakyamuni Hall
> Kokūzō Hall
> Jizō Hall
> Obstacle-Removing Hall
Transforming Dharma Body:
> Monju Hall
> Unsurpassed Attainment Hall
Equally-Permeating Dharma Body:
> Outer Vajra Hall

The teachings concerning the bodies of the Buddha, the mandala's many deities, and the sections of the mandala are also closely related to the Mikkyo view of consciousness. Kūkai wrote in the *Record of the Secret Treasury*:

> What are the bodies of the four types of Dharma Body in the mandala?
> Answer. Dainichi Nyorai in the central dais is the Dharma Body, the four Buddhas the *ōjin,* Shakyamuni the Transforming Body, and the serpent-gods and demons of the outer Vajra section the Equally-Permeating Body.[10]

Viewed through these several perspectives, the four-layered Tai-zō Mandala thus reveals itself as unfolding concentrically. This is, however, only a partial, surface view of the mandala. Actually it is three-dimensional, as is clearly illustrated by an associated practice known as the nine-layered A-syllable visualization (*kujū ajikan*). Also called the nine-layered moon disk visualization, this was a central visualization practice in the early Tai-zō Mandala ritual.[11] The *Commentary on the Dainichi-kyō* has a vague description of a nine-layered moon disk, and records of oral transmissions describe various nine-layered A-syllable meditations that are either concentric (like a bull's-eye), nine disked (the disks arranged one on top of the other), or eight-petalled (much like the Eight-Petalled Central Dais).

The concentric form of the nine-layered A-syllable visualization gives a view of the consciousness as nine concentric disks, while the nine-disked form shows a side view of similar disks one above the other. The eight-petalled form shows the A-syllable within a moon disk, symbolizing the ninth consciousness, at the center of an eight-petaled lotus with eight more A-syllables representing the other consciousnesses arrayed around it. This is an expanded view in which all consciousnesses are visible both individually and as an entire system.

By the process of transforming consciousness and acquiring wisdom (*tenjiki tokuchi*), the consciousnesses reveal themselves to be the five wisdoms ascribed to the five Buddhas (*gobutsu*) enthroned in the center of the mandala. The master Yūkai (1345–1416) wrote in his *Nikyōron-shō* (Summary of the Doctrine of the Two Teachings):

> According to their profound, secret meaning, the ten consciousnesses are as follows: The eight consciousnesses are the Buddhas of the eight petals. The ninth consciousness is the nine Buddhas of the eight petals and the central dais. The tenth consciousness is these nine Buddhas . . . and all the various subsidiary deities made into a single consciousness. Know that these, embraced by the nine deities, form the tenth consciousness.[12]

Kūkai's *Record of the Secret Treasury* describes the consciousnesses in relation to the deities of the Tai-zō Mandala in terms of the essential mind (*shinnō*) and all subsidiary minds (*shinju*). The essential mind is the core consciousness at the base of all the mind's activities, while the subsidiary minds are the various consciousnesses functioning under the essential mind. The two are not separate, but complementary.

The essential mind embraces the entirety of whatever the mind is doing or perceiving, while the subsidiary minds work in limited aspects. When the deities of the mandala are seen as embodiments of mind, therefore, Dainichi Nyorai represents the essential mind, while the other deities, his emanations, represent the subsidiary minds. In this view, the mind has five levels of meaning:

1. The essential mind of the central deity embraces all subsidiary minds in the One Consciousness (*isshiki*).
2. The eight major deities—the four Buddhas which are the major manifestations of Dainichi Nyorai, and the four Bodhisattvas which are their secondary manifestations—embrace all subsidiary minds, forming the eighth level of consciousness.
3. The central deity and eight major deities together embrace all subsidiary minds and form the ninth level of consciousness.
4. The numberless subsidiary minds of all the deities in the surrounding sections of the mandala are embraced in a single consciousness called the All-Embracing One Mind Consciousness (*issai isshin shiki*). This, joined to the ninth level, results in the tenth level of consciousness.
5. There are innumerable Minds and Consciousnesses. These result when innumerable subsidiary minds are added to the tenth level of consciousness.[13]

Viewed in terms of dynamic consciousness, the lotus of the central dais portrays a distinct movement. The northern lotus petal (to the left), seat of Tenkuraion, is the beginning of a counterclockwise movement that proceeds through Muryōju, Kaifuke-ō, and Hōdō. This spiral progression represents a deepening of consciousness that eventually reaches its greatest depth with Dainichi Nyorai in the very center.

This spiral development is defined by the five transformations (*goten*), the stages by which the innately enlightened mind unfolds to its highest development in the activity of skillful means. The five stages are also related to the five wisdoms and the five Buddhas, and are considered an unfolding of the Dharma Gate of the Three Phrases. In the form of the fivefold A-syllable (A ĀH AN AKU ĀNKU) they are used as a mantra in the Taizō Mandala practice.

The first stage is the awakening of mind, which is called the cause (*in*). This includes both innately enlightened mind and the realization of that mind. The second stage is that of correct practice (*gyō*) leading to realization of enlightened mind. The third stage is the "proof" (*shō*) of enlightened mind, which is enlightenment in the aspect of wisdom. The fourth stage is nirvana (*nehan*), which is enlightenment in the aspect of truth. The fifth stage is the ultimate activity of skillful means (*hōben*), which is the creative flowering of the enlightened individual.

This movement, from the microcosmic viewpoint, reveals the process by which the human mind undergoes infinite deepening. From the macrocosmic viewpoint, it shows the process by which Dainichi Nyorai appears in individual, physical manifestations in the phenomenal world without sacrificing the depth and clarity of the tenth consciousness.

The five wisdoms are differentiated among the five Buddhas just as are the specific activities of Dainichi Nyorai, but each Buddha, and each wisdom, is also endowed with the totality of the other four. Ultimately, all the subsidiary deities, including those at the periphery, reveal themselves as endowed with the full enlightenment of the center. Through such a network of subsidiary (yet essential) manifestations, the entire mandala shows itself to be fully permeated by the five wisdoms.[14]

In the course of the many changes and additions the mandala has undergone during its long history, the deities have never been arranged in a perfectly symmetrical system. It is not necessarily possible, therefore, to deduce the meaning of a deity from its location in the mandala. The four-layered concentric structure is an indication of certain important aspects of the Tai-zō, but this graphic structure alone does not fully explain the mandala. The many representations of Buddha-nature in the Tai-zō Mandala—including Hindu deities that predate Buddhism, deities originating within general Buddhism, and deities unique to Mikkyo itself—came together in a gradual process of evolution that is not fully documented or clearly understood. The hundreds of deities of the mandala do exist as an interrelated, organic system, but the esoteric meaning of this system cannot be reasoned out in its entirety by means of an intellectual construct imposed on the mandala from outside.[15]

The deities and beings function harmoniously in a larger unity as individual manifestations of the all-encompassing universal enlightenment symbolized by Dainichi Nyorai. The wisdom of the universal Buddha spontaneously gives rise to compassionate activity that wells up from the center and, becoming increasingly concrete and phenomenal, moves toward the periphery. Through mutual empowerment (*kaji*) with the peripheral gods and bodhisattvas and then with the more central deities, all beings move ever toward the center in an endless activity of deepening. In other words, the center undergoes infinite, un-ending transformations directed outward to all beings, and all beings move in-ward to enlightenment through mutual empowerment with the universal man-dala. No limits or boundaries separate the outward-moving from the inward, since each movement, as it extends, reveals itself as the other. At no time is there any cessation of activity.

OUTLINE OF THE KONGŌ-KAI MANDALA

Where the Tai-zō Mandala embodies the lotus-compassion that is the reality of all things as they are, the Kongō-kai ("Vajra-Realm") Mandala embodies the vajra-wisdom that illuminates the universe. *Kongō* (vajra) refers to the wisdom that is as adamantine and imperishable as the vajra. The *Kongōchō-gyō Kaidai* (Interpretation of the Kongōchō-gyō) gives the word *kai* four meanings: realm, being, body, and discrimination. Defining this further, the *Record of the Secret Treasury* says, "Realm means being. It is the body of those who wield the vajra."[16]

Realm (sometimes translated as *matrix*), therefore, means here the universe and its contents as unified in the light of discriminating wisdom, and the sub-ject of the Kongō-kai is the wisdom-body that concentrates all beings and forms into one through the combined five wisdoms. The Kongō-kai enfolds all beings and phenomena in the single being of Dainichi Nyorai, and the pictorial mandala embodies this universal entity.

The Kongō-kai is also sometimes known as the Nine-Assembly Mandala, the Moon Disk Mandala, the Wisdom Mandala, and the Western Mandala. Its textual basis is the *Kongōchō-gyō,* which, as seen earlier, is an assembly of many sutras. One section of the sutra describes seven mandalas, another describes two more. These nine were brought together into a single mandala with nine sections called assemblies (*e*).

In form, the Kongō-kai Mandala is a rectangle made up of nine almost square rectangles of equal size, each of which was originally an independent mandala. Moving from the center down and then clockwise, the nine submandalas are as follows:

Attainment Body Assembly (*jōjinne*)
Samaya Assembly (*sanmaya-e*)
Subtle Assembly (*misai-e*)
Offering Assembly (*kuyō-e*)
Four Mudra Assembly (*shiinne*)
Single Mudra Assembly (*ichiinne*)
True Meaning Assembly (*rishu-e*)

Descending into the Three Realms Assembly (*gōzanze-e*)
Descending into the Three Realms Samaya-Assembly (*gōzanze sanmaya-e*)

The central Buddha Dainichi, source of all the mandala's deities, manifests his own activity in the form of four further Buddhas enthroned in the four cardinal directions around the center. (In this mandala, west is at the top, north to the right, east at the bottom, and south to the left.) As in the Tai-zō, the mandala's primary deities, the Five Buddhas, embody the five wisdoms, but this mandala's deities are organized in five divisions (instead of three as in the Tai-zō). Each division has one of the five Buddhas as the central unifying symbol for an array of deities located throughout the nine assemblies. The five divisions are as follows:

Buddha Division (*butsu-bu*): The unifying essence of the entire mandala. The mandala's four other divisions are its manifestations. The central deity is Dainichi Nyorai. The essence of the Kongō-kai Dainichi Nyorai is symbolized in the moon disk.

Vajra Division (*kongō-bu*): The eternal life force. The central deity is Ashuku Nyorai.

Treasure Division (*hō-bu*): The equality in value of each and every element of the universal whole. The central deity is Hōshō Butsu.

Lotus Division (*renge-bu*): The unique individuality of each and every element of the whole, and the great compassion that supports this individuality. The central deity is Muryōju Butsu, also sometimes known as Kanjizai-ō Butsu. This deity is closely related to Amida.

Karma Division (*katsuma-bu*): The activity that creates the universal whole through all its individual elements. The central deity is Fukūjōju Butsu.

The mandala's nine assemblies contain a total of 1,461 deities of which 461 are individually identifiable as particular aspects of Dainichi Nyorai. All the deities of this mandala are seated on lotus thrones wholly enclosed by moon disks. The Kongō-kai takes its distinctive character from the Five Buddhas at the center, out of which all the rest evolve. As aspects of enlightened mind, these Buddhas are the Five Wisdoms, their primary symbol the five-pronged vajra.

The vajra, essential embodiment of wisdom, is depicted throughout the mandala, and is often found within a moon disk. Since wisdom acts through compassion, the vajra lies on a lotus flower within the moon disk. Where the lotus as the central symbol of the Tai-zō represents the body of compassion (which is the truth of all things as they are), here the moon disk symbolizes the Kongō-kai body of wisdom. The vajra, lotus, and moon disk together form the central symbol of the Kongō-kai. The five-pronged vajra as symbol of the five wisdoms appears throughout the practice associated with this mandala.

The deities of the mandala represent the endless unfolding of Dainichi Nyorai, who encompasses all deities and beings as manifestations of wisdom. Simultaneously, the mandala's deities lend the energy of their own individuality to the evolution of the whole, thereby enriching their individuality and the whole. These figures are engaged in an array of activities, some in deep samadhi, others teaching, bearing treasures, offering food, making music, singing, dancing, and so on. In these activities they offer their essential selves while sharing in a continuous process of mutual homage and empowerment. The deities here are distinctly individual, dynamic personifications of enlightened desire, and at their source are a wisdom and compassion founded in enlightenment.

THE NINE ASSEMBLIES OF THE KONGŌ-KAI MANDALA

Placed at the very center of the Kongō-kai Nine-Assembly Mandala, the Attainment-Body Assembly is, as its location indicates, the fundamental section of the mandala. The eight peripheral assemblies are for the most part elaborations or condensations of the Attainment-Body Assembly, and in fact the first four and last two assemblies are practically identical in structure. The Samaya Assembly (bottom center), for example, is identical to the Attainment-Body Assembly except that its deities are depicted in samaya form (as symbolic objects) rather than in human form.

The central assembly is surrounded by vajras in its wide outer border, and within is a circle of vajras, called the Great Vajra Disk, symbolizing the palace of the five Buddhas. Inside this circle, the five Buddhas are enthroned within individual moon disks. Between the disks are walls of vajras representing the five pillars of the palace that is said to stand atop a lotus on the peak of Mount Sumeru (Jap., Shumisen), the center of the cosmos.

The Four Great Gods shown holding the Great Vajra Disk represent the symbolic elements earth, water, fire, and wind (the element void being present in all). Each of the five Buddhas is surrounded by four subsidiary deities. Further manifestations of their activities extend into the second border, making a total of five Buddhas and thirty-two bodhisattvas in this area of the Attainment-Body Assembly.

In a practically undistinguishable mass filling the spaces in the second border are the one thousand Buddhas of the present age, representing the "three thousand Buddhas" of past, present, and future. These symbolize all the manifestations of all deities. (In the other eight sections of the mandala, only sixteen deities, representing the one thousand shown here, occupy the corresponding place.)

The outer border is occupied by the Twenty Gods of the Outer Hall (*gai-in nijitten*), many of whom are also in the Outermost Hall of the Tai-zō. In the four corners of this border and in the spaces between the Twenty Gods are vajras within halos.

The activity of the Attainment-Body Assembly will be described here in some detail, since it offers a pattern for the other assemblies as well. Shingon describes this activity as a mutual homage (*kuyō*) taking place between Dainichi Nyorai and the surrounding Buddhas and bodhisattvas. The five Buddhas interact continuously, and their interaction is made manifest in the forms of other bodhisattvas which in turn perform homage to the central deity.

This activity begins with Dainichi Nyorai manifesting the four Buddhas as follows:

> In the east (at the bottom) is Ashuku.
> In the south (to the left) is Hōshō.
> In the west (at the top) is Muryōju.
> In the north (to the right) is Fukūjōju.

The activities of the four surrounding Buddhas, becoming more concrete, are made manifest in the form of bodhisattvas, so that each of the four Buddhas is surrounded by four such subsidiary bodhisattvas. The resulting sixteen sub-deities are said to symbolize also the phases of the moon. Thus meditation on them attains the full moon of the mind, Dainichi Nyorai. These Sixteen Great Bodhisattvas (*jūroku daibosatsu*) are at the cardinal directions around the four Buddhas as follows:

1. Around Ashuku are bodhisattvas representing stages in the unfolding of wisdom:
   Vajra Being (Kongōsatta)
   Vajra King (Kongōō)
   Vajra Love (Kongōai)
   Vajra Bliss (Kongōki)
2. Around Hōshō are bodhisattvas representing initiation and encouragement:
   Vajra Treasure (Kongōhō)
   Vajra Light (Kongōkō)
   Vajra Banner (Kongōdō)
   Vajra Smile (Kongōshō)
3. Around Muryōju are bodhisattvas representing the further development of wisdom:
   Vajra Dharma (Kongōhō)
   Vajra Benefit (Kongōri)
   Vajra Cause (Kongōin)
   Vajra Language (Kongōgo)
4. Around Fukūjōju are bodhisattvas representing aspects of actual practice:
   Vajra Activity (Kongōgō)
   Vajra Protection (Kongōgo)

141

Vajra Fang (Kongōge)
Vajra Fist (Kongōken)

In response to the activity of Dainichi Nyorai, the four Buddhas manifest the Four Enlightenment (Haramitsu, from the Sanskrit meaning "attaining the other shore," or "perfection") Bodhisattvas. Arrayed at the four cardinal points around Dainichi Nyorai, they pay him homage. As sources of the subsidiary deities arising from the wisdoms of the four Buddhas, these four bodhisattvas are female in form. They are as follows:

Vajra Enlightenment (Kongō-haramitsu)
Treasure Enlightenment (Hō-haramitsu)
Dharma Enlightenment (Hō-haramitsu)
Activity Enlightenment (Katsuma-haramitsu)

In response to these bodhisattvas, Dainichi Nyorai manifests the Inner Four Offering Bodhisattvas, or goddesses (*tennyo*), who pay constant homage to the four Buddhas. Located in the intermediate directions between the four Buddhas, they are as follows:

Vajra Joy (Kongō-ki)
Vajra Flower-Garland (Kongō-man)
Vajra Song (Kongō-ka)
Vajra Dance (Kongō-bu)

Responding further to the activity of Dainichi Nyorai, the four Buddhas in turn manifest the Outer Four Offering Bodhisattvas, located in the four corners of the second border enclosing this assembly's central disk. They are as follows:

Vajra Incense (Kongō-kō)
Vajra Flower (Kongō-ke)
Vajra Lamp (Kongō-tō)
Vajra Powdered-Incense (Kongō-zukō)

Thus further energized, Dainichi Nyorai manifests the Four Absorbing Bodhisattvas, so called because they act to draw all beings into the universal being. Located at the midpoints on the four sides of the second border (between the Outer Four Offering Bodhisattvas), they are as follows:

Vajra Hook (Kongō-kō)
Vajra Cord (Kongō-saku)
Vajra Chain (Kongō-sa)
Vajra Bell (Kongō-rei)

The wisdom of Dainichi Nyorai pervades and sustains the mandala, and thus the universe. It is (as described also in Chapter Four) the Wisdom of the Nature of the Dharma Realm Body which, in becoming more concrete, is made manifest as the four wisdoms: the Great Perfect Mirror Wisdom of Ashuku, which reflects all things truly; the Wisdom of Equality of Hōshō, which sees Buddha and deluded beings, self, and others without discrimination; the Wisdom of Magical Perception of Muryōju, which unerringly penetrates delusions; and the Wisdom of Accomplishing Metamorphosis of Fukūjōju, which liberates all beings from suffering.

Further differentiations of these wisdoms are distinguished as the powers of the sixteen bodhisattvas (*jūroku-son no toku*) located around the four Buddhas. The unfolding interrelationships of the Four Enlightenment Bodhisattvas and the goddesses, where each deity offers up the entirety of its individual being, express the joy of seeking truth, the love of the spirit, and the creativity of art.

The organization and meaning of the next section, the Samaya Assembly, are identical to those of the Attainment-Body Assembly. Its name differs because its deities are depicted in samaya forms symbolic of each deity. Dainichi Nyorai, for example, is here depicted as a pagoda, Hōshō as a triple wish-fulfilling gem, and Kongōsatta as a vajra.

The structure of the Subtle Assembly (bottom left) is also identical to the Attainment-Body Assembly, except that here the deities are depicted in human form. A vertical three-pronged vajra forms the aureole behind the lotus throne of each deity. This section symbolizes the subtle vajra-wisdom that combines to form the wisdom of Dainichi Nyorai and then differentiates into the wisdoms of all deities. The Subtle Assembly depicts this wisdom being given to all beings.

The Offering Assembly (center left) is basically identical to the preceding section. Each deity is depicted holding in both hands the stem of a lotus bearing that deity's samaya form, as if offering its very being. Also known as the Activity Mandala or Offering Mandala, this section shows the activity of homage as an example for the practitioner. Evidently the deities of this section were meant to be shown in feminine form (like the goddesses in the Attainment-Body Assembly). This was not done in the painted version of the Kongō-kai, remaining instead a hidden aspect of the mandala.

The Four Mudra Assembly (top left) is also known as the Five Wisdoms Assembly and the Highest Four Mudra Mandala. The central disk depicts a large Dainichi Nyorai, surrounded in the cardinal directions by four vajra-bodhisattvas. In the intermediate directions are the Four Enlightenment Bodhisattvas, and in the four corners outside the disk are the Inner Four Offering Bodhisattvas, all deities from the central assembly, but shown here in their samaya forms. At the four corners of the outer border are vajras, and in the four sides are four lotus gates. These represent the remaining four Offering Bodhisattvas and Four Absorbing Bodhisattvas from the Attainment-Body Assembly. This arrangement, unique in the Kongō-kai Mandala, is a simplified

143

representation of the four preceding assemblies in one. It was made as an abbreviated form of those four assemblies, to be used for visualization in a special "fourfold attainment practice" performed before it.

The Single Mudra Assembly (top center), also known as the Highest Being Mandala, depicts only the figure of Dainichi Nyorai. The outer border is as in the preceding assembly, and the inner border is completely filled with lotuses. Treasure vases also holding lotuses are in the four corners. This "single deity mandala" is meant to be used in meditation on Dainichi Nyorai as embodiment of the universal Buddha-mind, wellspring of all beings and phenomena. The source sutra says that although the deity of this assembly is Kongōsatta, he is used to realize Dainichi Nyorai. In the painted mandala, therefore, the deity is shown as Dainichi Nyorai.

The True Meaning Assembly (top right) is also named the Kongōsatta (Vajra-Being) Assembly. This has the same outer border as the two preceding sections, with lotus gates in the four directions and vajras in the corners. The second border is filled with lotuses, as in the Single-Mudra Assembly, but here there are deities in the four cardinal and intermediate directions, the inner area being composed of nine rectangles. The primary deity, in the very center, is Kongōsatta.

Surrounding him in the cardinal directions are the four vajra-bodhisattvas of desire, sensation, love, and pride (as discussed briefly in Chapter Three), with corresponding bodhisattvas in feminine form in the four corners. At the corners of the second border are the Four Inner Offering Bodhisattvas, and on the sides between them are the Four Absorbing Bodhisattvas. The offering bodhisattvas represent offerings of flower garlands, song, dance, and joy; the vajra-bodhisattvas represent passions and emotions; and the absorbing bodhisattvas represent the oneness of self and deity. Human desires and delusions are here revealed as the energies of enlightenment.

The Descending into the Three Realms Assembly (center right), also known as the Unsurpassed Great Mandala of the Three Realms, is similar to the Attainment-Body Assembly. In the place of Kongōsatta, however, this assembly has Gōzanze, "descending into the three realms" and "subduer of the three poisons," the wrathful manifestation of Kongōsatta. Where the corners of the outer border in the Attainment-Body Assembly have vajras, in this assembly there are the fierce "illuminating kings" Fudō, Kongōyasha, Gundari, and Dai-itoku. In this section, Dainichi Nyorai assumes wrathful aspects to bring even the most stubborn beings to realization. The major deities, therefore, form the Wrathful Fist mudra.

The Descending into the Three Realms Samaya-Assembly (bottom right) is also called the Wrathful Secret Mandala. This is the previous assembly with the same deities (only the four "illuminating kings" being absent) depicted in their samaya forms. Skillful means are here shown in their wrathful aspect symbolized by samaya forms such as vajra and sword. Where the preceding assembly depicts Dainichi Nyorai's wrathful transformations of body, this assembly focuses on transformations of mind.

THE SPIRAL MOVEMENT OF THE
KONGŌ-KAI MANDALA

The common exoteric view of the highest wisdom (*hannya*) is as supreme truth itself, while skillful means (*hōben*), used in the phenomenal world, are impure and transitory. Mikkyo, however, does not distinguish wisdom and skillful means in terms of pure and impure, higher and lower, relative and absolute. Indeed, as the Three Phrases say, "skillful means are the ultimate." Skillful means are wisdom itself, embodied in concrete, phenomenal activity because it cannot remain aloof from the realities of life. The *Kongōchō-gyō* emphasizes skillful means.

Although the Kongō-kai Mandala appears at first glance to be a static composition of nine squares, it represents powerful energies in motion. The primary deities of the Attainment Body Assembly and their subsidiary manifestations carry on mutual homage in an unending cycle. This mutually empowering energy increases and intensifies until finally it bursts out of the vessel of the Attainment Body Assembly. In a spiral pattern—like a galaxy or a whirlwind—this energy moves through the assemblies of the mandala toward the phenomenal world. At the same time, beings on the periphery experience a complementary, inward–spiralling movement that tends ever toward the mandala's center.

The outward movement originating in the center is the movement of supramundane enlightenment into the world of phenomena. The nine assemblies exist in a relationship called the descending transforming gate (*getenmon*), in which they are seen as the successive centers of a pattern that revolves clockwise outward from the center in the following order:

Attainment Body Assembly. Existence.
Samaya Assembly. Form.
Subtle Assembly. Expression.
Offering Assembly. Activity.
Four Mudra Assembly. The indissolubility of the above four.
Single-Mudra Assembly. The single being of the universe.
True Meaning Assembly. Delusion transformed into enlightenment.
Descending into the Three Realms Assembly. Wrathful deities subduing
  obstinate delusions.
Descending into the Three Realms Samaya-Assembly. The inner mind of
  the wrathful deities.

145

The descending transforming gate portrays the descent of the wisdom of highest enlightenment into phenomenal beings. This is also called the "Dharma gate of the result [of enlightenment] directed toward the cause" (*jūka kōin no hōmon*). There is a simultaneous, complementary movement from the periphery toward the mandala's center, the movement of the phenomenal into the realm of enlightenment. This is called the "Dharma gate of the cause attaining to the result" (*jūin shika no hōmon*). For the practitioner, this is the return to the original self. It is also called the ascending transforming gate (*jōtenmon*). The nine assemblies are passed through in reverse order from the descending revolving gate, as follows:

1. Descending into the Three Realms Samaya-Assembly. In this and the next section, the esoteric practitioner awakens his enlightened mind and cuts through delusion.
2. Descending into the Three Realms Assembly.
3. True Meaning Assembly. Here the practitioner understands desire, the passions, and senses as the energy of enlightenment. Delusion is itself enlightenment (*bonnō soku bodai*).
4. Single-Mudra Assembly. Here the "unenlightened" individual takes on a perfect Buddha-body through the Five-Aspect Attainment-Body Visualization.
5. Four Mudra Assembly. Here the practitioner unfolds his innate four wisdoms through mutual empowerment with the four Buddhas.
6. Offering Assembly. The practitioner fulfills the requirements of esoteric practice.
7. Subtle Assembly. The practitioner attains true samadhi.
8. Samaya Assembly. The practitioner realizes the forms in which wisdom is expressed.
9. Attainment Body Assembly. The practitioner realizes the actuality of Dainichi Nyorai, symbol of ultimate wisdom.

The Kongō-kai Mandala thus depicts an evolution towards ultimate enlightenment. This mind of enlightenment, moving away from the center, takes on increasingly concrete form through skillful means, eventually assuming corporeal form in individual beings in a pattern that gives the mandala its clockwise movement. The deities of the "lower" assemblies can be seen as relatively more phenomenal than those of the "higher," but the figure enthroned at the center of each is Dainichi Nyorai. (In the only exception, the True Meaning Assembly, the central place is occupied by Kongōsatta, who is a direct manifestation of Dainichi Nyorai.)

Thus the single, central figure of the mandala as a whole is also at the center of every one of the nine assemblies. The energy of the Kongō-kai Mandala does not simply radiate outward from an unmoving center—rather, the whole pattern of energies represented by the center moves out in a spiral movement. This

146

motion of the mandala's center represents the dynamic wisdom-matrix of the universe.

The mandala reflects the nature of its source, the *Kongōchō-gyō,* which continued to be added to over several centuries, the mandala's assemblies being based on different sections of the sutra. In the historical evolution of the Kongō-kai Mandala, the center itself moved toward the "periphery." Drawing the energy of each successive center along with it, it increased in strength (as if increasing in momentum) as it moved outward.

The structure of the Kongō-kai is significantly different from that of the Tai-zō Mandala, in which a single Dainichi Nyorai forms the center of a concentric expanding movement. In the Kongō-kai Mandala, skillful means are portrayed in a complex spiral compounded of two opposite motions. From the point of view of the Buddha, the center is moving outwards, while from the point of view of the individual, the periphery is being drawn into the center.

Although the movement of the mandala may seem to end with one rotation, each single cycle contains within itself the beginning of the next. The evolution of the universe as seen in the mandala is the inexorable movement of living beings towards enlightenment. Each fulfillment of this potential leads to further expansion of potential in a never-ending spiral that ultimately fills the universe.

THE DUAL TAIZŌ-KONGŌKAI MANDALA

The dual mandala (*ryōbu mandara*) is the name for the Tai-zō and Kongō-kai mandalas as a single, comprehensive entity. These mandalas depict the teachings of Shingon's two fundamental sutras. The *Dainichi-kyō,* with its roots in the philosophy of the void, is a completely perfected system, "static" as is a gyroscope, while the *Kongōchō-gyō,* founded on the more practice-oriented teachings of yoga and consciousness-only, is more outwardly dynamic by nature. Where the *Dainichi-kyō* was completed in the seventh century, the subsutras that make up the *Kongōchō-gyō* were written over a period of several hundred years that did not begin until the seventh century. Further *Kongōchō-gyō* texts continued to be written up to the demise of Buddhism in India in the thirteenth century, so that Tibetan esoteric Buddhism, for instance, has more sutras in this lineage than does Japan. Later *Kongōchō-gyō* texts brought from China to Japan had relatively little influence on Shingon.

There are very few sutras relating to the Tai-zō Mandala outside of the *Dainichi-kyō* itself, whereas the Kongō-kai grew out of the multiple sutras in the lineage of the *Kongōchō-gyō.* This historical difference points to the differing natures of the two systems, and it may be interesting to look briefly at the mandalas in this light. The Tai-zō Mandala has a single center, with hundreds of

Buddhas, bodhisattvas, and other deities in concentric layers around it. Even at the mandala's outermost edge, however, Dainichi Nyorai dwells always as the unmoving center of the whole. The Tai-zō Mandala thus expresses the eternal universe of "bright mirror and still water." It is a portrait of the essential void-equality that pervades all things and beings.

The Kongō-kai, on the other hand, comprises nine mandalas each with its own center. Originally separate, each represents a historical evolution of doctrine. In earlier versions of the mandala (as known in Japan), the central figure of the Kongō-kai Mandala's central section is Dainichi Nyorai. In a subsequent development in India, however, Ashuku Buddha became the central deity, eventually to be replaced by Kongōsatta. Based on later texts than the preceding assemblies, the True Meaning Assembly of the Shingon Kongō-kai, where Dainichi Nyorai is represented by Kongōsatta, is a result of this kind of development.

The spiral movement of the Kongō-kai embodies a powerful centrifugal energy, and the concentric Tai-zō Mandala provides a balancing centripetal force. This is not to say that neither mandala contains anything of the dynamic pattern of its counterpart. The Kongō-kai expresses an inward moving, concentric energy in the activity of the Attainment-Body Assembly, for example, and the Tai-zō Mandala contains the spiral activity of the five Buddhas in the Eight-Petaled Central Dais.[17] The distinction is valid, however, in terms of the overall character of the two mandalas. The Tai-zō Mandala, concentric in form and apparently static, is nevertheless a wellspring of activity flowing out endlessly from a single source. The Kongō-kai Mandala, too, appears to be rigidly ordered and fixed, but it embodies an unending spiral activity.

The different perspectives of the two mandalas are expressed in many ways. The top of the Tai-zō Mandala is east, while the top of the Kongō-kai is west. When the mandalas are hung together, the Tai-zō hangs on the east wall facing west, and the Kongō-kai on the west wall facing the Tai-zō. Mandala practices and other rituals associated with the two lineages are fundamentally different. In the *Kongōchō-gyō* lineage, the movement in ritual practice tends to be from microcosm to macrocosm. Such movement is apparent, for example, in the visualization technique of expansion and contraction, which is not present in practices founded solely on the *Dainichi-kyō*. Where the mudra of universal homage in Kongō-kai practice is the Vajra *gasshō,* the same ritual of homage in Tai-zō practice employs the Lotus *gasshō.*

Similarly, purification techniques in the two practices are based on the particular manifestation in each mandala of Dainichi Nyorai as the wrathful deity that subdues delusion. The Kongō-kai practice employs a vajra-like mudra and the mantra of the fierce deity Gōzanze. The Tai-zō practice, however, employs the mantra and sword-holding mudra of the fierce deity Fudō, who wears the lotus crown of compassion and grasps the sword of truth in his right hand.

The two sutras, as we have seen, represent the teachings of different lineages, probably from different areas of India. When they arrived in China in the first half of the eighth century, they were considered to be of equal but separate status. Hui-kuo received the *Dainichi-kyō* from Shubhakarasimha's disciple Hsüan Ch'ao (Jap., Genchō) and the *Kongōchō-gyō* from Vajrabodhi's disciple Amoghavajra. It seems likely, though there is no definite proof, that Hui-kuo was the first Mikkyo master to learn the teachings of both lineages, and the first to systematize the dual mandala. The *Record of the Secret Treasury*, considered by many to be the oral teaching of Hui-kuo as recorded by Kūkai, contains an early mention of the term "dual mandala," also saying, "The Tai-zō is Truth [*ri*]. The Kongō is Wisdom [*chi*]."[18] Among the symbolic terms by which the two mandalas can be contrasted are the following:

Tai-zō	*Kongō-kai*
Centripetal force	Centrifugal force
Protective, nurturing	Active
Harmony	Development
Deepening	Expanding
Maternal	Paternal
Lotus	Vajra
Lotus	Moon Disk
Truth	Wisdom
Equality	Discrimination
Form	Mind
Five "Material" Elements	Consciousness Element

The two mandalas together thus signify the indissoluble unity of Truth and Wisdom, the inseparability of Matter and Mind, the resolution of mystical paradox. The Tai-zō symbolizes the totality of all that exists, the oneness of reality, while the Kongō-kai symbolizes the wisdom that knows truth in all its separate manifestations. In the Tai-zō, the moon disk representing wisdom rests on the lotus of compassion and truth, whereas in the Kongō-kai, the lotus is contained within the moon disk of Wisdom. The truth of the Tai-zō exists in the essential equality of all things as they are. The wisdom of the Kongō-kai, in contrast, is made manifest in discrimination between things. Both describe real aspects of the universe. Since they are both inseparable from compassion, however, the dual Taizō-Kongōkai mandala is an ideal pattern of harmonious activity. It is a unified portrait of the fundamental Buddha, which is none other than the infinite universe.

Symbolic Relationships in Mikkyo[19]

FIVE SECTIONS	Buddha	Vajra
FIVE BUDDHAS (*Kongō-kai*)	Dainichi	Ashuku
FIVE BUDDHAS (*Tai-zō*)	Dainichi	Hōdō
FIVE WISDOMS	Wisdom of the Nature of the Dharma Realm Body	Great, Perfect Mirror Wisdom
NINE CONSCIOUS-NESSES	Ninth	Eighth
FIVE ELEMENTS (*Bodily Locations*)	Water (*Abdomen*)	Fire (*Breast*)
FIVE DIRECTIONS	Center	East
FIVE COLORS	White	Red
FIVE SHAPES	Circle	Triangle
FIVE ENERGIES (*and Fingers*)	Faith (*Ring Finger*)	Progress (*Middle Finger*)
FIVE TRANS-FORMATIONS	Skillful Means as the Ultimate	Generating Enlightened Mind
RITUAL IMPLEMENTS	Pagoda	Five-Pronged Vajra

Treasure	Lotus	Karma
Hōshō	Muryōju	Fukūjōju
Kaifuke-ō	Muryōju	Tenkuraion
Wisdom of Equality	Wisdom of Magical Perception	Wisdom of Accomplishing Metamorphosis
Seventh	Sixth	First Five (*Senses*)
Earth (*Thighs*)	Void (*Crown*)	Wind (*Face*)
South	West	North
Yellow	Blue/Green	Black
Square	Teardrop (Lotus Leaf)	Half-Moon (Vajra)
Concentration (*Little Finger*)	Samadhi (*Thumb*)	Compassion (*Index Finger*)
Practice	Realization	Nirvana
Wish Fulfilling Jewel	Single-Pronged Vajra (*Lotus*)	Three-Pronged Vajra (*Vajra Wheel*)

SEVEN

The Scope and Complexity
of Shingon Ritual

Shingon Buddhism has a wealth of traditional ritual practices. Some sense of their number may be had by considering that the Kongō-kai and Tai-zō man- dalas contain some eighteen hundred deities, all of which, either individually or in groups, have associated practices. In addition, one deity may often be the focus of various different practices. Shingon rituals, therefore, exist in great numbers, although relatively few of these are practiced regularly.

Regularly practiced rituals are of many kinds. Apart from lay practices, such as pilgrimage and devotion (which are beyond the scope of this book), Mikkyo rituals can be classified in several ways. The scale of a ritual can be judged by the number of practitioners, from one up to twenty or thirty, and by the number of altar platforms (*dan*), each with its complicated array of ritual implements for specific purposes. Practices can also be classified by their ritual format. For instance, there are those based on use of either or both of the full mandalas; those centering on the particular activities of certain deities or groups of deities; and those based on the fundamental mudra–mantra combinations of the eighteen-fold practice (*jūhachi-dō*).

Rituals may also be classified by their purpose, the basic four being to avert misfortune, to increase benefit, to subdue negative influences, and to bring about harmonious relations. Outwardly, these purposes relate to material, secular benefit, such as healing or prosperity, but their underlying meaning derives from the goal of esoteric union.

Mikkyo places value not only on the quantity and variety of these practices, but more on the experiential knowledge distilled from various meditative traditions that is given systematic ritual form in them. Esoteric techniques based on the active use of body, speech, and mind can be combined in rituals of tremendous complexity, requiring painstaking attention to detail and spanning weeks and months of practice. They are combined with equal effect, however, in concentrated practices of great simplicity, which will be the subject of Chapter Eight.

152

REPRESENTATIVE MIKKYO PRACTICES

A representative three-secrets practice is initiation, an essential ritual for the Shingon priesthood. There are various levels of initiation, but the Dharma transmission initiation (*denpō kanjō*), signifying formal acceptance into the Shingon lineage, is a prerequisite for most advanced practice. This initiation is preceded by a rigorous course of study and preparation, culminating in the preparatory fourfold enlightenment practice (*shido kegyō*), itself composed of a series of complex rituals taking some one hundred days to complete. General descriptions of these rituals, which follow the basic format of most Mikkyo practice, will be given later in this chapter.

Types of practice commonly performed after initiation include the single deity ritual (*isson-bō*), a full-scale ritual using generally the same format employed in the above fourfold practice but focusing on one deity. This type ordinarily requires extensive preparation and time to complete. Among the single deity practices is that of Batō Kannon (Horse-headed Kannon), the only fierce form of this deity of mercy found in the mandala. This bodhisattva, above whose forehead is the head of a horse, embodies the deepest compassion, devouring human follies and delusions as a horse devours grass.

In another such ritual, the many different faces of Jūichimen Kannon (Eleven-headed Kannon) embody multitudinous manifestations of compassion. There is a ritual of Jizō (Earth Repository), who, as solid as the earth, is a treasury of compassion and potentiality as bountiful as all of nature. In the Hachi-ji (Eight-syllable) Monju ritual, the deity's mantra signifies all-pervading void wisdom. The practitioner visualizes this bodhisattva's seed syllable changing into the sword of wisdom and this into the figure of Monju, who holds in one hand the sword that cuts through ignorance, and in the other hand the book of wisdom.

When practiced in conjunction with the fire ritual (*goma*), the deity of this type of practice is usually Fudō Myō-ō. A rigorous *goma* practice known as the Eight-thousand Stick (*hassen-mai*) Goma, practiced regularly today, is a secret ritual with Fudō as the central deity. For the twenty-one days of the ritual, the practitioner eats a limited vegetarian diet, performing the Fudō *goma* three times daily. During this ritual, Fudō's mantra of liberating compassion is recited one million eighty thousand times. (This number, a multiple of the 108 delusions, and also of the 108 beads of the usual Buddhist rosary, is referred to in Mikkyo practice as one million.) On the last night and following day, the practitioner fasts and burns eight thousand sticks of offering wood. These represent the innumerable delusions of each of the eight consciousnesses being transformed in the flames of wisdom.

An important practice also in the single-deity format is the ritual of the *Wisdom-Truth Sutra* (*rishukyō-bō*). This sutra, of great importance in Shingon, expresses the Mikkyo affirmation of human desire as originally pure and in no way separate from the energy of enlightenment. The ritual can be performed in several forms (full to abbreviated, as well as centered on different deities), and may be performed on behalf of the practitioner or of petitioners—in other words, for esoteric benefit to self or others.

Of a different type are Shingon's large-scale rituals for public benefit. Two such major rituals practiced regularly are the "post-seventh day ritual" (*goshichinichi mishu-hō*) and the mandala offering (*mandara-ku*). The mandala offering (which has several varieties) is performed on special occasions, for example when a new Buddha-image is first installed, a new mandala is hung, a secret Buddha image is brought out to be viewed, or a memorial ritual is performed. In the full-scale mandala ritual, the two practices of the two main mandalas are performed simultaneously with up to thirty priests in attendance. Simply to watch the ritual from a distance is considered to bring merit, and serves as a form of initiation.

The post-seventh day ritual takes place every year beginning on the eighth day of the new year, lasting a week. Performed in Kūkai's time as a practice to protect and preserve the nation, it found considerable favor with the aristocracy, and was originally performed in a special Shingon hall within the imperial palace. Today it takes place in Kyoto's Tō-ji in the initiation hall, where head abbots and high priests come from all over the country to take part. It is still the custom for an imperial representative to attend (though today he wears a Western morning coat rather than robes). Shingon now performs this ritual to bring prosperity and benefit to all nations, as well as enlightenment to all beings.

The ritual itself is strictly secret, and the public can watch only the procession of high priests dressed in their colorful robes walking to the initiation hall. Within the hall, the priests perform complex three-secrets practices employing many altars—for mandala practice, the fire ritual, rituals to the outer protective deities of the mandalas—all performed simultaneously as a single practice for the benefit of all beings.

At the opposite end of the scale of size and complexity are two major three-secrets practices, the Morning Star meditation (*gumonji-hō*) and the A-syllable visualization (*ajikan*). These historically important practices follow a relatively simple format, and both embody the concentrated essence of esoteric practice. Where the Morning Star meditation is a rigorous practice involving long isolation from the world, the A-syllable visualization is suited to the novice and layman as well as to the advanced practitioner.

BASIC VISUALIZATION TECHNIQUES

Some of the basic Mikkyo visualization techniques—all used in conjunction with mudras and mantras, and all based on the process of mutual empowerment (*kaji*)—are hereby described.

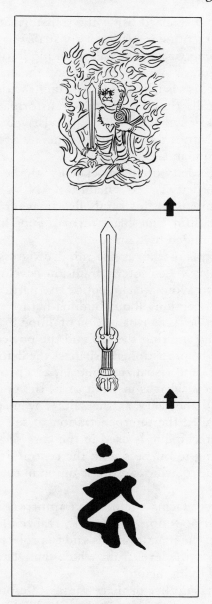

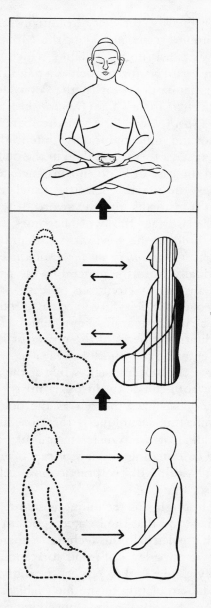

Transformation technique: (*Bottom*) The practitioner visualizes himself as the Sanskrit syllable KHAM. (*Center*) The syllable becomes the Sword of Wisdom (gamaya). (*Top*) Self becomes Fudō.

Image-manifesting technique: (*Bottom*) The deity enters the practitioner's body. (*Center*) The practitioner enters the deity. (*Top*) Self becomes deity.

155

Ordinarily, the deity in human form is visualized using the transformation technique (*tenjō-hō*). Here the Mikkyo practitioner begins by visualizing the deity's Sanskrit seed syllable, which he then visualizes as transforming into the deity's samaya form (such as a pagoda, vajra, or sword) representing the deity's essential nature. Finally, the samaya object is visualized as becoming the deity in human form. The *Dainichi-kyō* also calls this the syllable-transformation yoga (*tenji-yuga*). First visualized are Sanskrit syllables, which are relatively abstract and philosophical in content. The abstract then becomes concrete first in the samaya form, and then in the deity's human form.

In the case of Fudō, for instance, a fierce deity often associated with the fire ritual, the practitioner first visualizes the deity's seed syllable, KAN, which then transforms into the sword of wisdom (*riken*), his symbolic samaya form. In the last stage the sword becomes the wrathful, blue–black form of Fudō himself, holding the wisdom sword and surrounded by flames.

The *Commentary on the Dainichi-kyō* explains this as the mind progressing gradually from the general to the particular. The esoteric tradition developed this apparently circuitous process in part to avoid attachment to any particular aspect of the deity involved or to fixed conceptions about Buddha-nature.

The image-manifesting technique (*yōgen-hō*) is a visualization of union by the meditative process of the power of Buddha entering the self and the power of self entering the Buddha (*nyūga-ga'nyū*). The practitioner visualizes the deity as a projection of himself, while at the same time visualizing himself as a projection from the deity. Just as a mirror reflects what is in front of it, the practitioner visualizes the self as the deity and the deity as the self. The image-manifesting technique is therefore also called the interpenetration of self and Buddha, or the transfer technique. This technique is used in the core section (the culminating portion of practice leading to oneness with the central deity) of full-scale Mikkyo practice as a technique to achieve esoteric union in the secret of body.

Although this technique is said to be like facing the deity in a mirror, it is understood that the limited egocentric self does not, just as it is, realize union with the deity. In this technique, therefore, the practitioner is said to project the deity from a level of mind corresponding to the level from which the Dharma Body can be said to project the individual living being.

The circulation technique (*junkan-hō*) is another primary means of esoteric union. As in the "mind–conceiving concentrated recitation" (described in Chapter Five), the practitioner recites a mantra that links him and the deity in a chainlike cycle of recitation. The mantra is visualized issuing slowly from the deity's mouth as an interconnected series of syllables which gently enter the practitioner through the crown of his head. The syllables circulate through the practitioner's breast and, issuing from his mouth, reenter the deity through the navel, circulating through its breast before again issuing from its mouth to return to the practitioner in an unbroken cycle. This technique, focused on mutual enpowerment of practitioner and deity, is employed in the core section of Mikkyo practices to bring about esoteric union through the secret of speech.

In the syllable-disk visualization (*jirin-kan*), the practitioner first visualizes in his breast a moon disk with the deity's seed syllable or mantra at its center. Related syllables are then visualized emanating from the central syllable and ranging themselves around the circumference of the moon disk. When the central seed syllable is A, for instance, around it may appear the four syllables BA, RA, KA, and KYA (in that order) at the four cardinal points. The practitioner contemplates the meanings and relationships of the syllables as he visualizes them, before reversing the sequence and returning to the central syllable. (In practices associated with the Kongō-kai Mandala, the moon disk may be visualized as expanding to fill the entire universe.) Also called the "revolving syllable-disk" technique, this is employed in the core section of Mikkyo rituals to bring about esoteric union through the secret of mind.

In expansion visualization (*kakudai-hō*), the practitioner identifies with a symbolic image, then visualizes himself as this image gradually expanding to the size of the universe. After experiencing universe and self as one body, the practitioner gradually contracts the image back to its original size. This technique ordinarily employs a moon disk, a seed syllable within the moon disk, a vajra, or some other form symbolizing enlightened mind.

In the A-syllable visualization, for example, the practitioner contemplates a painted moon disk, lotus, and A-syllable, visualizes them within his breast, and contemplates their essential identity with the self. When the image is clear and unstrained, he expands it in gradual stages to extend farther and farther beyond his body. This expansion can be visual-

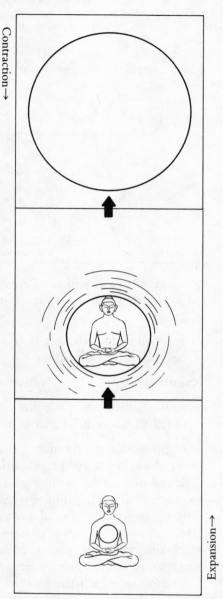

Contraction→

Expansion→

Expansion and contraction technique: (*Bottom*) The practitioner visualizes his mind in the shape of a moon disk. (*Center*) Self becomes moon disk. (*Top*) Moon disk expands to the size of the universe.

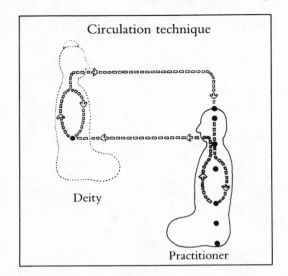

Circulation technique

Deity

Practitioner

ized as taking place on one plane, like concentric ripples spreading out on a still pond, or in three dimensions, like an expanding solid sphere. During this process the lotus and A-syllable merge into the single all-absorbing light of the moon disk.

Eventually, when the visualization fills the universe, the samadhi state in which there is no separate self or moon disk is said to be achieved, in which the practitioner becomes one with the universe. The image is then gradually contracted back to its original size within the breast. Kūkai's *Record of the Secret Treasury* explains the sudden entry into esoteric samadhi, a major aim of this technique, as follows:

> When you have filled the whole Dharma Realm with the moon disk, you must all at once forget both self and moon disk, dwelling solely in non-discriminating wisdom.[1]

Kakuban wrote in his *Musōkan-sho* (Praise of Formless Visualization):

> At the beginning of meditation, it resembles the moon, but after it expands to fill all, there is neither square nor circle.[2]

Although the moon disk at first expands gradually and continuously, at some point along the way the practitioner is said suddenly to forget self and moon disk and make a quantum leap into the realm of wisdom. If the expansion were to continue from beginning to end in the very same dimension, it would signify nothing more than an enlargement of the egocentric self. The Mikkyo meditator, however, is meant to pass through the state of no-self (*muga*) in order to reach the great self (*daiga*). Mikkyo ritual gives the mind a symbolic form to work with, to engage its energies, in order to bring about a spontaneous transformation in which the practitioner can experience the self on a macrocosmic scale.

In the permeation visualization (*shintō-hō*), the practitioner visualizes his exhaling breath as leaving his body through all its pores and spreading out into the universe. Then, with each inhalation, the energy of the universe enters the practitioner through his every pore, permeating his body. Shubhakarasimha wrote in his *Essentials of Meditation* that when one exhales, universal life energy "flows again from every single part of the body," and when one inhales, it "enters through the nose and circulates everywhere throughout the body, filling every vein and fiber."[3] The *Dainichi-kyō* says that this life energy "enters the entire body through every single pore and flows throughout the body, making it entirely pure."[4] Using this technique, the practitioner seeks to unite with the cosmic energy permeating all things.

These different elements are combined in systems of varying complexity. Such practice does not have its meaning as an arbitrary assemblage of mudras, mantras, and visualizations, however, but as a systematic combination of several different types of meditation technique in an organic whole.

The Concentration Points

In conjunction with the above techniques, Mikkyo employs certain specified locations on the body as concentration points[5] on which the practitioner visualizes seed syllables or symbolic images, and over which he forms mudras, as for example in the Five-Syllable Sublime-Body Visualization. This type of practice is called syllable-spreading visualization (*fuji-kan*). Mikkyo employs systems comprised of four, five, seven, nine, twelve, nineteen, and thirty-four concentration points. Some of these points are also located outside the body, for example on the altar before the practitioner, or in the earth below him.

Mikkyo most often employs the four points of heart, forehead, throat, and crown of the head (in their traditional order), but many variations occur.[6] In the permeation visualization, for instance, the body as a whole is employed as a kind of concentration point, and the eyes and other sense organs are also similarly used.

The concentration points may be used differently in different practices. In certain practices, for example, the heart, forehead, throat, and crown represent the wisdoms of the four Buddhas, and the practitioner is said to attain each of these wisdoms in turn by forming mudras at the corresponding points. Other practices (the Tai-zō Mandala ritual, for example) use forehead, throat, breast, and navel as the locations for visualizing the transformations of certain Sanskrit syllables. When the practitioner performs interpenetration with Dainichi Nyorai in the Kongō-kai Mandala ritual, he forms the appropriate mudra at heart, forehead, throat, and crown, associating them with the corresponding points of the deity.

In the RAN-syllable visualization (*ranji-kan*), a purification ritual, the practitioner forms a mudra at the breast, recites a mantra, and visualizes the syllable RAN on the crown of the head, in the heart, on the altar, and under the earth. In this visualization, the syllable becomes a red, triangular flame that burns away impurities.

In the three-secrets visualization (*sanmitsu-kan*), the palm of the hand, the tongue, and the heart are the three points of concentration on which the practitioner visualizes the UN-syllable. The syllable changes into a five-pronged vajra radiating a brilliant ignorance-dispelling light. In this way the body is prepared to manifest the universal three secrets.

The most common five-point system employs forehead, right shoulder, left shoulder, heart, and throat.[7] The seven-point system includes the left kneecap, the altar, right kneecap, heart, forehead, throat, and crown. The systems of four, five, and seven points are commonly used in "being-protecting techniques" (goshin-bō), in which the practitioner purifies his activities of body, speech, and mind while taking on the Buddha's protective energy as a preparation for the main portion of a particular practice. They are also used in the meditation hall visualization (dōjō-kan), in which the practitioner visualizes the creation of the sublime place of practice, an entire cosmos wherein the central deity is then visualized.

The nine concentration points are the forehead, right shoulder, left shoulder, heart, right armpit, left armpit, navel, right thigh, and left thigh. In the ritual of the Kongō-kai, the practitioner visualizes the "helmet and armor" of the Buddha on these nine points, protecting him from all evil and impurity. His hands forming the helmet and armor mudra, the practitioner recites a mantra, sending his mind to these nine points while visualizing, at the same time, the compassion of the Buddha protecting his body and mind like impenetrable armor.

As explained in the Dainichi-kyō, the twelve syllables of the Great King of Mantras are visualized on the following twelve points: crown, right ear, left ear, forehead, right shoulder, left shoulder, heart, upper back, navel, small of the back, both thighs, both feet. A nineteen-point system is used in a practice of Fudō, which often incorporates a fire ritual.[8] The practitioner visualizes these nineteen points both on himself and on the deity so that the two become one body. The Dainichi-kyō also gives a system of thirty-four points, rarely used today in actual practice, which the practitioner visualizes as covering his entire body, in this way making the body the very Dharma-teaching of the Buddha.[9]

The systems described above, together with the palms of the hands and the tip of the nose, include all the concentration points described in standard Mikkyo texts. These points belong to three groups: those extending throughout the body, those associated with the sense organs, and the "vital points." The concentration points that extend throughout the body are used as a means of visualizing syllables or symbols more concretely within one's entire body. The points associated with the sense organs—located, for example, on the eyes, the ears, the tongue, the entire skin surface of the body, and so forth—offer a means of relating the visualization to the bodily senses by which the world is perceived. The vital points are the heart, forehead, throat, crown, and abdomen.

Mikkyo considers all the senses as ways to know Buddhahood in the world and in the self, and esoteric practice uses the senses as means to enter a macrocosmic realm of being. The permeation visualization described earlier, for example, employs the entire surface of the body as a concentration point, as Shubhakarasimha's *Essentials of Meditation* suggests:

First regulate exhalation and inhalation, and pour the breath into and out of every single part of the body.[10]

The breath is visualized as a universal energy that flows in and purifies the entire body. The eyes serve similarly as concentration points. On entering the meditation hall, the practitioner visualizes radiant syllables on each eye. The right eye in this way becomes the sun, the left eye the moon, and through these pure eyes become visible a host of Buddhas filling the meditation hall. As to the nose, meditation texts often instruct the practitioner to direct the eyes, half-closed, to the bridge of the nose. The nose is here considered not as the organ of smell but as a point on which to focus the mind. The *Kongōchō-gyō* gives the following method for entering esoteric union:

Let your mind dwell in the great cylinder of the minute vajra at the tip of the nose, and bind the mind with the cord of concentration. . . .[11]

Mikkyo considers the "vital points" of heart, forehead, throat, crown, and abdomen to be most important. These are the points most often used, as well as the points held in common by most systems. The abdominal center (often called the navel) is considered the seat of the emotions and the source of subtle body energy.

The crown of the head plays an important part in the Mikkyo system. In Buddha images, the slight bump on this part of the head (called the *ushunisha*) signifies enlightenment. Esoteric texts call this center "the meeting place of the crown"[12] or "the seam in the bone at the crown."[13] The *Commentary on the Dainichi-kyō* advises the practitioner who has not attained full enlightenment to visualize "the syllable AN at the meeting place of the four directions on the seam in the bone at the crown of the head."[14] Visualization on this center is said to result in complete liberation.

The forehead center, actually a place between the eyebrows, is considered the location of the spiral tuft of hair that is one of the marks of a Buddha. A passage in the *Dainichi-kyō* says that the mudra of the secret of body is this tuft of hair, which is proof of Buddha-enlightenment, and the sutra gives a technique for attaining the power that is centered here. For the Mikkyo practitioner, this concentration point symbolizes the mind-eye that is to be opened.

The Mikkyo tradition has two terms for the heart, *karita* and *shitta*. The former is the corporeal heart, the latter the aspectless, metaphysical mind for which the bodily heart is a medium. These two "organs" are ordinarily referred to by the single Chinese character *shin,* which encompasses the meanings of mind, heart, and spirit. The bodily heart symbolizes the macrocosmic center from which the mind extends to fill all of creation. When, for example, the practitioner visualizes the moon disk of the mind (*shin gachirin*), representing innate enlightenment, he visualizes it within the breast. The core section of Shingon meditation, in which esoteric union by the three secrets takes place, employs the moon disk visualized in the breast as the medium for union with the deity. In the syllable-disk visualization (*jirin-kan*), described in the preceding section, the moon disk and seed syllables are visualized within the breast.

In the section of practice known as concentrated invocation (*shōnenju*), the practitioner employs the circulation visualization technique to move the mantra in an unbroken circle that passes through the concentration points of both practitioner and deity, thus attaining union in the secret of speech. In this regard, Mikkyo also places great importance on the throat, together with the mouth and tongue, as the region of the body where mantras are voiced—in other words, where the formless mantra transforms into voiced mantra, where perfect truth is made manifest in phenomena. It is through the throat center that subtle universal energies are said to flow together with the breath.

THE GENERAL FORMAT OF ESOTERIC RITUAL

The many different Mikkyo practices all involve union of Buddha (universe) and practitioner, and thus share a certain common structure. This format derives from the ancient Indian etiquette used to receive an honored guest. Mikkyo employs this etiquette on a symbolic level, the guest being the central deity of the practice, and the host, the practitioner.

In the first step of ritual, the practitioner prepares himself by purifying his body, arranging his clothing, and uniting his body, speech, and mind with the universal activity of the three secrets. This process is generally called the "being-protecting" technique (*goshin-bō*), and the section of practice in which it takes place is also called the "practitioner exaltation" technique (*shōgon gyōja-hō*). More or less the same steps are followed in all Mikkyo practices.

Next, as if preparing the ingredients for a sumptuous meal, the practitioner empowers the various offerings. After this, he purifies the area surrounding his "house," and fixes the place where the honored guest is to be received. This, called the realm-establishing technique (*kekkai-hō*), marks off the boundaries of the place of meditation. Since in the fourfold practice the practitioner is still a novice, the realm established by this technique is relatively small, covering only the altar. In more advanced practice it may be very large, as when Kūkai marked off the whole of the sacred mountain of Kōya-san as the realm. In some practices, it may cover just one fingertip.

In the section of practice often called the "meditation hall exaltation" technique (*shōgon dōjō-hō*), the inner room where the host will entertain the guest is cleaned and adorned. By means of this ritual, the practitioner creates the cosmic center of meditation using the meditation hall visualization (*dōjō-kan*). In this space is visualized the deity who is to be the guest.

All preparations completed, the host invites the guest to the place of reception, and sends a vehicle to bring the guest, who is welcomed on arrival with music (*shinrei*, the ringing of the five-pronged vajra bell). After closing the doors to prevent any outside disturbance (*kechigo-hō*, "establishing protections" technique), the practitioner uses the "offering and homage" techniques (*kuyō-hō*) to serve refreshments in the form of the various ritual offerings.

Conversation between host and guest gradually becomes more intimate, until, finally, the interchange of mind and mind becomes complete. This is the core section of practice in which esoteric union with the central deity takes place, the "self entering the Buddha and the Buddha entering the self" (*nyūgaga'nyū*). Various techniques are employed to bring about the experience of oneness with the deity in body, speech, and mind. This section is the heart of the entire practice.

Reluctant to bring the visit to an end, the host then provides parting refreshments (*gokuyō*, ending offerings) and, after opening the doors and removing the outer protections (*gekai*, "dissolving the realm"), sees off the guest with parting music. A vehicle is provided by which the deity is returned to his essential realm (*hakken*, "dispatch"). After the departure of the deity, the practitioner fixes the experience in his mind and body by repeating the beginning techniques of protective union with the universal three secrets.

Mikkyo ritual in general follows the above course, though the nomenclature may differ, and details of practice may vary depending on the deity being invoked. Mikkyo rituals are ordinarily performed before a painted or sculpted image of a deity. In the course of the ritual, the deity is invoked to empower the particular image with the essential reality it symbolizes. It is this essential "deity" with which esoteric union takes place. Three-secrets meditation usually involves different types of esoteric union at different stages of the practice, some repeated more than once, in order to continue deepening the samadhi experience.

RITUAL IMPLEMENTS AND OFFERINGS

Implements commonly used in Mikkyo ritual include various kinds of vajra (*kongō-sho*), sometimes translated as "thunderbolt." Originally weapons, they symbolize the diamondlike wisdom that destroys all delusion, and thus are the samaya form of many deities. While early vajras were actually sharp and pointed, like weapons, those used today are blunter, with rounded tips. They are most often made of bronze, sometimes alloyed with gold, silver, or iron, and more rarely of wood, bone, or crystal. When used ritually, the vajra is wielded like a weapon.

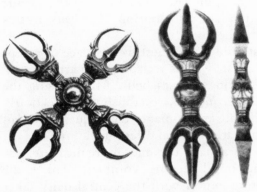

Three types of vajra brought from China by Kūkai.

Five-piece bronze altar set.

The three types of vajra most often used in Shingon today are single-pronged (*toko-sho*), three-pronged (*sanko-sho*), and five-pronged (*goko-sho*). The single-pronged vajra, signifying single universal truth, is the basic vajra form, with one sharply pointed prong on either end of the grip. The three-pronged vajra signifies the three secrets of body, speech, and mind, the three divisions of Buddha, Lotus, and Vajra in the Tai-zō Mandala, and so on.

The five-pronged vajra, with five prongs on either end, a total of ten, is interpreted in various ways. The five prongs signify the five Buddhas, for example, and the number ten, the ten directions. The five on one end may represent the five wisdoms of the Kongō-kai Mandala, the five at the other end the wisdoms of the Tai-zō, thus embodying in one ritual object the indissoluble dual mandala. One end of a vajra may signify the macrocosmic realm of the Buddha and the other end, the microcosmic realm of the individual, together symbolizing esoteric union. The five-pronged vajra is the samaya form of Kongōsatta as well as the central symbol of the Kongō-kai Mandala.

The vajra bell (*kongō-rei*), another important ritual implement, most commonly has a five-pronged vajra as its handle. This bell is rung to stimulate ("to startle into awakening") the enlightened energies of the practitioner and of the deities invoked during a ritual, as well as to create the welcoming and parting music offered to the deities.

The vajra tray (*kongō-ban*), a roughly triangular, three-legged bronze dish, is placed in front of the practitioner on the platform altar. A vajra bell stands in its center, with a five-pronged vajra lying to the front. A single-pronged and a three-pronged vajra are laid diagonally to the left and right of the bell. The vajra tray symbolizes the human heart, and thus also the enlightenment realized in the corporeal human being. The five-pronged vajra bell can be seen as a symbol of samadhi, in which wisdom is awakened.

A related ritual object is the karma-vajra (*katsuma-sho*), composed of two crossed three-pronged vajras. The two vajras represent Buddha and practitioner, their three prongs represent the three secrets, the combination representing the union of the three secrets of Buddha and practitioner. The total of twelve prongs can also signify the twelve links in the chain of karmic causation which, transformed, are the twelve causes of perfect enlightenment. Karma-vajras are placed on special lotus stands at the four corners of the platform altar.

The platform altar (*dan*) is a large, square wooden platform, most often facing south. It derives from the earthen platform mandala (as described in Chapter Six), and is the center of Mikkyo ritual. In the *Kongō-kai-shō* (Summary of the Vajra Realm), Kōzen (1121–1203) wrote:

> Sitting properly and making the ṣamadhi mudra, perform the interpenetration [*nyūga ga'nyū*] visualization. The deity and the self are not two, but separate. The deity dwells in the altar and the self dwells in the altar. Reciting the mantra together, the result is like Indra's net.[15]

Fire ritual at Tōji temple, Kyoto.

On the platform altar are placed the appropriate implements and offerings for the practice being performed. A separate ritual is required to prepare the altar. For the practice of the Kongō-kai Mandala, for example, there is a Kongō-kai altar arrangement, and for the Tai-zō Mandala practice, a Tai-zō arrangement (also used for most other practices). There are various kinds of platform altars for special purposes, such as that with a hearth for the fire ritual, the initiation platform, and the great altar (*daidan*) used for the dual mandala practice. The altar and its implements together are themselves a mandala of the universe.

The symbolic element of earth, which is related to the square shape, is represented by the A-syllable, and is associated with the Wisdom of All-Wisdom.

The square altar platform, though no longer made of earth, reflects this correspondence. The four sides of the great altar platform are considered to symbolize the four wisdoms, while the altar as a whole esoterically embodies the fifth Wisdom of the Nature of the Dharma Realm Body. A five-stranded cord (representing the five symbolic colors) is carved into the side panels around the platform between the upper and lower lotus petals as a symbol of the five wisdoms. The lotus's upward- and downward-pointing petals represent the complementary movements of enlightenment as depicted in the mandalas.

In front of the platform altar is placed a smaller platform (the *raiban*) on which the practitioner sits, to the left of which is a low table bearing still other ritual implements. According to the ritual being performed, there may be another such table with a further array of implements to the right, sometimes accompanied by a flat metal chime (*kei*), originating from the jade chimes of ancient China, suspended in a wooden frame.

Tall candle stands are placed just outside the four corners of the altar. On the corners themselves stand four single-pronged vajra stakes (*kongōketsu*), linked together by a five-colored cord. Inside the square formed by the cord, flower vases (*kebyō*) stand at each corner with one in the center. Along the four sides are arrayed various containers representing offerings to all Buddhas in each of the four directions. On a stand just behind the central flower vase is a "wheel treasure" (*rinbō*), a many-spoked metal wheel representing the invincibility of the Buddha in conquering ignorance. In front of the vase is a small pagoda (*tō*) symbolizing the very being of the Buddha, and in front of that is the vajra tray.

The pagoda originated in monuments erected to house the Buddha's relics, which are said to have been divided after his death and sent to eight different places. At Kuśinagara in Central India, where Shakyamuni entered his final nirvana, is the prototype of the pagoda, a tall grave-mound of heaped earth. The pagoda originated in the reliquary mound, but this evolved into various forms with different meanings. Mikkyo pagodas may, for example, enshrine Dainichi Nyorai or the Five Buddhas. The types placed on the platform came to be called altar platform pagodas (*dantō*), and today this includes, for instance, the reliquary (*sharitō*) and image-containing (*tahōtō*) pagodas; the five-storied type (*gorintō*) symbolizing the five elements; the lotus-shaped; wish-fulfilling-jewel-shaped; and treasure-vase-shaped stupas. These all symbolize the universal Dainichi Nyorai.

Along the front edge of the altar are placed the six containers (*rokki*), small metal bowls containing the offerings of water, powdered incense, and leaves (called *keman,* "flower garlands"). There are three bowls to the right and three to the left of a large, tripod incense burner (*kasha*) in the center. The three on the right are used in the opening offerings, while those on the left are for the ending offerings. Powdered incense, water used to purify the altar and implements, and a wooden wand (*sanjō*) with which the water is sprinkled are kept on one of the side tables.

The Sanskrit word *pūjā*, derived from a root meaning "to honor," is translated in Chinese characters as *kuyō* ("offering"). In early Buddhism, offerings were donations of food, clothing, money, and so forth, first presented to Shakyamuni and then later to the priesthood. The word later came to include homage, praise, and worship of the Buddha and other deities through the presentation of music, dance, mudras, and mantras, as well as material goods. Shingon offerings are of various kinds and combinations. One standard ritual format, the six-fold offering (*rokushu kuyō*), employs water, powdered incense, flower garlands, burning incense, uncooked rice, and light. These are offered twice, before the section of esoteric union and again at the end of a complete practice.

The water offering is often performed separately, the other five then becoming a single, separate set of offerings. In the *Commentary on the Dainichi-kyō*, the powdered incense is said to represent purity; the flower garland represents compassion; the burning incense signifies interpenetration throughout the Dharma universe; the food (uncooked rice) represents the nectar (*kanro*) of highest enlightenment, beyond birth and death; and the light signifies the delusion-destroying wisdom of the Buddha.

Mikkyo offerings to the deities are usually of two kinds, the "truth offering" (*rikuyō*), in which the practitioner visualizes the offerings while performing mudras and mantras, and the "material offering" (*jikuyō*), in which actual substances are offered following a prescribed ritual format. In most practices the visualized offering is performed first, followed immediately by the material offering. The purely internal offering, also called "mind-transporting offering" (*unjin kuyō*), is considered the highest form.

The ritual use of special offering water, known as *aka,* derives from the ancient Indian custom of receiving a guest with water for washing his feet. The *aka* is pure water, often taken from a well specially dug for the purpose. There is a separate ritual for drawing this water from the well, a special container in which the water is kept, and a special shelf on which this container is placed. Before being offered, it is sometimes scented.

In making the offering, the practitioner picks up the water container, holds it in fumes rising from the incense burner, and empowers ("does *kaji* with") it, using the appropriate mudra and mantra, to transform the water into its symbolic universal essence before offering it to the deities. In the opening offering the practitioner visualizes the water as washing the deity's feet, and at the end, as rinsing the deity's mouth. At the same time, it purifies the practitioner. The practitioner makes the offering by shaking three drops of water onto the altar from the tip of the wand. One interpretation has it that the practitioner makes this offering to the deity to wash away any obscurations that may dim the deity's radiance in the phenomenal realm. The water also washes away all distinction between the physical representation of the deity in the meditation hall and the essential deity summoned from the universal realm.

THE PREPARATORY FOURFOLD
ENLIGHTENMENT PRACTICE

The Preparatory Fourfold Enlightenment Practice (*shido kegyō*) consists of four rituals performed in a series as preparation for the Dharma-transmission initiation. The word *shido* means literally "four crossings," in the sense of "crossing over" beyond birth and death to enlightenment. The word *kegyō* means "added practice," referring to preparatory ritual performed before a main practice. The four practices are the eighteenfold practice, the Kongō-kai Mandala practice, the Tai-zō Mandala practice, and the fire ritual. The order in which they are performed may vary from school to school.

The basic fourfold preparatory system and its contents were apparently established by Kūkai based on oral transmissions from Hui-kuo. That system prescribed a series of initiations to be given to a candidate priest over a period of years, culminating at the age of fifty or so, the age then considered most suitable for receiving the Dharma transmission. At that time, each of the four practices took some 250 days, and they were separated by other intensive periods of meditation. In Japan, the ritual was elaborated and the time shortened. The four practices performed today follow a format established around the thirteenth century, and take some 100 days in all to complete.

The fourfold practice on Kōya-san is performed by student priests in a special training institute. Other such institutes also exist, some for women. Compared to the initiation candidates in Kūkai's time, students today tend to be younger, mostly in their early twenties. During their formal training on Kōya-san these student priests study *siddham*-style Sanskrit, sutra recitation (primarily of the *Wisdom-Truth Sutra* and *Kannon Sutra*), and a special form of chanted mantra called *shōmyō*. They attend lectures on doctrine and practice, and perform morning and evening rituals.

The major subject of doctrinal study is the *Nijūgokan Sho* (Twenty-Five Volumes of Writings), beginning with the *Jikkan-jō* (Ten Volumes of Texts), which consists of six works by Kūkai and Nagarjuna's *Treatise on Enlightened Mind*. The remaining fifteen volumes comprise sections of the *Dainichi-kyō* (two alternate versions include different sections) and the *Treatise on Mahayana*.

During the time of the fourfold practice, which begins in September and ends in December, the student priests concentrate only on this ritual. The practice takes place in a special hall equipped with altars and implements for many candidates. The Dharma-transmission initiation is held in January, followed by further lectures and advanced study.

The fourfold practice involves considerable ritual preparation such as, for example, recitation of the *Wisdom-Truth Sutra* and repeated performance of certain "being-protecting techniques" (*goshin-bō kegyō*). During the time of the entire fourfold ritual, minor rituals meant to purify and strengthen the practitioner accompany day-to-day activities of eating, sleeping, rising, bathing, and so on. The preparatory homage practice (*raihai kegyō*) is a ritual involving repetition over many days of full prostrations and esoteric confession preceding the four main practices.

The ritual of esoteric confession involves not confession of sins before another priest, but inner acknowledgment of one's limitations in mind and behavior. This is, therefore, considered another means to knowing the self as it truly is. The practitioner performs repeated prostrations, in each of which the entire body is cast down in reverence to the enlightened universe. Mikkyo does not consider sin as intrinsic to human nature, but views undue attachment to ideas of both good and evil as delusion. Since correct conduct is a necessary foundation for samadhi, however, the practitioner examines his own mind and behavior for preconceptions and limitations. Through such confession, the individual also acknowledges his indebtedness to society and the greater world.

A brief description of the course of the Eighteenfold Preparatory Practice is given below. It is followed by an even more abbreviated description of the Preparatory Fire Ritual (*goma*). The two intervening practices involve visualization of the mandalas and ritual union with their deities following a format similar to but considerably more complex than that of the eighteenfold ritual.

The hundreds of mudras, mantras, seed syllables, and visualizations employed throughout these rituals represent many levels of esoteric meaning both individually and in combination. Only a few of these meanings will be mentioned below. Offerings and ritual implements, too, have precise uses and meanings. The practitioner picks up each implement in a certain way, using prescribed mudra-like motions to manipulate it. Although certain basic sequences are repeated in different sections of the practice, and some of the same sequences are found in all the practices, the external, visible portion of ritual alone can be overwhelming in its richness and complexity.

During the time of the fourfold practice, the student priest performs each of the four major rituals over a period of about three weeks, three times daily, at 4 A.M., 10 A.M., and 2 P.M., each sitting lasting about two hours. In order to maintain the proper level of concentration throughout, the practitioner must ordinarily have considerable experience in meditation. Instruction by a qualified master is necessary.

THE EIGHTEENFOLD PREPARATORY PRACTICE

(For convenience, this ritual is divided into sections which, though traditional, are arbitrary and not necessarily marked in actual performance.)

The practitioner begins with ritual purification and contemplation of his oneness with Kongōsatta, who represents the enlightened Mikkyo practitioner. He then approaches the hall of meditation with hands forming a certain mudra, visualizing a fully opened eight-petalled lotus beneath his feet at every step. Before entering, he performs a ritual to awaken both the deity's active aspect and his own enlightened mind.

169

Purification and Preparation of the Practitioner. The practitioner performs prostrations before the image of the deity, Dainichi Nyorai, while reciting a mantra of homage to all Buddhas. He next purifies the universal elements within his body, and then, using the "being-protecting technique" (*goshin-bō*), further prepares the already purified body and mind. The practitioner visualizes the union of self and Buddha and the essential purity of the activities of body, speech, and mind, employing mantra recitation with mudras formed at various concentration points. This section ends with the mudra and mantra of "donning the protective armor" (*hikō-goshin*) of great compassion.

Empowerment of Offerings and the Vow of Practice. Here the practitioner dedicates the merit of his practice to the benefit of all beings, entreating the aid of all deities in completing the practice. Using the mudra and mantra of the wrathful deity Gundari Myō-ō, who subdues evil and delusion, he empowers ("does *kaji* with") the offering water and with it symbolically washes away delusion.

Through a series of complicated manipulations of ritual implements, recitations of syllables, and visualizations, the practitioner transforms impurities to reveal their essential purity. The other offerings undergo a similar process, followed by recitation of verses and prayers to all gods for protection. The practitioner recites the "five confessions," expressing the vows of all Buddhas and bodhisattvas.

The practitioner performs mudras and mantras to awaken the enlightened mind and realize the equality of self and Buddha, and then recites the five great vows, summarizing this entire section of the ritual:

> Living beings are numberless; I vow to liberate them all.
> Merit is boundless; I vow to accumulate all.
> The teachings are limitless; I vow to learn all.
> The Buddhas are numberless; I vow to serve all.
> Wisdom is peerless; I vow to realize the highest.

The merit of these vows is offered to the Buddhas and all beings, after which the verse of the mutual empowerment of the three universal powers is recited:

> The power of my meritful action,
> The power of Buddha-*kaji,*
> And the power of the universal Dharma Realm
> Dwell in all-pervading mutual homage.

Establishing the Realm. This section of the ritual prepares a sacred space, an internal realm of practice to welcome the Buddha. With a series of mantras and mudras, the practitioner visualizes creation of the altar boundaries and a protective fence of vajra-flames surrounding the altar within the mind.

Creation of the Sublime Meditation Hall. The practitioner visualizes the essential place of meditation, which is also the universe. He begins by visualizing a Sanskrit syllable becoming a palace with the mind–altar at its center. Above this, another syllable changes into an eight-petalled lotus, above which is the seed syllable of Dainichi Nyorai. This becomes a pagoda composed of the five elemental shapes, the samaya form of the Tai-zō Dainichi Nyorai, which the practitioner then visualizes as transforming into Dainichi Nyorai in perfect human form, the source of all deities and of the universal mandala.

In order to relate the visualized essential deity to his own being, the practitioner performs a ritual of empowerment at seven points on his body and recites a mantra. Ritual offerings to welcome the Buddha are then created by visualization.

Invitation and Summons. The practitioner invites Dainichi Nyorai to come to the meditation hall, using mudras and mantras to send a precious cart to bring the deity and his retinue into the sacred space, where they are ritually welcomed.

Establishing Protections. The practitioner sets up barriers against disruptive influences, using the moving mudra of a fiery delusion-subduing deity and visualizing an impenetrable barrier of flame around the sacred space, an unbreakable vajra net over it.

Ritual Offerings. In this section the practitioner entreats the help and protection of the deity and his retinue by a series of offerings. The first offering is water, then lotus thrones for the central deity and retinue, and welcoming music made by reciting a seed syllable and ringing the bell. The practitioner then makes the "five offerings" using the ritual implements on the altar.

The practitioner recites verses glorifying the Buddha's power and virtue and entreating aid, after which, using mudra and mantra, he visualizes an infinite offering to all deities throughout the universe. The verses of the three powers are recited again, uniting the merit of the offerings, of the Buddha, and of the universe.

Concentrated Invocation and Esoteric Union. The practitioner undergoes mutual empowerment with Dainichi Nyorai using a mantra invoking this supreme deity of the Kongō-kai Mandala and a mudra symbolizing the bodily union of self and Buddha, held at the breast to signify the moon disk of the true mind.

Next he performs empowerment using the rosary, which symbolizes the delusions of all beings. Delusions are visualized as being transformed instantly into wisdoms while reciting a mantra invoking union with the central deity 108 times using the circulation technique. The mantra is visualized emerging from the mouth of Dainichi Nyorai, entering the crown of the practitioner's head, circulating through his body, leaving from his mouth to enter the body of Dainichi, and so on, in an unbroken cycle.

The practitioner then repeats mutual empowerment with Dainichi Nyorai, and ends this section by performing the "diffused recitation," a long series of mantras of the central deity and his major manifestations.

Ending Offerings and Skillful Means. The practitioner makes parting offerings in gratitude to the deities, beginning with the five offerings, ending with water. The bell is rung as parting music. The merit gained in the ritual is directed to all beings in all realms of existence, and the protective barriers surrounding the mind-altar are dissolved one by one, using the earlier mantras and the same mudras performed with a different movement. A single "petal" from the flower offerings is placed on the altar, and the deities are visualized boarding this petal and returning to their cosmic dwelling place.

The ritual ends by invoking protective energies. The practitioner recites a mantra of homage while performing prostrations, then leaves the meditation hall.

THE PREPARATORY FIRE RITUAL

The fire ritual (*goma*) is placed last in the fourfold practice to eliminate all obstructions to the Dharma-tranmission initiation that follows. The *goma* is an adjunct ritual, ordinarily performed after a single-deity practice—in this case, the practice of Fudō. The fire ritual proper is made up of stages (*dan*) in which offerings are made to a particular deity or group of deities. While the simplest *goma* consists of only one stage, the offering to Ka-ten, god of fire, the *goma* of the fourfold practice has five stages. In the Shingon fire ritual the flames are the Buddha's wisdom-fire, which transforms the fuel of ignorance and delusion into wisdom.

The practice of Fudō and the subsequent five stages of *goma* take place in one session at the fire ritual altar (*goma-dan*), a square wooden platform upon which rests a round hearth. The altar, the opening ("mouth") of the hearth, and the hearth itself symbolize the equality of self and Buddha in body, speech, and mind, respectively. This altar holds many implements and offerings, all with particular symbolic meanings. As the offerings (sticks of wood, oil, grain, and other substances) are put into the flames within the hearth, the practitioner visualizes delusions entering the Buddha's wisdom-flame, where they immediately reveal their essential nature as the fuel of wisdom.

The central deity of this fire ritual, Fudō Myō-ō ("Unmoving Illuminating King") comes from the Wisdom-Holding Hall of the Tai-zō Mandala, and is a manifestation of Dainichi Nyorai in the terrifying aspect that, dwelling in adamantine enlightenment, cuts through the most stubborn delusions. Since

Goma ceremony at Kōyasan.

173

the Fudō ritual follows more or less the same format as the eighteenfold practice presented above, only the deity-visualization will be briefly described here:

After visualizing a pagoda symbolizing the universe, the practitioner employs several stages of syllable-transformations to visualize the anthropomorphic figure of Fudō, blue-black in color, surrounded by subsidiary deities. A looped cord in his left hand represents the skillful means that can bind the most ungovernable passions. Held upright in his right hand is the sword of the secret wisdom that cuts through delusion at the root. His wrathful qualities terrify and subdue all ego-obstructions, while his mantra expresses the liberating power of compassion. The practitioner fixes the deity within his body, in his mind, and on the altar before summoning the deity and retinue, after which he makes offerings, undergoes esoteric union, and so on.

On completion of the single-deity practice of Fudō, the practitioner begins the introductory ritual of the *goma* proper. The practitioner arranges the implements, performs homage to all Buddhas, burns incense, puts powdered incense on the hands, and so on, as in the eighteenfold practice described above. After rituals of mutual empowerment with Dainichi Nyorai and Fudō, he performs a visualization to unite the three secrets of Buddha, of practitioner, and of the *goma* hearth. The hearth's body, speech, and mind are the altar, the mouth of the hearth, and the hearth itself, respectively.

By complex ritual involving many implements, the practitioner empowers the offering of mustard seed (symbolizing the light of wisdom that destroys obstructions), and uses it with a fire mantra to prevent any negative influences from approaching the place of meditation. Then, forming the mudra of Ka-ten at his heart, forehead, throat, and crown, the practitioner invokes this tutelary deity of all *goma* practice. Taking the offering implements from the side tables and arranging them on the altar, he is now ready to enter the first of the preparatory *goma*'s five stages, the ritual to Ka-ten.

The practitioner arranges sticks of offering wood on the vajra tray and places eleven sticks of fuel wood, one representing fundamental delusion and ten representing delusions of conduct and perception, in the hearth. The practitioner sets the fuel wood on fire, visualizing this as lighting the flame of enlightenment. The flame is fanned while reciting a mantra invoking light, and visualizing a seed-syllable symbolizing the element wind. Water is sprinkled into the flames, and the fuel is empowered by reciting a mantra and wielding the three-pronged vajra.

The practitioner visualizes the wisdom-flame as a syllable that changes into a triangular flame, which then becomes the figure of Ka-ten. White in color, with four arms, the body of Ka-ten is cosmic flame. Placing a "floral tassel" on the burning fuel, the practitioner visualizes above it a throne surmounted by a syllable that first transforms into a ritual vase and then into the figure of Ka-ten, forming the mudra of fearlessness, holding a rosary, a wand, and a vase in his several hands, his body filled with flame.

Performing the mudra and mantra of summons, the practitioner visualizes Ka-ten being drawn into the hearth, and recites verses of invocation and welcome. The offerings then begin:

First, ladling water onto the hearth, the practitioner visualizes it rinsing the mouth of Ka-ten. In this and all the following offerings, the practitioner first performs the appropriate mudra and mantra, followed by the mudra used in the visualization of the deity. After this he recites further verses of invocation and welcome.

A small amount of powdered incense is thrown into the hearth. This is visualized as entering Ka-ten's mouth and filling his body and mind.

A mixture of oil (symbolizing delusions) and honey (wisdom) is offered with large and small ladles.

Offering sticks are placed in the hearth.

Ladles of rice, representing delusions in general, are tossed into the flames, first as an offering to the deity, then as a symbol of the internal process of overcoming delusion in the self.

Ladles of five grains symbolizing greed, anger, folly, arrogance, and doubt are next put into the flames. These are followed by separate offerings of "cut flowers," pellet incense, and grain incense, representing the "three poisons" of greed, anger, and folly. Another offering of oil follows.

The practitioner performs the mudra and mantra of universal offering to transform the offerings into the universal dimension, and empowers them by reciting the verse of the three universal powers. The mouth of the hearth is rinsed again, and a "floral tassel" tossed into a corner of the hearth to serve as the vehicle of Ka-ten's return to his essential realm. With the mudra and mantra of dispatching the deity, Ka-ten is visualized departing from the hearth. This completes the first stage.

Similar techniques are employed in the four following stages of the *goma,* comprising rituals to the following deities: Hannya Bodhisattva (chief deity of the mandala section from which Fudō comes); Fudō; all deities; and outer protective gods.

SHINGON INITIATION

All sects of Buddhism in Japan have ceremonies of formal commitment (*tokudo,* "crossing over") in which, after suitable preparation and study, a candidate enters the priesthood by cutting off his hair, receiving the precepts, and putting on a Buddhist's priest's vestment (*kesa*). The ritual of initiation, however, called *kanjō* in Japanese, is unique to the esoteric tradition. Of central importance to the continuation of the Mikkyo lineage, *kanjō* is treated in great detail in the *Dainichi-kyō* and other Mikkyo sutras and texts.

Kanjō literally means to sprinkle water on the crown of the head, deriving from an ancient Indian coronation ritual in which the head of a new king was sprinkled with water brought from "the four seas," signifying rule over his entire kingdom. In the general format common to most types of initiation, a master in the Dharma succession sprinkles water from five vessels, symbolizing the Five Wisdoms, on his disciple's head.

The various initiations differ in content, form, and purpose. The *Dainichi-kyō,* for instance, lists three kinds and five levels of *kanjō,* while other texts give many more. Not all are still practiced today, and some are primarily for laymen. Higher initiations can be classified as of three kinds according to ritual format. The first is the formal initiation ceremony using a full array of ritual implements before a special mandala altar. The second, no longer in use today, was conducted using a minimum of offerings and implements when material circumstances did not allow the first type. The last, "initiation based on mind" (*ishin kanjō*), uses no form or ritual, and is considered the highest kind of initiation.

Initiations are also classified in levels called the Five Realms (*goshu sanmaya*), referring to the depth of consciousness to which they are directed. The first, hardly an initiation in the usual sense, involves simply becoming aware of the existence of the mandala, and is called "looking at a mandala from a distance," as mentioned earlier in this chapter. This is a preritual *kanjō* signifying first contact with the esoteric teachings. Actual ritual contact with the esoteric teachings comes in the "bond-establishing" (*kechi-en*) initiation, in which the initiate is led before a mandala and casts a sprig of anise onto it to establish a Dharma-bond with a particular deity. This initiation is open to all laymen.

The third level, "mantra-receiving initiation" (*jumyō kanjō*), is for laymen who intend to devote themselves to Mikkyo. The candidate is led to a mandala, casts an anise sprig, and is given the mudra and mantra of his particular deity as the first step in formally becoming the disciple of a Mikkyo master. Also called "permission initiation" (*koka kanjō*) and "Dharma-learning initiation" (*gakuhō kanjō*), it results in permission to study and practice the esoteric teachings.

The fourth level is the "transmission of the Dharma" (*denpō kanjō*), in which a Shingon priest enters the path that may lead to becoming a teacher. This and the preceding two initiations were taken by the Indian patriarchs to China, where Kūkai received them from his own master, Hui-kuo. Guided through prescribed practices intended to open channels of communication to the deepest levels of mind, the initiate receives not only secret mantras and mudras, but also the Dharma lineage (kechi-myaku) of the generations of Mikkyo masters. Candidates must therefore meet strict standards of personal dedication and character, and undergo preparation through study and meditation (including the rigorous Preparatory Fourfold Enlightenment Practice). Before receiving the Dharma-transmission initiation, candidates also receive the esoteric precepts (*sanmaya kai*).

The *Dainichi-kyō* lists the following as basic requirements for the candidate:

To be a fit vessel of the Dharma, first, be far removed from all impurities; second, have reasoned faith [*shinge,* faith based on one's understanding of cause and effect]; third, be diligent and fearless; fourth, have deep faith [*jinshin,* faith beyond the limits of one's own understanding]; and fifth, be concerned always for the benefit of others.[16]

The Dharma-transmission initiation has been strictly maintained by Shingon, and is performed according to the ritual format Hui-kuo employed in initiating Kūkai. The initiate thus receives a pagoda and vajra, symbols of universal enlightenment, with appreciation of the unbroken continuity of the esoteric lineage. This ritual also results in the initiate being given the title of *ajari,* meaning master. Despite the exalted title, however, this provides only the basis for further training, and higher ranks of *ajari* exist. Only a person suited by capacity, affinity, and learning eventually becomes a master qualified to conduct this initiation and thereby transmit the Dharma lineage.

The fifth level comprises advanced initiations reserved for those admitted to the Dharma lineage. The mind-to-mind initiation (sometimes called "forehead-to-forehead" initiation) that uses no ritual or paraphernalia belongs to this level. This is a direct, intuitive transmission of teachings, not limited to any particular time, place, or format, and is an intensely individual process based on the unique relationship between teacher and student.

One advanced form of ritual initiation, called the "initiation of scholarly practice" (*gakushū kanjō*), takes place only on Kōya-san for a strictly limited group of senior priests who have undergone decades of study. In ancient times this was a way of advanced scholarly teaching in which problems were posed based on esoteric texts which the initiates would then respond to in the form of a debate. The initiate would have to win the debate in order to receive the degree of Great Ajari. This initiation is still practiced on Kōya-san, but the debate aspect has become formalized today, since scholarly studies are largely pursued in Shingon universities.

The various types of initiation differ in many points, but in all cases every element is prescribed. For example, tradition dictates precise details of participants' movements and positions throughout (including even how far to turn and in which directions, how far to step back and with which foot, and so on); the altar implements are placed on a laid-out mandala at specified locations and moved in specified ways during the course of the ritual. The number of candidates is limited to one, two, four, five, seven, eight, or ten under one master. Since initiation is counted among Mikkyo's most important rituals, its details are for the most part kept secret. A brief picture of the Dharma transmission initiation is, however, given below. Most initiation rituals (except the first and the fifth type) follow this general pattern, employing the usual ritual techniques.

As Mikkyo practice uses the many bodily senses, the initiation ritual likewise

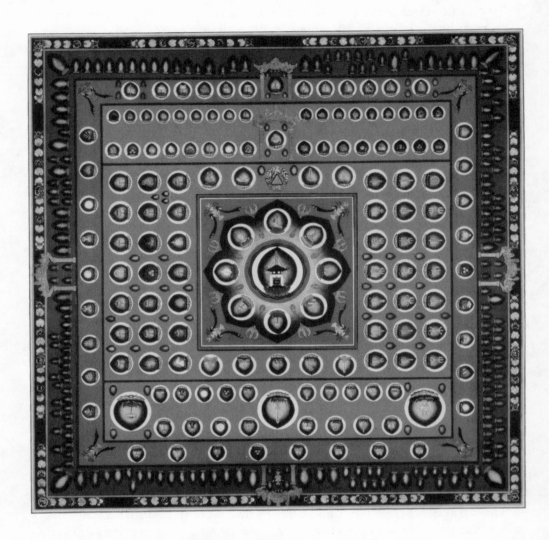

Painted floor mandala for Shingon initiation.

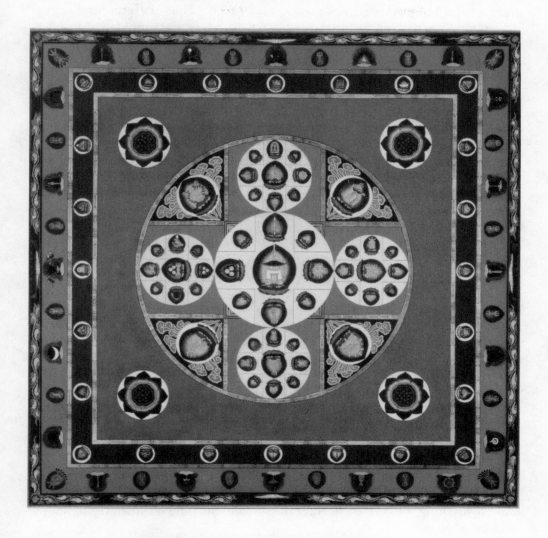

Painted floor mandala for Shingon initiation.

involves the tongue, eyes, nose, ears, and so on. Thus, before entering the closed initiation hall where the secret ritual takes place, the candidate rubs powdered incense on his hands to purify his entire body, and puts cloves in his mouth to cleanse the faculty of speech. His eyes are covered with a silken mask to cut him off from the outside world. Forming a mudra and holding a sprig of anise between his extended middle fingers, he recites mantras and meditates on the union in fundamental equality of his mind and the Buddha-mind. Stepping over an elephant-shaped incense burner, the candidate passes through a cloud of incense smoke and enters the initiation hall (*kanjō dōjō*). Within, the participants alternate in chanting verses praising the Buddha's virtue and power.

The ritual functions to make the candidate's entire body-mind into a symbol of enlightenment transcending time and space, and the initiation hall itself is said to become the Iron Tower. Casting the anise sprig onto the mandala spread out on the initiation platform, the candidate establishes a Dharma-relationship with the central Buddha, Dainichi Nyorai. The mandalas used in this initiation are of the type (*shiki mandara*) made to be laid out flat on the altar platform, the altar implements placed on them. They are abbreviated forms of either the Tai-zō or Kongō-kai, showing only fifty-three deities, all depicted in symbolic samaya form, with Dainichi Nyorai portrayed as a pagoda above a vajra resting on a lotus.

The master uses a special wooden wand (*sanjō*) to sprinkle on the candidate's head the water of the Five Wisdoms. The wand is made from a plum branch that grew toward the east, facing the sun, and its tip is carved into eight lobes. The water into which the wand is dipped is contained in five vessels, symbolizing the wisdoms. In sprinkling the water on the crown of the head, the master enacts Dainichi Nyorai's transmission of truth to the initiate, who is seen as Kongōsatta.

In a state of mutual empowerment with Dainichi Nyorai, the master sprinkles the water while reciting a mantra of the Five Buddhas, the initiate performing the mudras and mantras of related bodhisattvas. In this way the essence of the esoteric teaching is expected to enter the initiate, opening channels to the source of enlightenment.

Included in the Dharma-transmission initiation is a mudra shaped like a pagoda, with sequences of movement representing the closed pagoda door opening. This mudra, associated with the Tai-zō Mandala, represents the pagoda that is the samaya form of Dainichi Nyorai, and harks back to the Iron Tower, symbol of the first communication of the esoteric teachings.

Holding a five-pronged vajra within his hands in a mudra, the master turns it in prescribed ways, reciting verses and mantras, and passes the vajra to the initiate, who receives it with the same mudra. This sequence also involves visualization of a pagoda above the vajra.

The master also gives the initiate a mudra shaped like an upright five-pronged vajra, associated with the Kongō-kai Mandala, that is the samaya form of

Kongōsatta. In receiving the vajra mudra, the initiate confirms his identity with Kongōsatta. The initiate then receives the oral transmission of the esoteric practices appropriate to the circumstances of the particular initiation.

It is said that initiation affects the most profound level of the body-mind being. The change that takes place in *kanjō* is thus in a different dimension than that which comes from conscious work on improving the self by accumulating merit. Where the latter is a gradual process of building from the bottom up, initiation is an intuitive experience coming from the top down. It is meant to cut through all stages and processes directly to the inmost self in a way that the esoteric tradition says can be known fully only through direct experience.

EIGHT

Concentrated Three-Secrets Practices

The fourfold preparatory prac- tice, though not the most complex of Shingon rituals, illus- trates the way in which the
Mikkyo practitioner repeats three-secrets techniques to build
up in minute detail an inner uni- verse of esoteric union. Just as the
highest initiation has no set format, the ultimate Mikkyo practice is the "formless," spontaneous activity of wisdom expressed not in ritual but in the complexity of day-to-day life. It would be incorrect, therefore, to assume that any
meditation is more advanced or effective by reason of its difficulty, or that esoteric rituals are ranked in order from the simple to the complex.

This chapter presents two practices that, though relatively simple, penetrate
directly to the essence of the esoteric teachings: the Morning Star meditation
and the A-syllable visualization. The former is an intensive secret practice,
given only to priests in the line of Dharma transmission, and is, because of its
rigors, undertaken by only a few. The A-syllable visualization, on the other
hand, is regularly practiced in Japan by priests—and, today, the laity as well—
in different forms suited to varying circumstances.

THE MORNING STAR MEDITATION

The Morning Star meditation (*gumonji-hō*) is a practice in which the mantra of
the bodhisattva Kokūzō is recited one million eighty thousand times ("one million" in Shingon terms) over a set period of time. Though following the basic
pattern of the fourfold practice, it is extremely abbreviated and its ritual simplified as far as possible, emphasizing primarily the core section of ritual which
is concerned with esoteric union through mantra recitation. The Morning Star
ritual manual instructs the practitioner to become one body with the universal
Dharma realm. The practitioner uses only one mudra and one mantra in a concentrated meditation focused on direct experience of the universe through
union with the deity of the morning star.

The name *gumonji-hō* means literally "technique for seeking hearing-
retaining," meaning that this practice is supposed to result in the ability to re-
member everything seen and heard. The Morning Star meditation was, in fact,
practiced in Japan as early as the Nara period to develop the memory and aid in

memorizing sutras. Its esoteric purpose, however, is to deepen the samadhi state in order to experience the self as the universal void of potentiality. It is here called the Morning Star meditation because it involves visualization of the deity Kokūzō in the form of Venus, the morning star. A central Mikkyo meditation both in the past and today, it is one of the important secret practices (*hihō*) of Shingon.

The source text of this practice is the *Kokūzō Bosatsu Nōman Shogan Saishō-shin Darani Gumonji-hō* (Kokūzō Bodhisattva's Power-Filled Wish-Fulfilling Supreme-Mind Dharani Technique for Seeking Hearing and Retaining). This text was translated from the original Sanskrit by Shubhakarasimha in China in 717, and brought to Japan the following year. The Morning Star meditation was therefore known and practiced in Japan some time before Kūkai brought the Shingon lineage from China. It is considered to be among the early elements of "pure" Mikkyo to arrive in Japan.

Various ritual manuals of the Morning Star meditation were written in Japan based on Shubhakarasimha's Chinese translation. Although the ritual was formalized in Japan, it clearly originated in India, where, for example, at the beginning of the ritual the practitioner would seal milk, symbolizing the nectar of enlightenment, into a container. When opened at the end, the manner in which the contents had fermented was believed to indicate how successful the practice had been. In Japan, however, milk was uncommon, and during much of the year is as likely to freeze as to ferment, necessitating a change in this part of the ritual.

Shubhakarasimha's translation of the source text still exists, and its most important steps have been adhered to in the Japanese ritual manuals. Although the title of this text is long, the contents are brief, emphasizing recitation of the mantra "one million" times. Kūkai used this text to perform the Morning Star meditation, and Shingon considers this to be the practice by which he first experienced the nature of the esoteric teachings. An important practice not only in Kūkai's own life but in the history of Shingon, the Morning Star meditation traditionally has had a strong appeal in Japan. Kakuban, for example, performed it eight times—a prodigious feat.

The Morning Star meditation is not a required practice for Shingon priests, nor does it have any relationship to the system of seniority within the priesthood. Because of its rigors, however, there are relatively few priests today who have completed the Morning Star meditation. It seems to have been much more widely performed, though probably in less rigid forms, during the eighth century, when laymen were also initiated into its practice.

It is not known who transmitted the practice to Kūkai. Legend has it that a priest named Gonzō, among the first masters of the Morning Star meditation in Japan, was Kūkai's teacher. In any case, after encountering his nameless master, the young Kūkai sought out isolated places on the Pacific coast and amid the deep gorges on the mountainous island of Shikoku in which to practice the

Morning Star meditation. Kūkai wrote in the *Sangō Shiiki* (Indication of the Basis of the Three Teachings):

> Here a priest gave me the Morning Star meditation of Kokūzō. In the text was written, "If one follows this technique and recites this mantra one million times, the ability to memorize the words of all the teachings will be gained."
>
> Believing the words of the great master to be true, I hoped to kindle a blaze out of this flying spark. I climbed to the peaks of Tairyū Mountain in the country of Awa, and immersed myself in recitation at Cape Muroto in Tosa. In the echoing valleys the image of the Morning Star appeared.[1]

CELESTIAL BODIES AND MEDITATION ON THE UNIVERSE

Mikkyo actively employs celestial bodies for meditation on the Dharma Body. In the Morning Star meditation the focus of ritual is the mantra, while the subject of esoteric union is the universe itself symbolized by Venus. Shingon considers the Morning Star meditation to refer back to Shakyamuni's experience of seeing the bright morning star at the moment of his enlightenment under the bodhi tree. In the A-syllable visualization, the universe is symbolized by the A-syllable in a moon disk, or sometimes the moon disk alone. Specific deities of other planets and constellations also play important parts as "guardians" in many Mikkyo rituals (e.g., in the fifth stage of the *goma* ritual).

Mikkyo also has a number of star rituals (*hoshiku*), derived from Chinese Taoist astrology, performed to avert misfortune and to prolong life. Unlike the Morning Star and A-syllable meditations, these star rituals are for material benefit, but remain, nevertheless, representative esoteric practices. One such practice is that of the bodhisattva Myōken, who in Shingon is the deity of the Pole Star, the most exalted of all stars. Although depicted in many forms, in the Myōken Mandala this deity stands within a moon disk surrounded by his attendants, the seven stars of the Great Bear constellation, each of which embodies an aspect of Buddha-nature.

Within the Morning Star meditation hall hangs a painting of the deity Kokūzō Bodhisattva, whose qualities are also symbolized by the morning star. The actual planet is also used in the meditation, and is viewed through a special window. Although Venus is not always visible, the subject of the practice is not simply the planetary body but the dynamic cosmos which, in the esoteric understanding, is embodied in the painting as well. The practitioner employs the planet, the painting of the deity, and the visualized image of the planet-deity as means to experience suprapersonal truth.

In the painting used in the Morning Star meditation, Kokūzō is depicted in color on wood within a moon disk about one foot in diameter. His body is gold, radiating beams of light. Seated on a lotus throne, he wears the crown of the five Buddhas. His left hand holds the stem of a pale red lotus on which rests a blue wish-fulfilling gem emanating yellow flames. His right hand is extended, palm up, fingers bent down, in the wish-bestowing (yogan) mudra.

Kokūzō is a deity of wisdom, virtue, and good fortune, whose activity is to fulfill all wishes. His direction is south. The esoteric tradition considers this the direction from which all treasures come, and south is also associated with the Buddha Hōshō, whose name means "giving birth to treasure." Kokūzō's name literally means "repository of the void," void here indicating not merely nothingness, but the mysterious potentiality that gives rise to all phenomena. The samaya form of Kokūzō is the wish-fulfilling gem (nyoi hōshu). The samadhi of the Morning Star meditation focuses on this magical jewel, symbol of void-potentiality. The wish-fulfilling gem embodies Kokūzō's enlightened energy, the universe itself which evolves eternally in perfect freedom, oblivious to humans' attempts to delimit it in their own understanding.

In the Morning Star meditation the practitioner concentrates exclusively on the single practice of union with the deity, the planet Venus. Focusing his being in this way on the distant morning star (symbolizing the universe), he seeks to unite with the source of the mind.

THE PRACTICE OF THE MORNING STAR

The Morning Star meditation hall traditionally is built in an isolated, natural setting where the sky and stars are visible. (In ancient times it was also performed in the open.) Only a few temples exist in Japan today where this meditation may be practiced: Tairyū-ji in the Awa region on Shikoku, Kongō-ji in Kōchi, Mount Misen on the island of Miyajima in the Inland Sea, and the Shinbessho on Kōya-san.

The practice hall for the Morning Star meditation is built so that its east, west, and south sides are open and uncrowded, facing natural landscapes in the distance. The east side in particular must not be closed in by trees or other buildings. The hall is small, usually four and one-half tatami mats (about nine square feet) to six mats in area. High in the east wall is a small window through which the practitioner, who sits facing this wall, can see the stars. Hanging on this same east wall, the painting of Kokūzō is kept covered with a white cloth except during the time of meditation. The room is lit only by a small oil lamp which is kept burning throughout the ritual.

The source text for the Morning Star meditation contains a brief reference to a "wooden mandala," a four-legged wooden platform about forty centimeters square, which is still used today. Like the larger platform altars, it functions as a place to summon the deity from its essential realm.

185

Symbolizing the deity's enlightenment, the altar is immediately below the painting, and offerings are placed on a stand before it. To ensure its tranquillity and ease of concentration, the altar is not touched during the practice; neither is the water in the flower vase changed, though fresh water is added. The "flowers" are made from the leaves of the *kaya* tree (*Torreya nucifera*), and *kaya* oil is burned in the lamp. In fact, every ritual performed with the six offering implements employs some part of this tree.

In the past, the Morning Star meditation took one hundred days, but now ordinarily takes fifty days. The date for beginning the meditation is chosen by counting back from the day on which it ends, which must be marked by a solar or lunar eclipse. The closing ritual (*kechigan*) takes place at the exact time of the eclipse.

The number of recitations to be done each day is calculated precisely according to the length of the practice. If fifty days, for example, the practitioner must recite the mantra "twenty thousand" times (actually 21,600) daily. Each day has equal sittings of the same length and intensity, so that a continuous rhythm can be maintained throughout the practice. Special rituals mark the opening and closing days, but the ritual performed during all the intervening days remains exactly the same.

Since the mantra recitations must be counted, the practitioner uses a rosary and a device rather like a cribbage board with pegs, each of which stands for a certain number of recitations counted with the rosary. The rosary is made of *kaya* wood (or sometimes oak), and has only 54 beads instead of the usual 108. Although the ritual manual specifies a crystal rosary, crystal was found too heavy to be practical and was replaced with the wooden beads.

The Morning Star meditation is physically and mentally demanding. Practiced by a solitary meditator in the mountains over a long period of time, it may not be interrupted by illness or discouragement. It is not rare for practitioners to learn they are unable to bear its rigors. Its practice is not, therefore, taught indiscriminately, and its secrecy is strictly maintained. Since much of the Morning Star meditation is revealed only by direct oral transmission, only certain aspects are described here.

In outline, the ritual format is that of the usual single-deity practice, but differs in that only one mudra and one mantra are used throughout. The right hand forms the mudra of the wish-fulfilling gem, while the left hand forms the Vajra Fist at the hip. The mantra is that of Kokūzō. Since the practice comes under the category of a benefit-increasing ritual, the practitioner, following ancient distinctions maintained in few other rituals today, faces east and wears a yellow robe.

During the time of the practice, all activity such as eating, bathing, sleeping, and so on, is ritualized. Strict rules govern diet. Intake of salt, for example, thought to increase nervousness, is reduced before and during the practice. The morning meal consists of a simple rice gruel, and nothing may be eaten after noon, though the practitioner may drink water.

The general daily procedure during the Morning Star meditation is as follows:

Before entering the hall in the morning, the practitioner ritually worships the morning star (*myōjō-rai*), then performs a ritual of drawing two buckets of *aka* water from a well, one for the practitioner and one for the deity. Techniques of purification are used in which he scoops up water in his left hand, transfers it to the right, sips it, then washes his hands and face. The practitioner recites the mantra while visualizing himself purified within and without.

The mantra is NŌ BŌ AKYASHAKYARABAYA ON ARI KYAMARI BORI SOWAKA (In the name of Kokūzō Om Flower-Garland Lotus-Crown may it be accomplished).

Having prepared the offerings, the practitioner, wearing over his nose and mouth a white mask that is removed when the practice proper begins, enters the meditation hall. He performs obeisance to the deity, sits in half-lotus, and with a special stick raises the cloth covering the painting.

Being-Protecting Technique. The practitioner performs the mantra and mudra at five points of the body. He then visualizes Kokūzō and all the Buddhas absorbing him into themselves, causing all his delusions to vanish and his body-mind to become pure.

Water Sprinkling. Forming the mudra, the practitioner recites the mantra to empower the water, then sprinkles it on the offerings, the altar, and the floor.

After the ritual of powdered incense, the practitioner empowers the offerings and the altar. Recitation of prayers invoking the protection of the deities is followed by the rituals of purification of the three activities, all-pervading homage, awakening the enlightened mind, and so forth.

The practitioner establishes the sacred space for practice, and within it visualizes the "sublime meditation hall." With eyes closed, he contemplates Kokūzō's essential oneness with the painted image, after which he summons the deity to the altar.

Taking up the container of *aka* water, the practitioner manipulates it while visualizing the feet of the deity being washed. The deity, visualized seated on a flower, is welcomed by ringing the bell and making the five offerings. The universal offering and homage to all Buddhas follow. The practitioner then performs mutual empowerment with Kokūzō, reciting the mantra while forming the mudra at various parts of the body and contemplating his essential identity with the deity.

The core section of the Morning Star meditation then begins, in which the practitioner forms the mudra and recites the mantra while counting with the special rosary. In Kokūzō's breast he visualizes a moon disk in which the syllables of the mantra appear. Emitting a golden radiance, the mantra flows from the deity to enter the practitioner through the crown of his head, leaving through his mouth and reentering Kokūzō through the feet. Forming the same mudra throughout, the practitioner visualizes his recitation in this manner until the prescribed number is reached.

This complete, the practitioner performs "entry into the Dharma Realm," in which, with the same mudra held at the breast, he visualizes the moon disk and the syllables of the mantra gradually expanding to fill the universe, then gradually contracting back to their original size. After repeating mutual empowerment with Kokūzō, the practitioner performs the "diffused recitation" (with several hundred repetitions) to Dainichi Nyorai and four other deities.

Next the ending offerings are performed, followed by recitation of praises, the verses of all-pervading offering and of the mutual empowerment of the three universal powers, the five great vows, and homage to the Buddhas. The practitioner offers the merit gained by this practice to the benefit of all beings, after which he dissolves the protections surrounding the sacred space and dispatches the deity. After completing the being-protecting techniques, the practitioner leaves the meditation hall.

AN EXPERIENCE WITH THE MORNING STAR MEDITATION

Taikō Yamasaki describes his experience with this practice as follows:

I performed the Morning Star meditation at Mount Misen temple in Miyajima in 1955, from 10 October to 13 November, the date of a lunar eclipse. My master in this practice was the *ajari* Kanayama Bokushō.

I rose at two o'clock every morning, bathed, and then performed the ceremony to Venus and the ritual of drawing *aka* water, after which I entered the practice hall for two meditation periods totaling ten hours. During the practice I was isolated from the everyday world. The temple was surrounded by the great trees of a primeval forest, and stars in a clear sky were visible to me on awaking in the morning and before sleep at night.

At the beginning, I had pain in my legs and back from the long hours of sitting, making it difficult to concentrate on meditation. Gradually, however, my body and mind came into harmony, creating within me a feeling of lightness and tranquillity. During meditation, my body came to feel almost transparent, while my mind and what I saw around me were clear, like crystal. Far from being a hallucination, this came from increased clarity of consciousness—as though I had come to a place where heaven and earth join.

Coming out of meditation and leaving the practice hall, the sense of the vastness of the universe would remain, as though I were seeing the world for the first time. The trees were no longer separate from myself, but seemed a part of me, as though we were a single being. Although my emotions were involved, this was not an experience of ordinary, sentimental intimacy, but rather an experience of consciousness, a realization that one is made of the very same substance as everything else and that nothing in nature is unrelated to the self.

At night, after finishing the day's sitting, I would go up to the mountaintop and meditate in the open, feeling the stars in the late autumn sky surrounding me on all sides, as though I were hanging in space. This sense of unity with all things remained in my mind even after the practice ended and I returned to the world. A profound feeling of gratitude and a new appreciation for life came to affect everything I did.

Because the Morning Star meditation consists of a single three-secrets ritual that must be performed at an even, unbroken pace throughout, it requires great determination. Initiation into the practice is not granted unless the candidate fulfills requirements of ability, training, and experience in meditation. To meditate concentratedly for so many hours day after day is physically strenuous, demanding good health and emotional balance. This meditation is a serious practice not to be undertaken lightly, and I have heard many stories of people who experienced considerable difficulty with it.

For instance, it is difficult at first to adjust to solitary practice after life in the everyday world. Unexpected things happen in the mind. Delusions and attachments come welling up, and subconscious fixations can grow out of all proportion because one's concentration is so deep. I had hallucinatory experiences of such intensity that it is difficult for me to imagine a physically weaker or older person withstanding them.

Hallucinations can become intense during the practice because one is going directly to a deep level of the mind. They should not be cut off, however, but recognized for what they are without either enjoying them or fearing them. Shubhakarasimha wrote that he was offered the secret of invisibility while doing this practice. I experienced something similar when a mysterious priest "appeared" and offered to teach me a secret mudra. The image was so vivid that I had difficulty realizing that it was not real. I understand now how unfortunate it could have been had I had the slightest inclination to accept, since it would have disturbed the entire practice.

During the course of the practice the hallucinations gradually diminished, my concentration deepened, and eventually I came to experience continuous samadhi. All my senses became clearer and sharper, including my smell and hearing, to the point that I felt I could hear the sound of incense burning—an experience recorded in Mikkyo texts.

Taikō Yamasaki in meditation.

Meditation scroll with A-syllable.
Kamakura period (13th century),
Tōji temple, Kyoto.

The Morning Star meditation strengthens the inner spiritual faculties, and may produce unusual experiences, but the point of the practice, of course, is to experience truth.

THE A-SYLLABLE VISUALIZATION

The A-syllable visualization (*ajikan*) is an early Shingon meditation. Over the past thousand or so years, more than one hundred A-syllable visualization texts have been written in Japan, and a body of oral transmissions has been accumulated. The practice has many forms of varying complexity, emphasizing different techniques and aspects of Mikkyo doctrine, but in all cases centers on the sound, the form, and the meaning of the syllable A as a way to experience suprapersonal reality. As mentioned earlier, Mikkyo sees this syllable as an embodiment of the true nature of the myriad phenomena of the universe, transcending birth and death, ephemerality and permanence, the one and the many, past and future, in a single symbolic form.

The A-syllable visualization, like other three-secrets practices, has been transmitted in secret within the priesthood. During its long history it underwent many developments, and exists today in a variety of forms. Its line of transmis-

190

Monks practicing A-visualization at Kōyasan meditation hall.

sion is said to have remained unbroken over the centuries, and today the A-syllable visualization is taking a position as one of Mikkyo's major practices, for the laity as well as for the priesthood.

Complicated forms of practice require considerable ability in visualization and concentration. The Morning Star meditation, in which a single mudra and mantra are repeated over a long period of time, demands even greater concentration. The A-syllable visualization, on the other hand, can develop ability in meditation through gently graded stages, and so has been used as a preparation for more difficult practices. It is not, however, regarded as merely a preparatory exercise. A busy Shingon priest, in fact, often finds no time for regular practice of anything other than a brief, concentrated ritual—of which this is the principal example.

The most concise and versatile of Mikkyo's hundreds of ritual practices, the A-syllable visualization nevertheless fulfills the scope of the esoteric teachings. Kakuban wrote about the value of this practice in the *Ichigo Taiyō Himitsu-shū* (Single Collection of the Essential Secrets):

This visualization is the precious lord of all practices, the emperor of all samadhis . . .

Easy to perform, a way by which enlightenment is easily attained, this practice cannot be surpassed. . . . A person of great capacity for concentrated practice will become a Buddha in his very body.[2]

191

THE ALL-ENCOMPASSING SYMBOLISM
OF THE A-SYLLABLE

The doctrines and practices of Mikkyo, with their hundreds and thousands of texts and deities, may appear impossibly complicated on first approach. Without a firm grasp of the core of the teachings, the novice priest may find this complexity overwhelming. The essence of this vast number of sutras and texts, however, can be found in the *Dainichi-kyō* and *Kongōchō-gyō,* while the multitude of Buddhas and bodhisattvas can all be seen as manifestations of the central deity, Dainichi Nyorai.

The entire system of doctrine and practice set forth in the *Dainichi-kyō* is, in fact, symbolized in concentrated form in the single seed syllable A. The *Commentary on the Dainichi-kyō* says, "The A-syllable gate is the king of all mantras. . . ."[3] The sutra explains that all mantras are rooted in the A-syllable:

> The mind within all these mantras you must truly hear clearly. It is the A-syllable gate. To concentrate on the mind of all mantras is the highest. This is the place where all mantras dwell.[4]

In both exoteric and esoteric teachings this syllable was a symbol of the Dharma universe. This traditional meaning was maintained and enriched over the course of centuries in the contexts of different cultures. Originally the A-syllable was a negative prefix, and for this reason it was used in exoteric texts to represent the perfect truth which could not be expressed directly. Where exoteric teachings gave the A-syllable three meanings of negation, Mikkyo found in it the threefold affirmation of the universal void of potentiality, the unborn, and phenomenal form.

This single syllable thus came to represent the full range of Mikkyo teachings. As Kūkai wrote in the *Bonji Shittan Jimo Heishakugi* (Sanskrit Siddham Syllable-Mother Chart with Explanation of Meanings; a text on the orthographic elements that make up Sanskrit written syllables):

> The A-syllable is the wellspring of all the Dharma teachings. All teachings, including the exoteric and esoteric, arise from this syllable.[5]

The *Dainichi-kyō* says: "What is the Dharma teaching of mantra? It is said, in the A-syllable gate all things are originally unborn. . ."[6] The *Commentary on the Dainichi-kyō* explains this as follows:

> The A-syllable is the source of all Dharma teachings. In the sound made when the mouth first opens, there is always the sound of A. To be apart from the sound of A is to have no words. Therefore it is the mother of human speech.
>
> The languages of the three realms all depend on names. Names depend on syllables. Therefore, the *siddham* A-syllable is the mother of all syllables.

This you should know. The true meaning of the syllable A is also like this, its meaning penetrating all things.

What is this in the relative [*sho,* limited, phenomenal] aspect? There is nothing that is not born from a combination of causes, and all things born from cause have a beginning and a source. Examining now things that are born out of ultimate [*nō,* essential] cause, again these are born from a multitude of causes and develop and transform in accordance with their cause.

What then is at the root? Examining it in this way, we know the reality of the originally unborn. This is the source of the myriad things. In hearing all speech, one is hearing the voice of the A-syllable. In the same way, in looking at the birth of all things, one sees the reality of the originally unborn.

One who sees the originally unborn knows his own mind as it truly is, and knowing one's own mind as it truly is, is the Wisdom of All-Wisdom. Therefore the mantra of Dainichi Nyorai is just this one syllable.[7]

Also:

The sutra says, "If you practice the mantra of the world-liberating one of this unequalled phrase . . ." This means practicing the phrase of unequalled wisdom. The A-syllable gate is the king of all mantras, just as Shakyamuni is king of all Dharmas. Therefore it is called the mantra of the world-liberating one.[8]

The textual basis of the A-syllable visualization can be traced back to Nagarjuna's *Treatise on Enlightened Mind* and the *Dainichi-kyō.* There are more than one hundred extant Japanese ritual manuals of this practice, most of which are based on the *Ajikan Yōjin Kuketsu* (Record of Oral Instruction on the A-syllable Visualization). This, the earliest known text to deal with the practice, is said to contain the oral teaching of Kūkai as transcribed by his disciple Jichie (786–847). In it is written:

Just as the sea embraces a hundred rivers, the roots of all good are gathered in this single syllable. Therefore it is called the mantra of the ocean mudra samadhi. Thus if you visualize this syllable one time, it surpasses the merit of reciting simultaneously the eighty thousand Buddhist teachings.[9]

Mikkyo sutras and texts contain abundant explanations of the A-syllable, which is seen variously as a symbol of the void of potentiality, of the originally unborn nature of all things, and of Dainichi Nyorai—in other words, the ungraspable reality of the universe. For Shingon, recitation and visualization of the A-syllable therefore represent union with one's true mind. The *Aji-gi* (The Meaning of the A-Syllable), attributed to Kūkai, states:

The A-syllable is originally unborn, ungraspable void. This ultimate ungraspable void is endowed with a multitude of virtues and embraces the

truth of all Buddhas everywhere. Because it is based on mutual empowerment with the void, it embraces all Buddha-truths . . .[10]

In representing all language, the A-syllable also symbolizes the "speech" of
the Dharma Body, present in all things. In the *True Meaning of the Voiced Syllable,* Kūkai wrote:

The A-syllable is the beginning source of Sanskrit. In opening the mouth
and calling out, there is the sound of A. In other words, this is voice. The
voice of the A-syllable can call out any name, and expresses the name-
syllable of the Dharma Body. In other words, this is the voiced syllable.
What is the meaning of the Dharma Body? The Dharma Body means
that all things are originally unborn. In other words, it is truth.[11]

The *Dainichi-kyō* states:

Most secret of all secrets, I will explain the great mind of mantra wisdom.
I will now proclaim this for you. Hear me clearly with one mind. The
A-syllable is the mind of all mantras. From it flow forth the infinite all-
pervading mantras. Stopping all frivolous argument, it gives birth to skillful wisdom.[12]

Mikkyo thus crystallizes the entire universe in one esoteric symbol. The
seeming simplicity of the A-syllable, however, does not deny the rich diversity
every individual finds in himself and his surroundings. This is illustrated in another, related meditation, the "hundred-radiance all-illuminating king" (*hyakkō
henjō-ō*). This visualization practice centers on the syllable AN, which is written
like the A-syllable but surmounted by a dot-like orthographic element called
the "void point" (*kūden*). Around the AN, the practitioner visualizes an array
of some one hundred other Sanskrit syllables, representing further combinations of orthographic elements, in a disk that is made to rotate. The meditator
then visualizes the rotating syllable-disk transforming into a light which, shining like the sun, cuts through the darkness of ignorance. This is, in fact, a sun-
disk visualization.

The hundred-radiance all-illuminating king visualization is explained at
length in the *Dainichi-kyō* and in various Chinese commentaries, where the
AN-syllable is identified with Dainichi Nyorai. The AN-syllable visualization
(*anjikan*) has been practiced in Japanese Shingon, but there are considerably
fewer texts dealing with it than with the A-syllable practice.

Aspects of the Tai-zō Dainichi Nyorai are symbolized in the five syllables A,
ĀH, AN, AKU, and ĀNKU, representing, respectively, awakening the enlightened mind, practice, wisdom, nirvana, and skillful means seen as identical
to enlightenment. These syllables are used, for example, in the syllable-disk
visualizations of the fourfold practice. The A is the basis of the other four

syllables in orthographic form as well as in doctrinal meaning, and all are therefore regarded as "transformations" of the one essential A.

All Sanskrit syllables, therefore, are regarded as of equal importance in Mikkyo. All have their associated meanings, and any one of them can be visualized within the moon disk in a separate meditation. At the same time, however, every syllable is contained in the single A. This illustrates the characteristic Mikkyo view of the single universal truth as not existing apart from the myriads of individual beings and phenomena. Grounded in this core understanding of esoteric Buddhism, therefore, the Mikkyo meditator is able to venture freely in many directions to experience the numberless transformations represented in these fundamental symbols.

Techniques of the A-Syllable Visualization

It is a special characteristic of the A-syllable visualization that it can be done in simple abbreviated form, taking about ten minutes, or it can be done in expanded form with full use of ritual implements, involving more advanced techniques and taking about an hour. It can be practiced in the meditation hall or in any quiet room, with or without a painted A-syllable image, and is therefore suitable for practice by priests and lay practitioners alike. The simplicity of even the expanded practice, however, is in striking contrast to the major rituals patterned after the eighteenfold practice, as well as the Morning Star meditation.

For the "deity" of this practice, the meditator ordinarily uses a painting of a Sanskrit A-syllable superimposed upon a moon disk above a lotus flower. The lotus is usually white with eight petals, the A-syllable gold, and the disk white like the full moon. Some hanging scrolls used in this meditation have only a golden circle around the edge and no white inside, while others contain a red lotus flower or only an A-syllable shining in a light mist. In the A-syllable meditation, the practitioner contemplates the painted symbolic image, performs ritual empowerment with it, and visualizes it internally in graded stages. The A-syllable, lotus, and moon disk thus function as "living" symbols which, in the manner characteristic of esoteric practice, are meant to speak directly to the meditator's deepest consciousness.

Kūkai's *Record of Oral Instruction on the A-Syllable Visualization,* excerpted below, contains valuable information, although, as is often the case with early ritual manuals, it gives relatively little detail about actual techniques. Most later texts are based on this one and provide additional details in varying degrees.

First, if you desire to visualize this syllable, find a place where the ceiling and the four walls do not seem cramped and it is neither too dark nor too light, and sit there. If it is too dark, deluded thoughts will arise, and if it is too light, the mind will be distracted. At night, sit with a dim lamp hung behind you.

Place a cushion and sit in full or half lotus. Form the Dharma Realm Samadhi Mudra and have your eyes neither fully open nor closed. If they are open, they will move and distract you, while if they are closed, you will sink into sleep. Narrow your eyelids without blinking and fix both eyes on the bridge of the nose. If the tongue is put to the palate [just behind the teeth], the breath will quiet of itself. Do not shift or bend the lower back, but sit straight to aid the circulation. If the blood circulation is impaired, illness may arise, or the mind may become disturbed.

Being careful in these things, first form the Vajra *gasshō* and recite the Five Great Vows. Next recite the five-syllable mantra of the Tai-zō one hundred times. Then perform the visualization. First, visualize the syllable in its ultimate, essential aspect, then contemplate the truth of its limited, phenomenal aspect . . .[13]

Although concise, the A-syllable visualization incorporates the basic Mikkyo meditation techniques (described in Chapter Six) to varying extents. Generally, the meditator first prepares body and mind (as in the fourfold preparatory practice) for esoteric union, then, after entering the place of meditation, performs the "being-protecting technique," comprised of the rituals of purification of the three activities, equality with the deities of the three divisions of the mandala, and donning the armor of compassion. He next performs the ritual of awakening the enlightened mind and recites the vow of equality and the five great vows.

Following these, the practitioner recites the five-syllable mantra of Dainichi Nyorai, using the circulation technique. Oral teachings sometimes instruct the practitioner also to perform a breath-regulating technique in which he visualizes his mind as one with his breath, flowing in and out with every inhalation and exhalation. This may be changed gradually into the permeation technique, in which the practitioner visualizes his breath flowing through his entire body.

The practitioner then brings the image of the "deity" within his breast using the image-manifesting technique. He may also employ the transformation technique, internally visualizing the deity's seed syllable (A) and samaya forms (lotus and moon disk) transforming into the deity's anthropomorphic form— which in this case is the practitioner himself.

The A-syllable within the moon disk can also be replaced or augmented by other Sanskrit syllables representing different aspects of the A-syllable. By visualizing such syllables in turn within the moon disk, the practitioner brings the syllable-disk technique into this meditation. By expanding and then contracting the moon disk, the meditator incorporates the expansion technique. (This expansion visualization is performed only after the practitioner is able to maintain the internally visualized image clearly and without strain for the re-

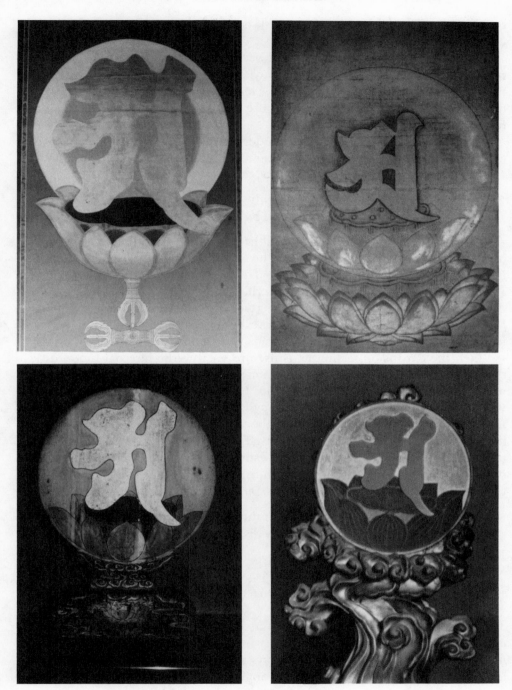

Various A-scrolls and disks.

quired time. Even then, the moon disk is never expanded any farther than is comfortable for the individual.)

The moon with its cool white light occupies a special place in esoteric doctrine and practice. The *Treatise on Enlightened Mind* says, "When I look at my mind, its form is like a moon disk,"[14] indicating that every individual is endowed with Buddha-nature which is pure and perfect, cool and radiant like the full moon.

This moon-like light of intrinsic Buddha-nature, however, is said not to be evident to a mind clouded with delusion. As Kūkai wrote in *The Meaning of the UN-Syllable*:

The sun, the moon, and the heavenly bodies have always been there in space, though they may be obscured by clouds and mists.[15]

Mikkyo meditation on intrinsic Buddha-nature has traditionally used images of the moon or even the moon itself. The moon disk visualization (*gachirin-kan*) is an ancient practice mentioned in the *Treatise on Enlightened Mind* and written about by Shubhakarasimha. Although the moon visualization apparently predates the A-syllable visualization, the two are not essentially different, since Mikkyo considers the A-syllable itself to be the originally unborn light of the moon disk.

When the expansion technique is used to enlarge the internal moon disk in the A-syllable visualization, the practitioner sees the A-syllable as the pure light of the moon disk alone. The lotus, too, becomes part of the same radiance in which all are essentially one. As a seed syllable it is the A; as the samaya form of Dainichi Nyorai it is the lotus and the moon disk; while as the anthropomorphic form it is the meditator himself. These forms, essentially the same, point to a single truth. To accomplish esoteric union with the moon disk is no different, therefore, from uniting with the A-syllable and lotus. The *Record of Oral Instruction on the A-Syllable Visualization* says:

The A-syllable is the seed syllable of the moon disk, and the moon disk is the radiance of the A-syllable. Moon disk and A-syllable are entirely one.[16]

THE A-SYLLABLE VISUALIZATION AND THE DUAL MANDALA

The A-syllable visualization and the painted and visualized image (*honzon*) used in it have been described in great variety in sutras, treatises, commentaries, and meditation manuals. This visualization exists in two forms, classified as belonging to either the Tai-zō or the Kongō-kai mandala systems. The former stresses the lotus of compassion, a central symbol of the Tai-zō system, and the latter the moon disk of enlightened mind of the Kongō-kai. When it is a Tai-zō practice, the practitioner visualizes an A-syllable painted within a moon disk that is above a lotus. When it is a Kongō-kai practice, both lotus and A-syllable are visualized inside the disk, and the expansion technique may be used. Since the central symbol of each is present in the other, this meditation is also understood as uniting both mandalas.

The complex doctrines and practices of Mikkyo were purposely condensed into the A-lotus-moon image of the A-syllable visualization, which belonged originally to the Tai-zō lineage. The historical development by which the A-syllable visualization was divided into two types, however, is not clear. Little is known with any certainty about the purpose in making this division, and no explanatory texts specifically differentiating the two forms of practice seem to have been written.

The many A-syllable visualization texts written over the past millennium are scattered among many temples throughout Japan, and many of the texts have been held secret. It is, therefore, no simple task to read and compare them all. This section will present materials from some texts illustrating the development of the two forms of A-syllable visualization.

The *Dainichi-kyō* and its *Commentary* contain many passages explaining various methods of meditation on the A-syllable. According to traditional Shingon doctrinal study, the A-syllable is the Dharma Body (*hottai*) of the *Dainichi-kyō*. This syllable is therefore treated throughout the sutra but in many varying ways and very simply. In the sutra it is said, for example:

How wonderful is the practice of mantra, endowed with vast wisdom. Visualizing this [the A-syllable] pervading all things, one becomes as noble as the Buddha.[17]

And further:

Make the A-syllable your inhalation and exhalation, and contemplate it at the three times [*sanji,* the times of day appropriate for meditation]. If the practitioner maintains this well, he will live a long life in this world.[18]

Other sections throughout the sutra deal in many ways with meditation involving this syllable, but the A-syllable visualization as known in Shingon is based primarily on the following passage:

Contemplate that lotus. It has eight petals and its stamens are outspread. On the flower dais is the A-syllable. It gives fiery wonder to the lotus. Its brilliance radiating everywhere to illuminate living beings, like the meeting of a thousand lightning bolts, it has the form of the Buddha's meritorious manifestations.

From deep within a round mirror it manifests in all directions. Like the moon in clear water, it appears before all living beings. Knowing this to be the nature of mind, one is enabled to dwell in the practice of mantra.[19]

In explaining this passage, the *Dainichi-kyō Sho* says:

199

When the practitioner first begins to study visualization, the mind is not yet pure and mature. If he is unable to perform the visualization, then he should first make a painting of the magical lotus.[20]

The sutra describes the A-syllable as being visualized above an eight-petalled lotus altar, and instead of being within a moon disk, it is within a round mirror. There is another passage later in the sutra, however, which does place it in a moon disk:

> Within that pure, round, full moon disk at the heart, manifest the A-syllable gate clear and bright, and make it the golden color of the omnipresent vajra.[21]

Although the sutra and its commentary do not present a systematic A-syllable visualization, it seems likely that passages such as those above provided the basis for the first development of painted A-syllable images for this practice in China. It should be remembered, too, that a moon disk visualization practice existed predating the A-syllable visualization.

The ninth-century *Record of Oral Instruction on the A-Syllable Visualization* describes an A-syllable visualization with all the ritual elements of a full meditation practice: exaltation of the practice hall, techniques for sitting in meditation, use of the Dharma Realm Samadhi Mudra, recitation of the Five Great Vows and of the five-syllable mantra of the Tai-zō Dainichi Nyorai, the painted image with A-syllable, lotus, and moon disk, explanations of these and of how to visualize the image internally, the technique of *nyūga-ga'nyū* visualization in which the practitioner and deity interpenetrate, expansion-contraction technique, and so on.

This text shows the A-syllable visualization developing, from its origin in the Tai-zō lineage, into a meditation encompassing the dual Kongōkai-Taizō mandalas. In this *Record of Oral Instruction on the A-Syllable Visualization* is written:

> In starting to speak, when our mouth opens our voice arises first from the A in our breast. Passing the throat, jaw, tongue, teeth, and lips, what emerges from these five places is the voice of the Buddhas of the Kongō-kai's five divisions teaching the Dharma. When we recite with the throat, tongue, and lips, it is the three divisions of the Tai-zō.[22]

This relates the visualization to the Tai-zō and Kongō-kai in terms of the three and five bodily points where the voiced syllable originates. The text thus clearly encompasses both mandalas in the A-syllable visualization.

Quoting from the *Renge Sanmai Kyō* (Lotus Samadhi Sutra, a sutra dealing with both mandala systems, but known only by references to it in other texts), the *Record of Oral Instruction on the A-Syllable Visualization* says:

Arrange the throne of the two mandalas within the breast. . . . If in this way one visualizes this syllable [the A] once, it will excel the merit of reciting the eighty thousand Buddhist teachings all at once.[23]

As described in the *Record of Oral Instruction on the A-Syllable Visualization*, the image of practice includes both the Kongō-kai type (although without the lotus), and the Tai-zō type with A-syllable within the moon disk above the lotus. Although both basic forms are described, the moon disk and lotus are not explicitly associated with the Kongō-kai and Tai-zō lineages. The text does, however, contain the following statements:

The A-syllable is the seed syllable of the moon disk, and the moon disk is the radiance of the A-syllable. Moon disk and A-syllable are entirely one.[24]

And:

The samaya form is the eight-petalled lotus.[25]

These passages place the A-syllable, lotus, and moon disk in an inseparable relationship of symbolic identity, providing a foundation for the later development of clearly defined A-syllable visualization practices focusing on the moon-lotus of the indissoluble dual mandala.

After the *Record of Oral Instruction on the A-Syllable Visualization*, many manuals on the subject came to be written, all with distinctive differences, but most of them continually referring back to this text by Jichie. Other ritual elements were later added, however, such as the triple prostration (*gotai tōji no sanrai*), the being-protecting techniques (*goshin-bō*), awakening enlightened mind (*hotsu bodaishin*), the samaya vows (*sanmaya kai*), and the mutual empowerment of the three universal powers (*sanriki kaji*). The central section concentrating on esoteric union was also expanded. The A-syllable visualization thus became a full ritual practice, complete in itself.

Several early A-syllable visualization texts are introduced below in chronological order, showing something of the development of the image symbolizing the dual mandala:

I. Ajikan Yōjin Kuketsu (Record of Oral Instruction on the A-Syllable Visualization; excerpted in the preceding section):

The eight-petalled lotus is the heart [*karita,* corporeal heart] mind. This is form. The mind [*shitta,* spiritual mind] dwells in this lotus. These two minds do not separate for even a moment, and therefore you should visualize the moon disk above the lotus. The moon disk is the mind (Skt., *citta*). The form of this mind is truly like the moon disk. The round form of the moon disk is like a crystal jewel. The seed syllable of the lotus is the A-syllable. Therefore you should visualize the A-syllable within the moon disk.[26]

What is described here is an A-syllable visualization of the Tai-zō form. The relationship of the lotus and the moon disk, however, is expressed not in terms of truth and wisdom, Tai-zō and Kongō-kai, but in terms of the physical heart ("mind") and the mind beyond form.

Also in the same text:

Within your breast is the moon disk. It is like the moon on a clear autumn night. Within it is the A-syllable. The A is the seed syllable of the moon disk, and the moon disk is the radiance of the A-syllable . . .

At first, visualize the moon as one *chū* [a forearm's length, or about sixteen inches] in size, then later gradually expand it to fill the three thousand worlds and the palace of the Dharma realm.[27]

This expansion-contraction visualization, performed with the A-syllable in the moon disk, identifies this practice as being in the Kongō-kai lineage. Here, however, there is no lotus.

2. *Ajikan Hossoku* (Principles of the A-Syllable Visualization). Written by Seizon (1012–1074), this text has been transmitted in the Chūin school. It is translated in its entirety later in this chapter, so only a brief excerpt is given below:

Visualize: In my mind is a white, perfectly bright moon disk. Within the moon disk is a lotus. Above the lotus is an A-syllable.

. . . Visualize the A-syllable, lotus, and moon disk gradually growing larger by degrees. Visualize it filling the innumerable worlds and the Dharma Realm. Then, suddenly, forget deity and mind both, and dwell for a while in nondiscrimination.

Then visualize that the all-pervading A-syllable, lotus, and moon disk gradually contract back to the original size of one *chū* . . .[28]

Here also it is the Kongō-kai form, with lotus and A-syllable within the moon, incorporating, as well, the characteristic Kongō-kai expansion-contraction technique.

3. *Ajikan Shidai* (A-Syllable Visualization Manual). By Shōkaku (1057–1129):

First draw the eight-petalled white lotus one *chū* in size. On that lotus altar draw the moon disk. Within the moon disk paint a golden A-syllable.[29]

This is the Tai-zō form, described here as part of an A-breathing visualization (*asokukan*) in which the syllable A is recited with the practitioner's inhalation and exhalation. Shōkaku also wrote, in his *Ajikan* (A-Syllable Visualization):

All living beings originally have within their breasts an eight-petalled corporeal heart [*nikudan*]. Its shape is like that of the lotus . . .

This lotus should be unfolded through visualization. This is the mind-lotus. The moon disk on the flower altar of this lotus is the mind moon disk. . . . Therefore, the mind-lotus and the mind-moon are not two. They are the lotus-moon of indissoluble truth-wisdom. The lotus is truth, the moon wisdom.[30]

In these two works Shōkaku does not treat the Kongō-kai form, but in employing the Tai-zō form, he identifies the lotus as truth (Tai-zō), the moon as wisdom (Kongō-kai), describing the two as indissolubly united.

4. *Ajikan* (A-Syllable Visualization). Kakuban (1095–1143) wrote several works with this title, dealing with both Kongō-kai and Tai-zō forms. In one text he writes:

If the practitioner wishes to practice the A-syllable visualization, first draw an eight-petalled white lotus one *chū* in size, and above that lotus altar paint a moon disk. Within the moon disk paint a white A-syllable.[31]

This is the Tai-zō form. In another text (quoted below by Raiyu), Kakuban gives a practice using the Kongō-kai form. Kakuban does not, however, offer any explanation of the obvious differences between the two forms of central image for A-syllable visualization.

5. *Ajikan.* By Myōe (1173–1232):

Within one's breast is an eight-sectioned corporeal heart [*nikudan*]. Before realization, this appears as an eight-petalled mind-lotus altar. Above this mind-lotus is an A-syllable. This transforms to become the moon disk . . .

Within one's mind is a white eight-petalled lotus. Above the lotus is a moon disk one *chū* in size. Inside the moon disk is a golden A-syllable. It emits a white radiance illuminating the infinite world and removing ignorance and delusion from within all living beings. You should visualize this syllable.

The moon disk is like an empty quartz sphere. The moon disk is wisdom. The A-syllable is truth.[32]

This deals primarily with the Tai-zō form. The first part describes use of the transformation technique to visualize the A-syllable above the lotus transforming into a moon disk. The last part expresses the indissoluble truth-wisdom relationship in terms not of lotus and moon disk but rather of A-syllable and moon disk.

6. *A-UN Gō-kan.* (Unified A-UN Syllable Visualization). By Dōhan (1178–1252). This text gives a practice in which the practitioner visualizes the syllables A and UN with his breath. The A-syllable is not given pictorial form, and the lotus and moon disk are not employed, but since this meditation does deal with the originally unborn A-syllable, it is presented here as one type of A-syllable visualization. It presents the indissoluble Taizō Kongōkai in terms of A and UN rather than lotus and moon:

At all times, the exhalation is the A-syllable and the inhalation the UN-syllable. . . . The A-syllable is the perfect entirety of the Tai-zō, the UN-syllable the Kongō, the unchanging wisdom-seed . . .

Mouth open and lips meeting, make the two syllables, the A-UN of exhalation and inhalation, follow upon each other. These two syllables are indissoluble truth and wisdom, the two mandalas in one, a subtle gate of visualization.[33]

7. *Aji Hishaku* (Secret Explanation of the A-Syllable). By Raiyu (1226–1304). This is probably among the earliest texts specifically identifying the two forms of the A-syllable visualization. In it is written:

Abbreviated A-Syllable Visualization. Master Kakuban. Within the mind moon disk is an eight-petalled lotus. On the lotus altar is a certain single A-syllable. . . . [This passage, referred to above, is, with the exception of the words *Abbreviated* and *a certain,* identical to a passage in Kakuban's *Ajikan.*]

Another abbreviated visualization. [Referring to the *Ajiyōryakukan* (Essentials of Abbreviated A-Syllable Visualization), by Jitsuhan (d. 1144).] Jitsuhan said, "Truly the Shingon practitioner must always perform visualization. Within the breast is the heart-mind (*karita-shin*). Its form is like that of an unopened lotus. . . . Above that altar is a single round brightness, and within that round brightness is a single A-syllable. . . ."

Question. In the lotus and moon of these A-syllable visualizations, is there any difference of higher and lower?

Answer. They are dual teachers, and each has profound meaning. To visualize the A-syllable above the lotus altar within the disk signifies the Kongō. To contemplate the A-syllable in the moon disk above the lotus signifies the Tai-zō. Ask further about the nondual single mind. . .

Question. Lotus and moon are respectively Tai-zō and Kongō, without difference in worth. Why then must the lotus be visualized on the moon for the Kongō and the moon visualized above the lotus for the Tai-zō?

Answer. It is said, the three realms are all endowed with truth and wisdom. However, since in the Kongō this wisdom is the source, the round brilliance of original wisdom is visualized first. Truth inevitably manifests through wisdom, and thus the lotus is visualized on the disk.[34]

Raiyu writes that the lotus represents the truth of the Tai-zō, and the moon, the wisdom of the Kongō-kai. When the lotus is outside the moon, therefore, it is the central image of the Tai-zō form of A-syllable visualization, and when the moon encloses the lotus, it is the Kongō-kai *honzon.* The text makes this distinction without offering any further explanation.

The various A-syllable visualization texts give different forms of central image belonging to either the Kongō-kai or Tai-zō lineages. These texts, however, do not clearly state which lineage they are in, nor do they go beyond Raiyu's above explanation in dealing with differences in practice of the two basic types. Some later writings associate the painted images with the deity thrones in their respective mandalas, but still without commenting on differences in actual practice.

A-syllable visualizations given in the *Dainichi-kyō* and its commentary are presented in terms of the symbolic power of the lotus. The *Commentary,* for example, states in such a connection:

> The worldly lotus grows forth from filth and mud. Though its place of origin may be called evil, the lotus is nevertheless pure in body and nature, its magical colors beyond compare. Just as it is unstained by impurity, so too are ordinary beings.[35]

Other texts and manuals in the Tai-zō lineage also stress the lotus in their explanations of this practice. The *Record of Oral Instruction on the A-Syllable Visualization,* for example, says:

> Living beings have an eight-part corporeal heart. . . . The lotus petals are the skillful means of great compassion.[36]

Conversely, texts dealing with the Kongō-kai A-syllable visualization explain the central image in terms of the moon and of radiant light. Kakuban, for example, wrote:

> Within and without it is bright and pure. . . . Emitting the radiance of the five wisdoms, it pierces the darkness of the nine consciousnesses.[37]

Another point of difference in the Kongō-kai and Tai-zō A-syllable visualization methods (and other meditations as well) is that while many of the former include expansion-contraction visualization, this technique is rarely found in Tai-zō lineage practices. This reflects an essential difference in the two systems.

Many different kinds of visualization are given throughout the *Dainichi-kyō,* but expansion-contraction techniques are nowhere mentioned. This applies also to most other texts in the Tai-zō lineage. Many sutras in the *Kongōchō-gyō* lineage, however, do give expansion and contraction visualization as part of such practices as, for instance, the Five-Aspect Attainment-Body Visualization (*gosō jōshingan*). The expansion-contraction technique is clearly characteristic of Kongō-kai visualization practice.

In the *Record of Oral Instruction on the A-Syllable Visualization,* written before formal division of A-syllable visualizations into the two types, the expansion-contraction technique is given as part of the visualization of the A-syllable within the moon disk (here without any lotus at all). In connection with this, which would later become identified as the Kongō-kai form, the text also describes symbolic virtues of the moon disk.

In another section in the same text, where the visualization has the lotus outside the moon disk, the text enumerates the symbolic virtues of the lotus, but gives no expansion and contraction technique. As a general rule, therefore, there is no expansion-contraction associated with the lotus, which represents the Tai-zō system, but it does take place with the moon disk, which symbolizes the Kongō-kai.

The lotus represents the corporeal heart and the purity of self-nature, or, in other words, the sanctity of life. By meditation on the symbolic lotus, the practitioner seeks to realize the mysterious source of all reality. At the same time contemplating the A-syllable of the originally unborn, the practitioner seeks to experience the radiant beauty of the universe and all it contains. This is the Tai-zō A-syllable visualization.

By visualizing the expansion and contraction of the mind moon disk, the practitioner seeks to experience the infinitude of the universe. The Kongō-kai A-syllable visualization consists in realization of the unity of self and universe.

These two forms of meditation, expressing the dual philosophies of equality in truth and discrimination in wisdom, developed into the combined Kongō-kai-Taizō A-syllable visualization. The manifold meanings of the A-syllable have been discussed and enumerated at length in Mikkyo, and understanding of the philosophical aspects of the A-syllable is considered an important element of ritual practice. However, as the practitioner is advised in the *Record of Oral Instruction on the A-Syllable Visualization:*

> When meditating, do not think particularly about meanings and principles. Just visualize vividly the form and color as they should be.[38]

THE NINE-LAYERED A-SYLLABLE PRACTICE AND THE TAI-ZŌ

As briefly described in Chapter Five, the four-layered Tai-zō Mandala and its Eight-Petalled Central Dais can be explained in terms of Mikkyo doctrines of the Buddha-bodies, the levels of consciousness, and so on. Through these approaches the mandala is shown to unfold concentrically. This is, however, only a surface view of what is actually a multidimensional mandala. A key unlocking this profound aspect of the Tai-zō Mandala is the nine-layered A-syllable visualization (*kujū ajikan*).

Also called the nine-layered moon disk visualization, this was originally a central ritual in Tai-zō Mandala practice. When the Tai-zō practice was abbreviated for inclusion in the fourfold preparatory practice, however, the nine-layered A-syllable visualization was removed, and subsequently has been given little attention.

The scriptural basis of the nine-layered A-syllable practice is in the *Dainichi-kyō,* which gives a visualization involving a five-disk mandala of earth, water, fire, wind, and space. The following passage from the sutra describes the water disk visualization, which later developed into an independent meditation practice:

206

The light of the moon on an autumn evening is pure and white. The mandala, like this, proclaims how rare and marvellous are the Buddhas.

Contemplating its pure whiteness, create a round disk in nine layers that dwells in the midst of a thick mist and removes all passion and suffering. Make it pure milk-white like a jewelled garland, like crystal, like the light of the moon, and let it flow in everywhere, filling all places.[39]

The *Dainichi-kyō Sho* makes clear that the "round disk in nine layers" means a nine-layered moon disk:

It is pure white and incomparable, like moonlight on an autumn night. In this mandala, the disks must indeed be layered, made like a nine-layered moon disk. Make it as a thick and subtle cloud-white mist, and dwell in its midst. By performing this technique, any deluded passions that arise will all perish.[40]

The "nine-layered A-syllable visualization" is first named as such in the *Tai-zō Bonji Shidai* (Tai-zō Sanskrit-Syllable Practice), said to have been written by Kūkai. This text describes the visualization as taking place twice during the Tai-zō Mandala practice. The first reference is as follows:

Next, the nine-layered A-syllable visualization.
Inner five-pronged vajra mudra.
Visualize the first syllable gate clearly and distinctly. The round disk in nine layers is void and perfectly white.[41]

And later in the practice:

Next do the interpenetration [*nyūga ga'nyū*] visualization.
Same [referring to the samadhi mudra].
In the center of my mind is a nine-layered full moon.
At the place of the nine deities.
Above that is an A-syllable. Because this is the originally unborn and ungraspable [*honpushō fukatoku*] A-syllable, the self-nature of my mind is also originally unborn and ungraspable.[42]

The steps described in both passages above are the same as in earlier ritual texts, but here for the first time the nine-layered A-syllable visualization is given as an independent ritual. The second quote is describing the central section of the practice, where esoteric union takes place by interpenetration of practitioner and deity, here performed by means of the nine-layered A-syllable visualization.

This is no longer merely the water disk portion of a five-element visualization, as it is in the *Dainichi-kyō* and early ritual manuals. Instead, its placement indicates that it has become a meditation practice by which union with the essence of the entire Tai-zō Mandala can be attained. In terms of doctrine, this was possible because the seed syllable of the water element (BA) was later replaced by the A-syllable, the symbolic origin of all syllables and the seed syllable of the entire Tai-zō Mandala.

The phrase "the place of the nine deities" appears in the final passage above. The text gives the precise number of layers not merely to describe the visualized image but in order to link it with the nine deities of the mandala's center. The *Hajigoku Giki* (Hell-Destroying Ritual Text), an early Mikkyo text said to have been translated by Shubhakarasimha, states, "The nine-layered moon disk manifests the nine deities of the eight petals." Further on in the same text is written:

> The three consciousnesses are, first, the . . . sixth consciousness; second, the . . . seventh consciousness; third, the . . . eighth consciousness. Added to these now is the fourth, the stainless pure consciousness. This is the true meaning of the nine-layered mind moon disk.[43]

The clear identification of the nine-layered moon disk with the deities of the Eight-petalled Central Dais gives the nine-layered A-syllable visualization central importance in the Tai-zō practice. This understanding went through further philosophical development in Shingon. Kakuban wrote in the *Shingachirin Hishaku* (Secret Explanation of the Mind Moon Disk):

> The greater meaning of the two realms [Tai-zō and Kongō-kai] is that both manifest the mandala through the moon disk. In the Tai-zō, the nine-layered full moon manifests the nine deities of the inmost enlightenment of the ninth consciousness [implying the tenth]. In the Kongō, it manifests the perfect brightness of the five divisions [of the Kongō-kai Mandala] and the Buddhas of the self-realized five wisdoms.[44]

In the *Taizōkai Nenju Shidai Yōshūki* (Summary of Essentials of the Tai-zō Realm Ritual; a commentary on a similar text by the tenth-century master Gengō), the master Gōhō (1306–1362) wrote:

> That text says, within the pure moon disk that is bright and full in your mind, visualize a brightly manifested A-syllable. . . .
> The entire meditation practice depends on this visualization. That perfectly full, pure moon disk is the nine-layered moon disk. The master of the Enmei-in temple [Gengō], grasping this meaning, places this visualization in the section of the syllable-disk visualization.[45]

These texts clearly state that that the nine-layered A-syllable visualization is the heart of the Tai-zō practice. Later records of oral transmissions contain various explanations of the nine layers, consciousnesses, and deities in a three-dimensional relationship. The associated nine-layered A-syllable visualizations differ in detail, but can be classified in three major groups: concentric, nine-disked, and eight-petalled. All involve nine layers which are specifically linked with the deities of the Eight-Petalled Central Dais, thus symbolically encompassing the entire Tai-zō Mandala.

In the concentric form, which is variously called "large and small nine layers," "the bull's eye," and so forth, the practitioner visualizes nine concentric moon disks, smaller within larger. The center represents the ninth consciousness, the disk outside it the eighth, and so on toward the periphery in descending order. It is visualized as shallower at the periphery and deeper at the center (or, lower at the periphery and higher at the center).

As discussed in Chapter Five, the various doctrines applied to explain the structure of the Tai-zō Mandala all treat the center as primary and of a "higher" order in relation to the periphery, which is relatively more phenomenal. The "bull's-eye" form of the nine-layered A-syllable visualization, which has the ninth consciousness at the center of a concentric representation of all the consciousnesses, is well suited to visualization within the practitioner's breast, allowing practice of the Tai-zō Mandala in its symbolic entirety without the necessity of performing more complex visualizations.

In the nine-disked form, the disks are visualized one on top of the other, as in a nine-storied pagoda. They may be visualized as being all of the same size or as becoming progressively smaller towards the top. This might be called a side view of the nine layers, whereas the concentric form is a frontal view that does not show as distinctly the relative vertical positions of the nine consciousnesses. The nine-disked form, however, shows clearly that the Tai-zō Mandala is meant to function in more than just one or two dimensions, and through the nine-layered A-syllable meditation, the practitioner visualizes himself as embodying the multidimensional mandala.

In the eight-petalled form, the A-syllable within a moon disk is visualized as the ninth consciousness at the center of an eight-petalled lotus with eight more A-syllables as the other consciousnesses arrayed on the petals around it. If the concentric form offers a frontal view and the nine-disked form a side view, then this is an expanded view. When the nine layers are visualized concentrically, the higher layers partially cover the layers beneath them. Using the eight-petalled form, however, the practitioner visualizes the ninth consciousness in the center and the others around it so that each is visible individually while the whole is also visible as an interrelated system embracing the entire Tai-zō Mandala.

In early Tai-zō Mandala practice, the nine-layered A-syllable visualization was generally performed twice, once near the beginning of the practice (somewhere between the "exaltation of the practitioner" and the "establishment of the realm"), and again in the central section of esoteric union (as part of the interpenetration or syllable-disk visualizations). The *Summary of Essentials of the Tai-zō Realm Ritual,* the most comprehensive explanation of the Tai-zō practices, says this about the first:

> As a rule, it is said that since the mysterious gate of the three secrets and the four mandalas is opened in the mind-ground of the unborn A-syllable, one must continually dwell in this visualization at the beginning, middle, and end of the practice. However, it may also be condensed into one visu-

alization either at the beginning or the end. . . . This is because visualization of the A-syllable in the nine-layered moon disk accomplishes entry into Buddha-equality.[46]

Gōhō, however, gave no further explanation. In a later passage about the visualization performed near the end of the Tai-zō practice he wrote only:

> I was told that the explanations relate to the meditation done at the beginning. At this point, it should be performed according to the oral instruction of one's master.[47]

There is a definite potential for confusion in the rich and complicated Tai-zō practice. The nine-layered A-syllable visualization performed near the beginning can, therefore, be considered a preliminary overview of the entire practice, an outline of what the practitioner will be experiencing as he goes through the many ritual steps that follow. The visualization placed near the end of the Tai-zō practice, then, would serve to consolidate and unify the whole of the preceding ritual.

SEIZON'S TEXT ON THE A-SYLLABLE VISUALIZATION

Seizon (1012–1074), an eminent Shingon master and Abbot of Tō-ji temple, was author of many Mikkyo texts. Among these is the *Ajikan Hossoku* (Principles of the A-Syllable Visualization), a ritual manual traditionally transmitted within the Chūin school.[48] The text is given below in its entirety:

PRINCIPLES OF THE A-SYLLABLE VISUALIZATION

Paint the form of the moon disk to be one *shaku*, one *sun*, and two *bu* [in all, a little more than one foot in diameter]. Within the disk paint a lotus. Above that paint an A-syllable. Hang this painting [*honzon*] so that the [vertical] distance between the center of the A-syllable and the [practitioner's] seat is about one *shaku* six *sun* [about nineteen inches] and the [horizontal] distance between the painting and the practitioner is from eight *sun* [about nine and one-half inches] to four *shaku* [just under four feet]. This distance, and the placing of a cushion on the seat, should be left to the will and comfort of the practitioner. Sit in half-lotus.

Forming the Dharma Realm Samadhi Mudra, rock the body back and forth and from left to right two or three times so that the mind is not drawn to any part of the body. The ears and shoulders should be aligned, the nose and navel even. Both eyes should remain directed to the bridge of the nose. If the tongue is pressed against the palate, the breath will pass quietly through the throat. One should sit upright, the body neither tilting to the side nor slumping, in order to aid the circulation.

Next, while reciting the mantra of universal homage, pass the rosary through the hands two or three times. Then place it over the left arm.

Next, the being-protecting technique.

Next, place both hands together in *gasshō*. Recite the Five Great Vows:

SHUJŌ MUHEN SEIGAN DO

Living beings are numberless; I vow to save them all.

FUKUCHI MUHEN SEIGAN SHŪ

Merit is boundless; I vow to accumulate all.

HŌMON MUHEN SEIGAN GAKU

The teachings are limitless; I vow to learn all.

NYORAI MUHEN SEIGAN JI

The Buddhas are numberless; I vow to serve all.

BODAI MUJŌ SEIGAN SHŌ

Wisdom is peerless; I vow to realize the highest.

JITA HOKKAI DŌ RIYAKU

Self, other, and the Dharma Realm benefit equally.

Next, with the rosary, recite the five syllables [of Dainichi Nyorai] A BIRA UN KEN one hundred times.

Next, form the Dharma Realm Samadhi Mudra and hold it before the navel. Visualize: In my mind is a white, perfectly bright moon disk. Within the moon disk is a lotus. Above the lotus is an A-syllable. The A-syllable, lotus, and moon disk in the mind of the deity, and the A-syllable, lotus, and moon disk in my mind, and the A-syllable, lotus, and moon disk in the minds of all beings are one in equality. Visualize them as a single, indissoluble body.

Open your eyes and observe the painting, then close your eyes and visualize it within the mind. Visualize in this way, with eyes open and then closed, a few times.

Next, visualize the A-syllable, lotus, and moon disk gradually growing larger by degrees. Visualize it filling the innumerable worlds and the Dharma Realm. Then, suddenly, forget deity and mind both, and dwell for a while in nondiscrimination.

Then visualize that the all-pervading A-syllable, lotus, and moon disk gradually contract back to the original size of one *chū* [about sixteen inches]. Reverently visualize it resting within the breast. At this time, forget body and mind and dwell only in nondiscrimination.

After this, when tired, cease the samadhi mind. Using the rosary, recite your prayer.

Next, the being-protecting technique.

Next, placing both hands together, visualize: the Buddha that was summoned is reverently dispatched to its original palace in the Pure Land, and the Buddha of one's own mind is reverently dispatched to its original palace in one's mind. After this, dwell in the mind of great compassion.

211

Then leave the meditation hall.
End.

Oral Explanation.
When the visualization is finished but before one stands, rub the body slowly from the head down to the feet to aid circulation. Then stand. Irregular circulation gives rise to illness.

During the visualization, self and deity are not-two. Dwell in nondiscrimination. At other times, above all, the deity [meaning also the painted image] should be exalted at the summit of the Dharma Realm. It is to be respected and revered. The self dwells in the first place of the first stage.

The first stage is the place of Kongōsatta. It is not the first stage spoken of before in the exoteric teaching. It is the first stage of this [esoteric] Buddha-Vehicle. The Shingon practitioner always visualizes the deity as Dainichi Nyorai and knows the self as Kongōsatta.

The above is the honored record of Seizon. However, the last lines [further indented above] were added by a later person and are not in the old text.

The master says the distance between the painting and the practitioner, between eight *sun* and four *shaku,* should be according to the will and comfort of the practitioner. The height of the painting should allow the A-syllable to be at eye-level.

[A note of caution: Advanced visualization techniques such as mantra circulation, expansion-contraction, and so on, require various safeguards against dangerous errors. This A-syllable visualization, therefore, should only be attempted under the guidance of a qualified master.]

MEANINGS OF THE A-SYLLABLE AND MOON DISK

In the *Single Collection of the Essential Secrets,* Kakuban expanded on the esoteric meanings of the A-syllable as follows:

The Meaning of Equality. The meaning of the A-syllable is that there is no higher or lower in things. Since body is originally equal and without discrimination, mind and body are also originally equal in nature, not distinguishable as profane or holy. Buddha-nature and the *sendai* [Skt., *icchantika,* a being considered in early Buddhism to be incapable of becoming a Buddha] are one truth and equal.

The Meaning of Nondiscrimination. The meaning of the A-syllable is that all things are without discrimination. Since it is pure and without stain, mind and body too are originally neither separated nor stained. Originally pure, they are one in essence and in form.

The Meaning of Not Born and Not Dying. The meaning of the A-syllable is that all things are unborn and undying. Apart from discrimination and nondiscrimination, the body-mind is the original life that dwells in the eternal nirvana of the discriminated particular and the nondiscriminated substance of transformation together.

The Meaning of Originally Unborn. The meaning of the A-syllable is that all things are originally unborn. If delusions are unborn, then the pure Dharma is also unborn, and the body-mind is uncreated. Neither coming into being nor extinguishing, it dwells eternally in the waveless sea of mind.

The Meaning of No Beginning. The A-syllable is not exhausted or depleted by anything. Since all things are originally endowed with it without beginning, the body-mind, also originally endowed with it, is without beginning or end. It is the eternal reality that pervades the Dharma Realm.

The Meaning of Not-Dwelling. The meaning of the A-syllable is that all things have no dwelling place. They do not dwell in birth or in death and do not stop in nirvana. The body-mind likewise has no dwelling place, and is not limited by impurity or purity. Truly it fills the Dharma Realm and there is no place to which it does not extend.

The Meaning of Immeasurable. The A-syllable is in all things without measure. Since the myriad things are A, the A-syllable is also immeasurable. Since one's mind pervades the Dharma, mind is all things, and if all things are immeasurable, then mind also is immeasurable.

The Meaning of No-Self. The meaning of the A-syllable is that all things have no dual [small and great, impure and pure] self. Since the human self is unborn, the Dharma self is void. Since one's mind is A, all beings are also A. If A and A are without self, then the single A is the true self.

The Meaning of Not Created. The A-syllable dwells eternally uncreated in all things, and all created things exist in the A-syllable. The delusion of the created does not manifest itself apart from the single A, and the uncreated truth manifests itself through the three poisons [delusions].

The Meaning of No Darkness. The meaning of the A-syllable is that all things are without darkness. Since the body is apart from ignorance and eternally radiant, the mind is apart from ignorance. This is called Dainichi: the eternal dawn after the long night of birth and death.[49]

Mikkyo uses the moon disk, too, as a symbol of immeasurable powers and virtues. Employing the metaphor of the moon's waxing and waning to explain the unfolding of Buddha-nature, the *Record of Oral Instruction on the Ajikan* ascribes to the moon the three virtues of purity, freshness, and brightness. Kakuban, in the *Single Collection of the Essential Secrets,* expands on its symbolic meaning as follows:

Perfect. Even as the moon is round and perfect, one's mind lacks nothing. Endowed with myriad powers and virtues, it fulfills the wisdom-seed.

Contemplating the roundness of the moon, visualize the perfect form of the mind. Complete in bountiful wisdom, these two disks are the dual perfection of the innate Buddha.

Stainless. Even as the moon is stainless and white, one's mind is the unstained Dharma. Forever apart from things of darkness, it always bestows undefiled goodness. Contemplating the whiteness of the moon, visualize the spotlessness of the mind. Self-nature is pure and white, the source of innate power and virtue.

Pure. Even as the moon is pure, one's mind is without defilement. The nature of the self is pure, neither wanting anything nor stained by anything. Contemplating the absolute purity of the moon, visualize the pure nature of mind. Originally without desire and without stain, the mind is the original Pure Buddha.

Cool. Even as the moon is cool, one's mind is apart from heat. Extinguish the fire of anger with the water of compassion. Bathed in the moon's cool light, the compassionate water of the mind is calmed and the measureless flames of anger are extinguished at once.

Luminous. Even as the moon shines brightly, the radiance of one's mind is bright and clear. Originally apart from the darkness of delusion, the mind is eternally free. The moon of the mind shines clearly within one's breast, and the darkness of the five hindrances disappears. When the round mirror shines within the mind, its radiant wisdom illuminates all.

Uniquely Precious. Even as there is but one moon, so one's mind is uniquely precious. It is the object of all Buddhas' reverence, it is that in which the myriad teachings are founded. In the palace of the mind is the peerless Nyorai, the King of Mind, and all the subsidiary beings arrayed around him are his manifestations.

The Middle Way. Even as if one were placed at the moon's center, so is self-nature far from any boundaries. Eternally perfecting the Middle Way, it forever transcends prejudice and attachment. Apart from the limitations of superficial teachings, it dwells in the center of mantra. Passing beyond the land of the ōjin [the Buddha who manifests itself in response to particular historical circumstances] one enters the palace of the Dharma Body.

Swift. Even as the moon is never delayed, so one's mind is swift. Turning the wheel of the secret, one cuts off delusions in an instant. If one's mind is directed to the Pure Land, the ten directions are not far. Riding a vehicle of divine power, one instantly becomes a Buddha.

Moving. Even as the moon moves and changes, one's mind transforms eternally. Passing through the water of mind, one makes waves that benefit all beings. Turning the wheel of the true law, one breaks through the darkness of evil and delusion. Power and virtue are without limit, never ceasing to benefit self and others.

Omnipresent. Even as the moon is visible in all places, so one's mind is everywhere tranquil. When the water of change and causation becomes still, one's mind reflects in all things everywhere. Without dividing its single substance, the mind manifests itself in the nine realms, and without taking on multiple bodies, it is present in the lands of the ten directions.[50]

KAKUBAN'S "A-SYLLABLE VISUALIZATION"

In his *Ajikan* (A-Syllable Visualization) Kakuban offers his insights in the following verses:

Amid dreams, phantoms, bubbles, shadows, sparks from a stone—
Amid going, returning, sitting, lying down, foolish thoughts—
On the seat of meditation, the mind should not be open,
In the chamber of samadhi, the mind should not be closed.
Natural wisdom does not come from without,
Nor is the wisdom-without-a-teacher gained by oneself.
One's mind is the Dharma Realm, apart from existence and nonexistence.
Clear and tranquil, there is not one thing.
Not going and not coming, it shows going and coming.
Birth and death are originally void and without cause.
Without form, consciousness embraces the void.
Not apart from birth and death, it is apart from birth and death.
Without grasping nirvana, it gains nirvana.
Freely concealing and revealing itself, it is like the moon in water.
The common man and the saint are one, and there is neither delusion nor
    enlightenment.
Eternally dwelling, never changing, it cuts off beginning and end.
All things are subject to change and nothing is created.
Outside the teaching, the formless sings the meaning of the Dharma.
Even if Buddhas and patriarchs do not transmit it, the universe is endowed
    with it.
Although the source of mind is void and serene, it is more adamantine than
    the vajra.
The void-sword of the A-syllable cuts through birth and death.
The wisdom-water of the BAN-syllable gives rise to all things.
The life-wind of the UN-syllable permeates the void.
The innate mind-lotus blossoms of itself.[51]

EDITOR'S POSTSCRIPT

In all major Shingon temples throughout Japan, whatever the school, the *Hannya Rishu-kyō* (the Wisdom-Truth Sutra) is chanted every morning and evening.

The morning service begins while it is still dark and ends as the altar candles gutter out and the first rays of the rising sun touch the world. This short sutra contains the essence of Shingon thought. It is in praise of the purity of desire. Desires are the basis of human life, according to the text; even more, they are the very "speartips" of the life of the universe.

Human desires are, by their nature, unsatisfiable; worse, they are the root of suffering; and yet, the sutra tells us, without them, and without the fundamental desire to live, there can only be death. This will-to-live is no other than the Great Desire of the universe itself, wherein finite life merges with infinite being. Such is the wisdom-truth of this sutra.

As the sun rises, the chant ends. A fitting end, as well, to the labors and deficiencies of this book, the last words are:

It is good. . . .
It is good. . . .

Notes

The following abbreviations are used.

AJI: *Ajikan Hiketsu-shū,* edited by Kakuban et al. (Rokudaishindo, 1913).

J: *Jikkan-jō,* by Kūkai, rev. ed. (Kōya-san University, 1966).

KAZ: *Kōgyō Daishi Zenshū,* edited by Shōsei Kobayashi (Kaji Sekai Shisha, 1935).

KD: *Kōbō Daishi Shodeshi Zenshū,* edited by Hase Hōshū (Rokudai Shinpō-sha, 1942).

KS: *Kōgyō Daishi Senjutsu-shū,* edited by Miyasaka Yūshō (Sankibō–Bussho-rin, 1977).

KZ: *Kōbō Daishi Zenshū,* 3rd ed., rev., edited by Inaba Yoshitake et al. (Mikkyō Bunka Kenkyū-sho, 1965).

SZ: *Shingon-shū Zensho,* edited by Shōkai Wada (Kōya-san University, 1937).

TSD: *Taishō Shinshū Daizōkyō,* edited by Takakusu Junjirō et al. (Taishō Issai-kyō Kankō-kai, 1924–1934).

1. Origins and Development of Esoteric Buddhism in India and China

1. The *Hanju Sammai-kyō,* translated into Chinese in the Later Han by Lokarakṣa (Jap., Shirukasen).
2. The *Keshaku Darani Jinshu-kyō,* translated into Chinese in the third century by Chih-ch'ien (Jap., Shiken).
3. The *Dai Kichigi Jinshu-kyō,* translated into Chinese in the late fifth century.
4. The *Muri Mandara Shu-kyō,* translator unknown; a variant version of the *Hōrōkaku-kyō.*
5. The *Sengan Senbi Kanzeon Darani Jinshu-kyō.*
6. Divākara (Jap., Jibakara), an Indian who had studied at Nālandā, was active in Lo-yang and Ch'ang-an. Two others were Devaprajñā (Jap., Daiunhannya), and Paramitī (Sanskrit uncertain; Jap., Haramitei). Maṇicinta (Jap., Hō-shiyui), from northern India, came to Lo-yang in 693 and concentrated on translation and ritual practice. The texts he translated were mostly esoteric. The priest Śikṣānanda (Jap., Jissha'nanda; 652–710) translated many sutras, including esoteric ones, in Lo-yang, where he worked with Bodhiruci (Jap., Bodairushi; 572–727), who was especially favored by the Empress Wu, and I-ching (Jap., Gijō; 635–713). Both Bodhiruci and I-ching translated several esoteric Buddhist sutras.
7. Among them were a new version of the *Kegon-kyō,* the *Daijō Rishu Ropparamitsu-kyō,* and the *Shugokokkai-shu Darani-kyō.* Kūkai recorded these teachings in his *Sanjū-jō Sakushi* (Thirty-Volume Copybook).
8. The eight Japanese priests best known for journeying to China in the early Heian

219

period to receive esoteric Buddhist texts and teachings are grouped together as the *nittō hakke*. These (with affiliation and years in China) are: Saichō (Tendai; 804–805), Kūkai (Shingon, 804–806), Jōkyō (Shingon; 838–839), Engyō (Shingon; 838–839), Ennin (Tendai; 838–847), E-un (Shingon; 842–847), Enchin (Tendai; 853–858), and Shūei (Shingon; 862–865). Another Shingon priest who might have been included among these, had his plans succeeded, was Shinnyo (dates unknown), son of the emperor Heizei (r. 806–809). Named the crown prince under emperor Saga (r. 809–823) in 810, he was deposed in a political struggle, took orders, and became Kūkai's disciple. Shinnyo went with Shūei to China, where after studying in Ch'ang-an he received permission to travel on to India. He set out westward, passing through Yunnan, and, according to a later report, died in Southeast Asia.

2. Historical Background of Shingon Buddhism in Japan

1. Katsumata Shunkyō, "Kūkai Izen no Mikkyō," *Daihōrin* 50:2, p. 93.
2. The *Fukū Kenjaku Jinpen Shingon-kyō,* which was in Japan by 753. See Katsumata Shunkyō, "Nara Jidai no Mikkyō," in Miyasaka Yūshō et al., *Mikkyō no Rekishi* (Tokyo: Shunjū-sha, 1977), pp. 181ff.
3. Katsumata ("Nara Jidai no Mikkyō," pp. 169–175) lists the Mikkyo sutras found in this record, with translators and dates of translation, as well as the dates they were copied in Japan. Among the conclusions he draws are the following:
   The listed Mikkyo texts total about 130 in about 280 volumes, indicating that of those then in China, only a few had not yet been brought to Japan. This is about one-fourth of the 612 Mikkyo texts in the present canon.
   As to the dates of transmission and translation, there are relatively few early in this period, then a sudden increase from Sui into T'ang. This probably reflects the development of Mikkyo in India.
   The texts listed are mostly of the miscellaneous category, of which the majority in China had made their way to Japan during the Nara period. Very few pure category texts had been taken to Nara Japan. Of the twenty-six such texts translated by Shubhakarasimha, there were only four; of the twenty-five by Vajrabodhi, likewise only four; of the seventy-two by Amoghavajra, only one. The new esoteric teaching established in China by these three masters had had no occasion as yet to be taken to Japan.
   The copying of Mikkyo texts in Nara Japan took place mostly after 735. If these texts were in fact brought by Dōji and Genbō (who returned in 718 and 735), that would explain why few works by Amoghavajra were included among them.
4. *Shōryō-shū,* KZ, 3, p. 456.
5. Matsunaga Yūkei (*Mikkyō no Rekishi,* pp. 176–178) discusses various dates assigned to the establishment of the Shingon sect, from as early as 807 to as late as 835, and concludes that the most appropriate relates to the gathering of disciples and the formation of a Shingon religious organization. This is dated in part by Kūkai's *Yuikai* (Admonishments) of 813, in which he addresses his disciples concerning the proper practice of Shingon. He had given esoteric initiation to a large

number of priests the previous year, so it is likely that Kūkai had a number of disciples by this time. This is also close to his writing in 813–814 of the *Benkenmitsu Nikyō-ron* (Treatise on the Exoteric and Esoteric Teachings), which established a scriptural and doctrinal rationale for Shingon in the context of all other Buddhist teachings.

6. *Shōryō-shū*, KZ, 3, pp. 407ff. This has also been published in the *Sangō Shiiki—Shōryō-shū*, edited by Watanabe Shōkō and Miyasaka Yūshō, in the *Nihon Koten Bungaku Taikei* (Tokyo: Iwanami, 1965).

7. *Shōryō-shū*, KZ, 3, p. 402.

8. Kūkai is said to have had ten great disciples (*jū daideshi*): Shinzei (800–860), Jichie (also Jitsue; 786–847), Dōyū (d. 851; he was also a patriarch of the Kegon school), Shinga (801–879), Enmyō (d. 851), Gōrin (767–837), Taihan (778–837), Shinnyo (dates unknown), Chisen (789–825), and Chūen (d. 837).

9. See note 8 for Chapter 1 about the nittō hakke.

10. In the late tenth century new Buddhist texts and teachings were taken from India to Sung China. Among the new texts translated by the Indian Shih-hu (Jap., Sego) around this time was the thirty-volume version of the *Kongōchō-gyō*, the *Issai Nyorai Shinjitsu-shō Daijō Genshō Sammai Dai Kyō-ō-kyō*. The Chinese translation of this sutra was taken to Japan in the twelfth century. As a text of the later esoteric development in India, it contained material unfamiliar to Mikkyo in Japan, and so was not immediately incorporated into Shingon. Study of it in Japan seems not to have begun until the time of the priest Gōhō (1306–1362) of Tō-ji.

11. Raihō (1279–1330), Gōhō (1306–1362), and Genpō (1333–1398); each has the character *hō*, meaning "treasure," in his name.

3. Mikkyo: The Esoteric Teaching

1. *Dainichi-kyō*, TSD, 18, p. 12.

2. *Benkenmitsu Nikyō-ron*, cited in Togano-o Shōun, *Shingon-shū Tokuhon, Kyōgi-hen*, (Wakayama: Kōyasan, 1948), p. 133, as KZ, 1, p. 505.

3. *Benkenmitsu Nikyō-ron*, cited in Togano-o, *Shingon-shū Tokuhon, Kyōgi-hen*, p. 133, as KZ, 1, p. 505.

4. *Kenmitsu Fudō-sho*, KS, I, p. 3.

5. *Kongōchō Gohimitsu-kyō*, cited in Togano-o, *Shingon-shū Tokuhon, Kyōgi-hen*, p. 122, as TSD, 20, p. 535.

6. *Dainichi-kyō Sho*, TSD, 39, p. 592.

7. *Sokushin Jōbutsu-gi*, KZ, 1, p. 511.

8. *Dainichi-kyō*, cited in Togano-o, *Shingon-shū Tokuhon, Kyōgi-hen*, pp. 81ff, as TSD, 18, p. 1.

9. *Shōji Jissō-gi*, cited in Togano-o, *Mandara no Kenkyū*, p. 422.

10. *Sokushin Jōbutsu-gi*, KZ, 1, p. 507.

11. *Rishu-kyō*, TSD, 8, p. 243.

12. *Dainichi-kyō Sho*, TSD, 39, p. 782.

13. *Hannya Shingyō Hiken*, KZ, 1, p. 554.

14. Ibid.

15. *Unji-gi,* KZ, 1, pp. 546ff.
16. *Shōji Jissō-gi,* KZ, 1, p. 521.
17. *Dainichi-kyō Sho,* Section 7, cited in Togano-o, *Mandara no Kenkyū,* p. 454.
18. *Dainichi-kyō Sho,* cited in Togano-o, *Shingon-shū Tokuhon, Jisshū-hen,* p. 32, as TSD, 39, p. 657.
19. *Dainichi-kyō,* cited in Togano-o, *Shingon-shū Tokuhon, Kyōgi-hen,* p. 68, as TSD, 18, p. 10.
20. *Shōji Jissō-gi,* KZ, 1, p. 521.
21. *Aji Mondō,* KS, 1, p. 235.
22. *Dainichi-kyō,* TSD, 18, p. 20.
23. *Dainichi-kyō Sho,* TSD, 39, p. 701.
24. *Shugokokkai-shu Darani-kyō,* TSD, 19, pp. 32ff.
25. *Unji-gi,* KZ, 1, p. 537.
26. *Dainichi-kyō,* TSD, 18, p. 1.
27. *Dainichi-kyō Sho,* TSD, 39, p. 580.
28. *Dainichi-kyō,* TSD, 18, p. 1.
29. *Dainichi-kyō Sho,* TSD, 39, p. 588.
30. Ibid.
31. *Kongōchō-kyō Giketsu,* TSD, 39, p. 808.
32. *Kyō-ō-kyō Kaidai,* KZ, 1, p. 719.
33. *Gyokuin-shō,* SZ, 21, p. 28.
34. Sung translation of the *Kyō-ō-kyō,* cited in Togano-o, *Shingon-shū Tokuhon, Kyōgi-hen,* p. 28, as TSD, 18, p. 368. Togano-o relates this to the Tibetan version he also quotes (in Japanese, and in parallel with the Sung text) in *Mandara no Kenkyū,* p. 309.

4. The Ten Levels of Mind

1. *Nehan-gyō,* quoted by Kūkai in the *Hizō Hōyaku,* KZ, 1.
2. *Hizō-ki,* KZ, 2, p. 42.
3. *Sokushin Jōbutsu-gi,* cited in Togano-o, *Shingon-shū Tokuhon, Kyōgi-hen,* p. 87, as KZ, 1, p. 508.
4. *Nikyō-ron,* KZ, 1, p. 490.
5. Ibid., p. 505.
6. *Jūjūshin-ron,* KZ, 1, p. 398.
7. *Shakuron Myōmoku,* SZ, 40, p. 168.
8. *Dainichi-kyō Sho,* TSD, 39, p. 600.
9. *Unji-gi,* KZ, 1, p. 536.
10. *Dainichi-kyō Sho,* TSD, 39, p. 606.
11. *Musō-kan,* KAZ, 2, p. 157.
12. *Matsudai Shingon Gyōja Yōjin,* KAZ, 2, p. 183.
13. *Bodaishin-ron,* quoted by Kūkai in KZ, 1, pp. 455, 464.
14. *Ajikan,* unpublished manuscript, p. 4.
15. *Mui Zen-yō,* TSD, 18, p. 945.
16. *Dainichi-kyō Sho,* TSD, 39, p. 587.

17. *Dainichi-kyō*, TSD, 18, p. 1.
18. *Dainichi-kyō Sho*, TSD, 39, p. 579.

5. The Secret Activities of Body, Speech, and Mind

1. *Sokushin Jōbutsu-gi*, KZ, 1, p. 507.
2. Ibid., p. 513.
3. *Dainichi-kyō Sho*, cited in Togano-o, *Shingon-shū Tokuhon, Kyōgi-hen*, p. 96, as TSD, 39, p. 583.
4. *Hannya Shingyō Hiken*, KZ, 1, p. 554.
5. *Goshōrai Mokuroku*, KZ, 1, p. 95.
6. *Dainichi-kyō Sho*, cited in Togano-o, *Shingon-shū Tokuhon, Kyōgi-hen*, p. 80, as TSD, 39, p. 620.
7. *Dainichi-kyō, Guen-bon*, cited in Togano-o, *Mandara no Kenkyū*, p. 480.
8. *Dainichi-kyō*, TSD, 18, p. 1.
9. *Dainichi-kyō Sho*, TSD, 39, p. 580.
10. *Shingon Myōmoku*, TSD, 77, No. 2449.
11. *Dainichi-kyō*, TSD, 18, p. 1.
12. *Dainichi-kyō Sho*, TSD, 39, p. 583.
13. *Sokushin Jōbutsu-gi*, KZ, 1, p. 571.
14. *Dainichi-kyō Sho*, Section 5, cited in Togano-o, *Mandara no Kenkyū*, p. 476.
15. *Hizō-ki*, KZ, 2, p. 36.
16. *Dainichi-kyō Kaidai*, KZ, 1, p. 638. On the same page of this text is also written:

> Empowerment was, of old, called the protective, supporting activity of the Buddha-mind, and was also called *kabi* [*ka*, increasing, and *bi*, putting-on]. However, this did not yet express the full meaning.
>
> *Ka* is so named because it involves coming and going, transferring and entering. The meaning of *ji* is that it absorbs and does not scatter.

17. *Dainichi-kyō Kaidai*, KZ, 1, p. 637.
18. *Sokushin Jōbutsu-gi*, KZ, 1, p. 516.
19. *Nenji Shingon Rikan Keihaku-mon*, KZ, 2, p. 182.
20. *Dainichi-kyō Sho*, cited in Togano-o, *Shingon-shū Tokuhon, Jisshū-hen*, pp. 23f, as TSD, 39, p. 714.
21. *Dainichi-kyō Sho* [No. 15]: Cited in Togano-o, *Mandara no Kenkyū*, p. 487.
22. *Shōji Jissō-gi*, KZ, 1, p. 521.
23. Ibid., p. 524.
24. *Hizō-ki*, KZ 2, p. 157.
25. *Dainichi-kyō Sho*, TSD, 39, p. 783.
26. Ibid.
27. Ibid., p. 621.
28. Ibid., p. 651.
29. *Hannya Shingyō Hiken*, KZ, 1, p. 561.
30. *Unji-gi*, KZ, 1, p. 546.

31. *Kongōchō Giketsu,* summarized and cited in Togano-o, *Shingon-shū Tokuhon, Jisshū-hen,* p. 13.

32. *Shiui Yōryaku-hō,* cited in Togano-o, *Shingon-shū Tokuhon, Jisshū-hen,* p. 135, as TSD, 15, p. 299.

6. The Dynamic Mandala

1. *Goshōrai Mokuroku,* KZ, 1, p. 95.
2. *Dainichi-kyō Sho,* TSD, 39, p. 625.
3. *Jūjūshin-ron,* KZ, 1, p. 397.
4. *Sokushin Jōbutsu-gi,* KZ, 1, p. 513.
5. *Dainichi-kyō,* TSD, 18, p. 1.
6. *Dainichi-kyō Sho,* TSD, 39, p. 585.
7. *Dainichi-kyō Sho Gijutsu,* SZ, 20, p. 111.
8. In another version:

    Buddha Division: Hall of the Eight-Petalled Central Dais, All-Pervading Wisdom Hall, Shakyamuni Hall, Monju Hall, Wisdom-Holding Hall, Kokūzō Hall, Unsurpassed Attainment Hall.

    Lotus Division: Kannon Hall, Jizō Hall.

    Vajra Division: Vajra-Wielding Hall, Obstacle-Removing Hall.
9. *Dainichi-kyō,* TSD, 18, p. 1.
10. *Hizō-ki,* KZ, 2, p. 42. This gives a general principle, but one difficult to apply throughout the whole mandala. The Buddha Tenkuraion in the Eight-Petalled Central Dais, for instance, cannot always be identified with the Accepting Dharma Body, and the relationship of the mandala's sections—other than the central, the Shakyamuni, and the outermost sections—to the Buddha-bodies is not entirely clear. Some scholars of the medieval period in Japan related the Self-Proving Dharma Body to the Eight-Petalled Central Dais and the mandala's first layer; the Accepting Dharma Body to the second layer; the Transforming Dharma Body to the third layer; and the Equally-Permeating Dharma Body to the fourth layer. However, this approach, too, raises difficulties in interpretation. In any case, it is clear that the center of the Tai-zō Mandala is primary, essential, and of a "higher" order relative to the periphery; and this principle applies also to the doctrinal system of the bodies of the Dharma Body.
11. The nine-layered A-syllable visualization will be further described in Chapter Seven.
12. *Nikyōron-shō,* SZ, 3, p. 17.
13. In typical Mikkyo fashion, the five wisdoms are correlated with the five Buddhas, five elements, nine consciousnesses (actually understood as ten, but often described as nine for convenience in relating to other doctrines using the number nine, such as the nine central deities), and so on. A passage from the *Hizō-ki* (KZ, 2, p. 42) cited in Chapter Three is given here in fuller form:

    Question. Exoteric Buddhism sets forth eight levels of consciousness, but how many does Mikkyo set forth?

    Answer. One, or eight, or nine, or ten, or innumerable levels of consciousness.

Question. What are these minds?

Answer. When the deity of the fundamental mind of the central dais [of the Tai-zō] embraces all the subsidiary manifestations of mind, this is called the one consciousness. When the deities of the eight petals embrace all the subsidiary manifestations of mind, this is called the eighth consciousness. The deities of the eight petals and the central dais together embrace all the subsidiary manifestations of mind, and this is called the ninth consciousness.

Without moving any of the nine consciousnesses, a tenth beyond them embraces all the subsidiary manifestations of mind of Buddhas and all beings and things in one consciousness. This is called the tenth consciousness. This is the all-inclusive single-mind consciousness.

14. The five wisdoms represent the wisdom attained by the Mikkyo practitioner through awakening of innately enlightened mind, while at the same time they are the central enlightenment of Dainichi Nyorai. The five wisdoms are differentiated among the five Buddhas (and among the sections of the mandala) as are the specific activities of Dainichi, but each Buddha, and each wisdom, is also endowed with the totality of the other four. Ultimately, all the subsidiary deities at the periphery also reveal themselves as endowed with the full enlightenment of the center. For example, in the mandala subsystem in which Ashuku is the central deity, this Buddha embodies the Wisdom of the Nature of the Dharma Realm Body, just as Dainichi Nyorai symbolizes this wisdom in the Tai-zō Mandala as a whole. The four bodhisattvas who are emanations of Ashuku's particular energies then embody the other four wisdoms. Through such an ever-expanding network of subsidiary (yet essential) manifestations, the entire mandala is perceived to be fully penetrated by the five wisdoms.

15. Concerning the arrangement of deities in the Tai-zō Mandala's center, the *Dainichi-kyō* says only, "From the center of this flower dais appears Dainichi Nyorai" (TSD, 18, p. 6). Apparently the central dais was originally occupied only by Dainichi, and the four Buddhas and four major bodhisattvas were placed on the surrounding lotus petals on the basis of later commentaries on the sutra. The five Buddhas fit into a system relating them to levels of consciousness, wisdoms, and so on. The bodhisattvas, however, though embodying specific activities of the Buddhas, cannot be fitted precisely into the same system of interrelationships. Their placement is not fixed by their doctrinal or symbolic meaning.

16. *Hizō-ki,* KZ, 2, p. 9.

17. The five transformations (*goten*) exist in two primary aspects in the Tai-zō, similar to the patterns found in the Kongō-kai Mandala. One, the ascending transforming gate, represents the transformations achieved through practice, and shows the practitioner going through the five stages in order from the cause to the result of enlightenment. This is "the mind awakened from the east" (*tōin hosshin*), so called because it is seen beginning with the eastern Buddha of the mandala's center and passing through south, west, and north to reach, finally, the center. This shows the course of Dainichi Nyorai's enlightenment, beginning with Ashuku.

The converse of the above unites both innate and realized aspects of the enlightened mind, and is called the descending transforming gate. This is "the mind awakened from the center" (*chūin hosshin*), so called because here the Buddha of the center represents the awakening mind of enlightenment. The succeeding stages of attainment are then identified with the Buddhas of east, south, west, and north, respectively. Here Dainichi Nyorai, passing through the stages of enlightenment, reveals the fulfillment of skillful means as an outward movement.

18. *Hizō-ki,* KZ, 2, p. 9.
19. This chart has been adapted from that on p. 220 of the *Mikkyō Jiten,* edited by Taikō Yamasaki, Ryūken Sawa et al. (Kyoto: Hōzōkan, 1975).

7. The Scope and Complexity of Shingon Ritual

1. *Hizō-ki,* KZ, 2, p. 13.
2. *Musōkan-sho,* KAZ, 2, p. 157.
3. *Mui Zen-yō,* TSD, 18, p. 945.
4. *Dainichi-kyō,* TSD, 18, p. 642.
5. Prof. Yamasaki uses the term *seishin shūchū ichi* in referring to these points.
6. Other four-point systems employ the point between the eyebrows (forehead), the throat, the breast, and the navel; or heart, forehead, throat, and navel.
7. Other five-point systems include: crown, forehead, heart, throat, and shoulders; or heart, forehead, throat, crown, and entire body; and forehead, left and right nipples, heart, and lower body.
8. The nineteen points are: four different points on the crown, both ears, both eyes, both nostrils, mouth, tip of the tongue, both shoulders, throat, both nipples, heart, navel, both armpits, lower back, both calves, both knees, and both feet.
9. The thirty points are: hollow of the throat, point of chin, both sides of the neck, inside the throat, four points on the tongue, both shins, pancreas, lower back, both buttocks, anus, lower abdomen, both hands, both sides of the torso, back, breast, both arms, both elbows, upper chest, sexual organ, both eyes, forehead, outside corners of both eyes, lips, both ears, both cheeks, the crown, and the entire body.
10. *Mui Zen-yō,* TSD, 18, p. 945.
11. *Kongōchō-gyō,* TSD, 18, p. 236.
12. *Dainichi-kyō,* TSD, 18, p. 174.
13. *Dainichi-kyō Sho,* TSD, 39, p. 174.
14. Ibid., p. 706.
15. *Kongōkai-shō,* SZ, 32, p. 188.
16. *Dainichi-kyō,* TSD, 18, p. 4.

8. Concentrated Three-Secrets Practices

1. *Sangō Shiiki,* KZ, 3, p. 324. This has also been published in the *Sangō Shiiki–Shōryō-shū,* edited by Watanabe Shōkō and Miyasaka Yūshō, in the Iwanami *Nihon Koten Bungaku Taikei.*
2. *Ichigo Taiyō Himitsu-shū,* KAZ, 2, p. 170.
3. *Dainichi-kyō Sho,* TSD, 39, p. 642.
4. *Dainichi-kyō,* TSD, 18, p. 17.

5. *Bonji Shittan Jimo Heishakugi*, KZ, 2, p. 724.
6. *Dainichi-kyō*, TSD, 18, p. 10.
7. *Dainichi-kyō Sho*, TSD, 39, p. 651.
8. Ibid., p. 642.
9. *Ajikan Yōjin Kuketsu*, KD, 1, p. 472.
10. *Aji-gi*, KZ, 4, p. 219.
11. *Shōji Jissō-gi*, KZ, 1, p. 524.
12. *Dainichi-kyō*, TSD, 18, p. 38.
13. *Ajikan Yōjin Kuketsu*, KD, 1, p. 470.
14. *Bodaishin-ron*, J, p. 212.
15. *Unji-gi*, KZ, 1, p. 543.
16. *Ajikan Yōjin Kuketsu*, KD, 1, p. 470.
17. *Dainichi-kyō*, TSD, 18, p. 18.
18. Ibid., p. 19. Among other references to the A-syllable in this sutra are the following:

    In order to subdue the scattered winds, make the A-syllable your body and hold the KA-syllable gate in your mind (Ibid., p. 13).

    Spreading the A-syllable on all parts, maintain this for three myriad [*rakusha*] times (Ibid., p. 19).

    Make the A-syllable your body and place the great void point [*kūden*, a dot used in writing certain Sanskrit characters; associated with the void] at your head (Ibid., p. 20).

    Sit comfortably and visualize the A-syllable. Contemplate it at the root of your ear. When a full month of this continuous concentration has passed, truly the ears will be purified. (Ibid., p. 21.)

19. Ibid., p. 21.
20. *Dainichi-kyō Sho*, TSD, 39, p. 706.
21. *Dainichi-kyō*, TSD, 18, p. 52.
22. *Ajikan Yōjin Kuketsu*, KD, 1, p. 472.
23. Ibid.
24. Ibid., p. 470.
25. Ibid., p. 474.
26. Ibid., p. 475.
27. Ibid., p. 476.
28. *Ajikan Hossoku*, manuscript in author's collection.
29. *Ajikan Shidai*, AJI, p. 29.
30. *Ajikan*, AJI, p. 35.
31. *Ajikan*, KAZ, p. 383.
32. *Ajikan*, AJI, p. 39.
33. *A-UN Gō-kan*, AJI, p. 19.
34. *Aji Hishaku*, Vol. 1, p. 7, of three-volume text by Raiyu published in 1653. *Shingon Shū Zensho*, edited by Shokai Wada (Koya-san University Press, 1937).
35. *Dainichi-kyō Sho*, TSD, 39, p. 706.

36. *Ajikan Yōjin Kuketsu*, KD, 1, p. 475.
37. *Ajikan*, AJI, p. 19.
38. *Ajikan Yōjin Kuketsu*, KD, 1, p. 476.
39. *Dainichi-kyō*, TSD, 18, p. 20.
40. *Dainichi-kyō Sho*, TSD, 39, p. 702.
41. *Tai-zō Bonji Shidai*, KZ, 2, p. 249.
42. Ibid., p. 285.
43. *Hajigoku Giki*, TSD, 18, p. 913.
44. *Shingachirin Hishaku*, TSD, 79, p. 39.
45. *Taizōkai Nenju Shidai Yōshūki*, SZ, 13, p. 59.
46. Ibid., p. 60.
47. Ibid., p. 516.
48. *Ajikan Hossoku*, manuscript in possession of the author.
49. *Ichigo Taiyō Himitsu-shū*, KAZ, 2, p. 166.
50. Ibid., p. 163.
51. *Ajikan*, KS, 1, p. 234.

APPENDIX

Japanese Names and Terms with Sanskrit or Chinese Equivalents

Japanese	*Sanskrit and/or Chinese*
A	A
A, ĀH, AN, AKU, ĀNKU	A, Ā, AṂ, AḤ, ĀH
A BA RA KA KYA	A VA RA HA KHA
A BIRA UN KEN	A VĪRA HŪṂ KHĀṂ
Ai Kongōbosatsu	Rāga Vajrabodhisattva
ajari	*ācārya*
Ajikuṭa	Atikūṭa
aka	*argha*
amara-shiki	*amala vijñāna*
AN	AṂ
Anan	Ānanda
anmara-shiki	*amala-vijñāna*
araya-shiki	*ālaya-vijñāna*
asahanaka sanmaji	*āsphānaka-samādhi*
Ashuku Nyorai	Akṣobhya Tathāgata
Ashura	Asura
BAN	VAṂ
Batō Kannon	Hayagrīva
binaya	*vinaya*
Birushana	Vairocana
Bishamon-ten	Vaiśravaṇa
bodai	*bodhi*
Bodairushi	Bodhiruci
bodaishin	*bodhicitta*
Bon-ten	Brahmā
bosatsu	*bodhisattva*

busshin	buddhakāya
Buttochō	Fo T'u-ch'eng (Fotucheng)
chi	*jñāna*
Chikudonmara	Dharmarakṣa
Chikuhōgo	Dharmarakṣa
Chi-ten	Pṛthivī
Chitsū	Chih-t'ung (Zhitong)
chūgan	Mādhyamika
Dai-itoku	Yamāntaka
daijō	Mahāyāna
dai mandara	Mahā Maṇḍala
Dainichi Nyorai	Mahāvairocana Tathāgata
Daijizai-ten	Maheśvara
darani	*dhāraṇī*
Darumakikuta	Dharmagupta
Donkakara	Dharmakāla
Donmuran	Dharmarakṣa
Donmusen	Dharmakṣema
Donmushin	Dharmakṣema
Don'yō	T'an-yao (Tanyao)
engaku	*pratyeka-buddha*
Enma-ten	Yama, Yamarāja
Fudō Myō-ō	Acala Nāha
Fugen Bosatsu	Samantabhadra Bodhisattva
Fukū	Amoghavajra
Fukūjōju Butsu	Amoghasiddhi Buddha
Fukūkenjaku Kannon	Amoghapāśa
Fū-ten	Vāyu
ga	*ātman*
gan	*praṇidhāna*
gasshō	*añjali*
Gatten	Candra
Genchō	Hsüan Ch'ao (Xuanchao)
Genjō	Hsüan-tsang (Xuanzang)
Gijō	I-ching (Yijing)
giki	*vidhi, kalpa, tantra*
Gishin	I-chen (Yizhen)

Gisō	I-ts'ao (Yicao)
goma	*homa*
goun	*pañca skandha*
Gōzanze Myō-ō	Trailokyavijaya
Gundari Myō-ō	Kuṇḍalī
Hakushirimittara	Śrīmitra
Hannya	Prajñā
hannya	*prajñā*
Hannya Bosatsu	Prajñāpāramitā Bodhisattva
haramitsu	*pāramitā*
hō	*dharma*
hōben	*upāya*
Hōdō Butsu	Ratnaketu Buddha
Hō-haramitsu	Ratna-pāramitā
Hō-haramitsu	Dharma-pāramitā
hōjin	Saṃboghakāya
Hōken	Dharmabhadra
hō mandara	Dharma Maṇḍala
honpushō	*ādyanutpāda*
Hōshō Butsu	Ratnasaṃbhava Buddha
hosshin	*dharmakāya*
Hōten	Dharmabhadra
Ichigyō	I-hsing (Yixing)
in	*mudrā*
ingei	*mudrā*
Ishana-ten	Īśāna
issai chichi	*sarvajñāna*
Issai Nyorai Henchi-in	Tathāgatajñāna-mahāmudrā
issendai	*icchantika*
jiga	*ātman*
jihi	*maitrī-karuṇā*
Jikoku-ten	Dhṛtarāṣṭra
Jizō Bosatsu	Kṣitigarbha Bodhisattva
Jogaishō Bosatsu	Sarvanivaranaviskambhi Bodhisattva
Jūichimen Kannon	Ekādaśamukha
kai	*dhātu, śīla*
Kaifuke-ō Butsu	Saṃkusumitarāja Buddha

231

Kakumitsu	Buddhaguhya
KAN	HĀM
Kanjizai Bosatsu	Avalokiteśvara Bodhisattva
Kanjizai-ō Butsu	Avalokiteśvararāja Buddha
kanjō	*abhiṣeka*
kanro	*amṛta*
karita shin	*hṛdaya*
Karura	Garuda
Kashō	Kāśyapa
Ka-ten	Agni
Katsuma-haramitsu	Karma-pāramitā
katsuma mandara	Karma Maṇḍala
katsuma-sho	*karma-vajra*
Kegon	Hua-yen (Huayan)
Keika	Hui-kuo (Huiguo)
kiridaya	*hṛdaya*
KIRIKU	HRĪH
kō	*kalpa*
Kokūzō Bosatsu	Ākāśagarbha Bodhisattva
Kōmoku-ten	Virūpākṣa
kongō	*vajra*
Kongōai	Vajrarāga
Kongōbu	Vajranṛtā
Kongōchi	Vajrabodhi
Kongōdō	Vajraketu
Kongōge	Vajrayakṣa
Kongōgo	Vajrabhāṣā, Vajrakarma, Vajrarakṣa
Kongōharamitsu	Vajra-pāramitā
Kongōhō	Vajradharma, Vajraratna
Kongō-in	Vajrahetu
Kongōji	Vajradhara
Kongōka	Vajragītā
kongō-kai	*vajradhātu*
Kongōke	Vajrapuṣpā
Kongōken	Vajrasaṃdhi
Kongōki	Vajralāsī, Vajrasādhu
Kongōkō	Vajradhūpā, Vajrāṅkuśa, Vajrateja

Kongōman	Vajramālā
Kongōō	Vajrarāja
Kongōrei	Vajrāveśa
Kongōri	Vajratīkṣṇa
Kongōsa	Vajrasphoṭa
Kongōsaku	Vajrapāśa
Kongōsatta	Vajrasattva
Kongōshō	Vajrahāsa
Kongōtō	Vajrāloka
Kongōyasha	Vajrayakṣa
Kongōzō-ō	Vajradhara
Kongōzukō	Vajragandha
kū	*śūnyatā*
Kubira	Kubera
kudoku	*guṇa*
Kujaku Myō-ō	Mahāmāyūrī Vidyārājñī
Kumarajū	Kumārajīva
Kuyō	Navagraha
kuyō	*pūjā*
Makabirushana	Mahāvairocana
Makakashō (cf. Kashō)	Mahākāśyapa
Man Kongōbosatsu	Māna Vajrabodhisattva
mana-shiki	*mano-vijñāna*
mandara	*maṇḍala*
Miroku Bosatsu	Maitreya Bodhisattva
Mokkenren	Maudgalyāyana
Monju Bosatsu	Mañjuśrī Bodhisattva
muga	*nirātma*
Mugyō	Wu-hsing (Wuxing)
Mujaku	Asaṅga
mumyō	*avidyā*
Munishiri	Muniśrī
Muryōju Butsu	Amitābha Buddha
Muryōju Butsu	Amitāyus Buddha
mushikishin sanmai	*āsphānaka-samādhi*
myō	*vidyā*
Myōken Bosatsu	Sudṛṣṭi Bodhisattva

Nanpa-ten	Dhūrdhara
nehan	*nirvāṇa*
Nitten	Āditya
nyoi hōshu	*cintāmaṇi*
nyorai	*tathāgata*
ōjin	*nirmāṇakāya*
rakan	*arhat*
RAN	RAM
Rasetsu-ten	Rākṣasa
Rengeshō	Padmasaṃbhava
rinbō	*cakra*
ritsu	Skt., *vinaya;* Ch., *lü*
Ryūchi	Nāgabodhi
Ryūju, Ryūmyō	Nāgārjuna
sammai	*samādhi*
sanmahachi	samāpatti
sanmaji	samādhi
sanmakita	samāhita
sanmaya	samaya
Sego	Shih-hu (Shihu)
sendai	*icchantika*
Seshin	Vasubandhu
Shakamuni	Śākyamuni
Shari	Śāriputra
shi	*śamatha*
Shiken	Chih-ch'ien (Zhiqian)
shiki	*vijñāna*
shin	*citta*
shingon	Skt., *mantra;* Ch., chen-yen (*zhenyan*)
Shintai	Paramārtha
shira	*śīla*
shittan	*siddhaṃ*
shōjō	Hīnayāna
Shōkanjizai Bosatsu	Āryāvalokiteśvara Bodhisattva
Shōkannon Bosatsu	Āryāvalokiteśvara Bodhisattva
shōmonjō	*śrāvakayāna*
shuji	*bīja*

Shumisen	Sumeru
Soku Kongōbosatsu	Kelikila Vajrabodhisattva
Soriya	Sūrya
sotoba	*stūpa*
Subodai	Subhūti
Sui-ten	Varuṇa
Taimen-ten	Abhimukha
tairaku	*mahāsukha*
Taishaku-ten	Indra
tai-zō	*garbhakoṣa*
ten	*deva*
Tendai	T'ien-t'ai (Tiantai)
Tenkuraion Butsu	Divyadundubhi Meghanirghoṣa Buddha
Tensokusai	T'ien-hsi-tsai (Tianxizai)
tō, tōba	*stūpa*
UN	HŪṂ
ushunisha	*uṣṇīṣa*
Yoku Kongōbosatsu	Iṣṭva Vajrabodhisattva
yuga	*yoga*
yuishiki	*vijñaptimātratā*
zen	Skt., *dhyāna;* Ch., *ch'an* (chan)
Zenmui	Śubhakarasiṃha
zenna	*dhyāna*
Zōjō-ten	Virūḍhaka

Index

Affirmation of self, 72–75
Aji-gi (Kūkai's), 193–194
Aji Hishaku (Raiyu's), 204
Ajikan (A-Syllable Visualization)
  Kakuban's, 203, 215
  Myōe's, 203
  Rikan's, 102
Ajikan Hossoku (Seizon's), 202, 210–212
Ajikan Shidai (Shōkaku's), 202
Ajikan Yōjin Kuketsu (Kūkai's), 193, 195,
  198, 200–201, 213
Aji Mondō (Kakuban's), 80
Amaterasu, 53
Amoghavajra, 12, 18, 19, 20, 85–87,
  119, 120
Analysis of the Kongōchō-gyō (Amoghavaj-
  ra's), 87–88, 119–120
Annen, 35
Anuttarayoga (*mujōyoga*), 13–14
  "father" tantras, 14
  "mother" tantras, 14
Asaṅga, 90
Aśoka, King, 6
A-syllable, 117–118
  "originally unborn," 79–80, 118
A-syllable visualization, 154, 157–158,
  182, 184, 190–191
  dual mandala and, 198–206
  meaning of, and moon disk, 212–215
  symbolism of, 192–195
  techniques of, 195–198
  texts on, 201–215
A-Syllable Visualization Manual (Shōkaku's), 202–203
Atikuta, 17
Atiśa, 14–15
A-UN Gō-kan (Dōhan's), 203

"Becoming the Buddha," (*jōbutsu*), 61,
  66

Benkenmitsu Nikyō-ron (Kūkai's), 58, 94,
  96
Bodaishin-ron (Nagarjuna's), 70, 102, 105,
  168, 193, 198
Bodhiruci, 17
Bodhisattva, doctrine of the, 6, 7
Body, speech, and mind, 30–31, 96
  secret activities of, 106–122
  Shingon practices of, 30, 32
  See also Three Secrets
Brahmanism, 4–5, 6, 10
Buddha, 6, 7, 86
  Amida, 7, 39, 41, 76
  cosmic (primal), 8, 12, 15, 82
  Shakyamuni, 5, 6–7, 58–59, 67–68,
    76, 81–82, 87, 121, 123–124, 166,167
  See also Dainichi Nyorai
Buddha-nature, 61, 74–75, 121
  as Wisdom of All-Wisdom, 67–68, 84,
    99, 125–126
Buddhism
  Chinese schools of, 3, 58–61
  early, 5–6, 64, 71, 75, 167
  Emperors of Japan and, 19–20, 22,
    28–29, 32, 35–37, 41–44
  exoteric, 57–59, 60, 61, 75, 108
  Japanese schools of, 37–49
  Kings of India and, 6, 9, 11, 13
  Mahayana, 3, 6–13, 51, 58, 61, 66, 76
  persecution of, 13, 15, 22, 48
  proper goal of, 5
  Shinto and, 48
  Theravada, 58
  Tibetan, 13, 14
  Vajrayana, 14
  See also Esoteric Buddhism; Mikkyo;
    Shingon Buddhism

Cautions for Future Shingon Practitioners
  (Kakuban's), 101

Chan (Ch.) school, 61
Chandragupta I, King, 9
Chen-yen (Ch.) school, 3, 58. *See also*
    Shingon Buddhism
Chih-t'ung, 17
Chinese Buddhism, schools of, 3, 58–61
Ch'ing-Lung Temple, 21, 28
Chishaku-in Temple, 46, 48
Chōkaku, 43
Chū-in school, 38, 210
Commentary on the Dainichi-kyō (I-
    hsing's), 18–19, 65, 80, 82, 83, 156,
    161, 167, 192, 199, 205, 207
Commentary on the Flower Garland Sutra
    (Nagarjuna's), 120
Compassion, 105
    and skillful means, 105
    and tai-zō mandala, 125, 198
    and wisdom, 105, 111
Consciousness
    definition of, 91
    eight levels of, 90–95
    ninth, tenth, and innumerable levels
        of, 92–95, 97–98
    and wisdom, 93–95
Consciousness-only school (*yuishiki*), 9,
    66, 71, 81, 90–91, 96
    Kongōchō-gyō and, 66

Daichido-ron (Nagarjuna's), 8
Daigo-ji Temple, 37, 42, 43, 47, 49
Daijō Kishin-ron (Nagarjuna's), 70
Daikaku-ji Temple, 36, 43, 49
Dainichi-kyō, 3, 4, 8, 11–12, 18–19, 24–
    25, 27, 35, 81–85, 156, 159–161,
    168, 175–176, 192–194, 199, 205,
    206
    on Dharma-Body, 67, 105
    on five elements/five syllables, 69
    on Tai-zō mandala, 84–85
    on Universal A-syllable Body, 71, 80
    and the Void school, 66
Dainichi-kyō Sho, 18–19, 82–84, 125,
    156, 161, 167, 192, 199, 205, 207
    on mantra recitation, 77, 80
    on meaning of *kalpa,* 98–99
    on meditation, 101, 103
    on Six Great Elements, 65
    on Tai-zō mandala, 125–126
    on Three Secrets, 106, 109, 110, 113,
        115, 117–118

Dainichi Nyorai, 8, 12, 42, 62–64, 82,
    85–86, 122, 166, 170–174, 192
    as Amaterasu, 53
    as Amida Buddha, 41
    as Dharma Body, 63–64
    and Dharma-transmission initiation,
        180
    enlightenment of, 94
    and Kongosatta, 86–87
    mantra of, 193, 198
    as Shakyamuni Buddha, 59
    and Shingon lineage, 18, 87
    and six great elements, 69, 71
Darani Jikkyo, 11, 17, 113
Deities
    as aspects of wisdom, 93–95
    esoteric Buddhist, 23–24, 30, 62–64,
        117
    Hindu, 10, 62–64, 72
    local, 30
    as seed syllable, 117
    Shinto, 53
Delusion, 72, 172
    three types of, 88, 98–99
    wisdom and, 72–74, 89, 171
    See also Kalpa(s)
Denpo-in school, 41, 42
Desire, 72–75
Dharani (Skt.), 7, 8, 75, 76. *See also*
    Mantra
Dharmabhadra, 22
Dharma Body (*hosshin*), 42, 59–62,
    64–66, 108–110
    enlightenment of, 104
    Dainichi Nyorai as, 63–64
    universality of the, 61, 105
Dharmagupta, 12
Dharmakāla, 16
Dharmakṣema, 16
Dharma lineage, 56, 86–89
    and "Legend of the Iron Tower,"
        87–89
Dharma master, 56
Dharmapala, King, 13
Dharmarakṣa, 16
Dharma-transmission initiation, 153,
    168, 176, 177–181
Diamond Sutra, 7–8
Dōgen, 40
Dōhan, 42, 203
Dōji, 24, 25

Dōshō, 24
Dual mandala (ryōbu mandara), 35, 53, 81, 122, 147–151
  and A-syllable visualization, 198–216
  symbolism of, 151

Eight Great Patriarchs (Shingon), 18, 87
Eisai, 40
Eison, 50
Empowerment (kaji), 106–107
  mutual, 70, 74, 101, 105, 110
  mystery of, 110–112
Enchin, 35
Engyō, 33–34
Enlightened universe, 70–71, 128
  as Dainichi Nyorai, 70, 71
  and delusion, 72, 73–74
Enlightenment, 84, 106, 123–125
  communication of, 58, 60
  of Dainichi Nyorai, 94–95
  definition of, 61
  delusion and, 72, 73
  of the Dharma Body, 104
  energy of, 111
  of Shakyamuni, 121, 123–124
Ennin, 34, 35
En-no-Gyōja, 25, 51
Esoteric Buddhism
  in China, 15–22
  in India, 3–15
  in Japan, 23 ff.
  in Tibet, 4, 14
Esoteric sutras, 24–25
  primary, 3, 4, 8, 24–25, 81–86
Essentials of Meditation (Shubhakara-simha's), 100–101, 102, 158, 161
E-un, 34

Fire ritual (goma), 4, 10, 74, 169, 172–175
  in Brahmanism, 4, 10
Five Realms of Initiation (goshu sanmaya), 176–181
Five wisdoms (gochi), 94–95, 137
Flower Garland Sutra, 8
Formless Meditation (Kakuban's), 101
Fo T'u-ch'eng, 16
Fourfold preparatory practice
  eighteenfold practice, 168, 169–172
  fire ritual, 168, 172–175
  Kongō-kai Mandala practice, 168, 171
  Tai-zō Mandala practice, 168, 171

Four Universal Mandalas (shiman sōdai), 70
Fudō, 54, 156, 172–175
Fujiwara, Yoshifusa, 35, 36

Gasshō mudra, 114
Gembō, 24
Gen-yu, 46
Gohimitsu Giki, 73
Gōhō, 88, 208, 210
Gopala, King, 13
Goshorai Mokuroku (Kūkai's), 28, 108, 123
Great Bliss (tairaku), 72–73
Guhyasamaja Tantra, 14
Gupta dynasty, 9–11
Gyokuin-shō (Gōhō's), 88

Hannya Haramita Shin-gyō. See Heart Sutra
Hannya Rishu-kyō, 12–13
Hannya Shingyō Hiken, (Kūkai's), 74–75
Harṣa, King, 11
Hase-dera Temple, 46, 47, 48
Heart (Mikkyo tradition: "two heart-minds")
  karita, 89, 161–162
  shitta, 89, 161–162
Hevajra Tantra, 14
  and mother tantra, 14
Hideyoshi, 45–46
Hijiri (itinerant saints), 39, 47, 51
  Kōya-, 40, 44
Hinduism, 6, 9, 10, 13
Hirosawa school, 37–38
Hizō Hōyaku (Kūkai's), 32
Hokke-kyō. See Lotus Sutra
Hōnen, 40
Hosshō, 42, 43
Hsüan-tsang, 17
Hsüan Tsung, Emperor, 17–18, 19, 22
Hua-yen (Ch.) school, 58, 60–61
Hui-kuo, 20–21, 28, 87, 168, 176, 177

I-chen, 21
Ichigo Taiyō Himitsu-shū (Kakuban's), 191, 212, 213
I-ching, 17
I-hsing, 18–19, 83
Incantation, 3, 4, 8
  in Brahmanism, 4–5
  in early Buddhism, 4–6

Incantation (*continued*)
  in esoteric Buddhism, 3, 4, 23
  See also Mantra
Indication of the Basis of the Tree Teachings
  (Kūkai's), 27, 184
Indrabhuti, King, 13
Initiation (*kanjō*), 153, 175–181
  Five Realms of, 176–181
Innyū, 97
Interpretation of the Dainichi-kyō (Kūkai's),
  86, 111
Ippen, 40
Ise shrine, 53
Islam, 13, 15
I-ts'ao, 21

Japanese Buddhism
  Azuchi-Momoyama period, 45
  Heian period, 26–40, 42, 52, 54
  Kamakura period, 40–43, 53
  Meiji Restoration, 48–49
  Muromachi period, 43–45, 53
  Nara period, 23–26
  Sengoku period, 45
  Southern/Northern Courts period, 43
  Tokugawa (Edo) period, 45–48
Japanese Buddhism, schools of, 37–49
Jichie, 33, 38, 193
Jikkan-jō, 168
Ji school, 40, 44
Jitshuhan, 50
Jōdo (Pure Land school), 40
Jōdo Shin (True Pure Land school), 40
Jōgon, 47
Jokyō, 33–34
Jōyo, 39
Jujushin-ron (Kūkai's), 32, 97

Kajū-ji Temple, 49
Kakuban, 41–42, 59, 79, 101, 183
  and A-syllable visualization, 158, 191,
    203–205, 208, 212–215
Kakukai, 42
Kalacakra Tantra, 15
Kalpa (*kō*), 98–99
  definition of, 98
  three types of, 98–99
Kanbutsu Sanmai-kai-kyō, 120
Kangen, 38
Kaniṣka, King, 6

*Kanjizai Bosatsu Tabatari Zuishin Darani-
  kyo,* 120
Kanjō. See Initiation
Kannon, 24, 54, 76, 120
Karma-vajra (*katsum-sho*), 165
Kegon-kyō. See Flower Garland Sutra
Kenmitsu Fudō-sho (Kūkai's), 59
Kōbō Daishi, 3, 35, 38–39. *See also*
  Kūkai
Kokūzō bodhisattva, 25, 182–183
  and Morning Star Meditation, 183–
    186, 188
*Kokūzō Bosatsu Nōman Shogan Saishō-shin
  Darani Gumonji-ho,* 183
Kongōbu-ji Temple, 36, 38, 41–42, 46,
  48
Kongōchō Gohimitsu-kyō, 60
Kongōchō-gyō, 3, 4, 8, 11, 12, 18, 19, 35,
    85–86, 113, 120, 121, 161, 192
  and consciousness-only school, 66
  definition of, 85
  and Kongo-kai Mandala, 86
  and Kongosatta/enlightened con-
    sciousness, 69
  and "Legend of the Iron Tower,"
    87–88
Kongōchō-gyō Giketsu (Amoghavajra's),
    87–88, 119–120
Kongō-kai mandala, 81, 138–151, 152,
    157, 165, 171, 198–206, 210–212
  and moon disk/enlightened mind, 198
  nine assemblies of, 140–145
  outline of, 138–140
  spiral movement of, 145–147
Kongō-kai-shō (Kōzen's), 165
Kongō-kyō. See Diamond Sutra
Kongosatta, 8, 68, 73–74, 86, 169, 212
  and Dainichi Nyorai, 86–87
  and Dharma-transmission initiation,
    181
Koshin, 44
Kōya-san, 30–33, 38–42, 45–46
  Kukai at, 30–33
  restoration of, 39
Kōzen, 165
Kūkai, 3, 20–21, 25, 26, 59, 60, 66, 70,
    86, 87, 94, 95, 106, 108
  and A-syllable meditation, 192,
    193–195, 198, 207
  biography of, 26–27

as calligrapher, 28–29, 32
and fourfold preparatory system, 168
at Kōya-san, 30–33
and Morning Star meditation, 183–184
and Shingon, 3, 26–33, 50
Kumarajiva, 16

"Legend of the Iron Tower," 8, 86–89
List of Items Brought from China (Kūkai's), 108, 123
Lotus Sutra, 8, 76

Madhyamika (Chūgan) school, 8, 9
Mahavairocana, 4–5, 63–64. See also Dainichi Nyorai
Mahayana sutras, 7–8, 76
Mandala
  definition of, 123
  Kongō-kai, 20, 81, 138–152, 157, 165, 171, 198–206, 210–212
  Tai-zō, 20, 81, 125–138, 147–151, 152, 165, 171, 194, 198–210
  Taizo-kongokai, 147–151, 198–206
  types of, 126–128
Mantra, 61, 75–79
  definition of, 75
  dharani (Skt.), 7, 8, 24, 75, 76
  paritta (Pali), 5, 75
  speech and, 116–119
  Vidya (Skt.), 8, 75, 76
  See also Incantation
Matsudai Shingon Gyōja Yōjin (Kaku-ban's), 101
The Meaning of the A-Syllable (Kūkai's), 193–194
The Meaning of Becoming a Buddha in This Body (Kūkai's), 66, 69, 70, 106–107, 110, 111–112, 124
The Meaning of the UN-Syllable (Kūkai's), 75, 80, 99, 198
  and Three Secrets, 119
Meditation, 101–103, 106–107
  A-syllable, 182, 184, 190–191, 195–198
  goal of, 110–120
  Morning Star, 25, 27, 52, 182, 183–188
  on the universe, 184–185
  See also Samadhi
Meditation techniques (Mikkyo), 196–198

Meiji Restoration, 48
Mikkyo, 3–22, 56–62
  and exoteric Buddhism, 56–59, 60, 61, 75, 76, 78
  four major characteristics of, 57–62
  as Indra's net, 56
  ritual, 3, 4, 10, 34–37, 42, 54
  ritual texts, 5, 56, 201–215
  See also Esoteric Buddhism
Mind
  secret of, and internal visualization, 119–122
  ten levels of, 90, 95–98
Moon disk
  and five stages of samadhi, 100–101
  meaning of, 212–215
  visualization, 198–212
Morning Star Meditation (gumonji-hō), 25, 27, 52, 154
  definition of, 182
  practice of, 183–188
Mountain worship, 39, 51–55
  Honzan school of, 52
  Tōzan school of, 52
Mount T'ien-tai, 18, 27
Mount Wu-t'ai, 20, 27
Mudra (ingei), 61
  definition of, 112
  levels of meaning of, 114–115
  secret of body and, 112–115
Mui Sanzō Zenyō (Shubhakarasimha's), 100–102, 158, 161
Muniśri, 28
Muslim conquest, 13, 15
Musō-kan (Kakuban's), 101
Musōkan-sho (Kakuban's), 158
Mutual empowerment. See Empowerment
Myoē, 203
Myōken bodhisattva, 184

Nagabodhi, 12, 87
Nagarjuna, 8–9, 12, 70, 87–88, 168, 193
Nalanda, 11–12, 13
Nation-Protecting Lord Dharani Sutra, 80, 100–101
Natural Wisdom (Jinenchi-shū), school, 25, 51–52
Negoro-ji Temple, 42, 45–46
Nembutsu recitation, 39–40, 44, 51

"New teachings" (*shingi-ha*) school, 42,
47–48
  Buzan, 46, 48
  Chizan, 46, 48
Nichiren school, 40
Nijūgokan Sho, 168
Ningai ("Rain Priest"), 37
  and Ono school, 37–38
Ninkan, 44
Ninna-ji Temple, 36–37, 42, 47, 49
Ninshō, 50–51
Nobunaga, Oda, 45, 46

Odantapuri, 13
Offerings (ritual), 166–167
Ōgo, 46
"Old teachings" (*kogi-ha*) school, 42,48–49
Onkō (Jiun Sonja), 47
  and Unden school, 53
Ono school, 37–38

Padmasambhava, 13, 14
Pagoda (*tō*), 88, 166
  Kōya-san, 88
  symbolism of, 89, 117
Paritta (Pali), 5, 75
Persecution of Buddhism
  in China, 21–22
  in India, 13, 15
  in Japan, 48
Pilgrimage, 54–55
  Shikoku, 54–55
  thirty-three station, 54
Platform altar (*dan*), 165–166
Popular beliefs, 44, 49–55
Praise of Formless Visualization (Ka-
  kuban's), 158
Prajna (priest), 12, 21, 28
Precepts, 47
  samaya (Skt.), 50, 57
  sila (Skt.), 57
  vinaya (Skt.), 57, 176
Precious Key to the Secret Treasury
  (Kūkai's), 32
Preparatory Fourfold Enlightenment
  Practice, 62, 168–175, 182
  definition of, 168
  See also Fourfold preparatory practice
Principles of the A-Syllable Visualization
  (Seizon's), 202, 210–212
Pure Land school, 40, 54

Questions and Answers on the A-Syllable
  (Kakuban's), 79–80

Raikō, 109
Raiyu, 41–42, 204–205
*Record of the Oral Instruction on the A-Syl-
  lable Visualization* (Kūkai's), 193,
  195, 198, 200–201, 213
Record of the Secret Treasury (Kūkai's),
  111, 116–117, 136, 158
Rikan, 102
Ritual Manual of the Five Secrets, 73
Ritual
  in Brahmanism, 4–5, 10
  in early esoteric Buddhism, 3, 4–7,
  9–11, 23, 24, 54
  See also Shingon ritual
Ryōzen, 27

Saicho, 26, 28
  and Kukai, 29
Saidiji Temple, 49, 50
Śākyamitra, 124
Samadhi (*sammai/sanmaji*)
  A-syllable visualization, 158, 215
  Morning Star meditation, 183, 185,
  189
  stages of, 99–103
Sanbu-sho (Kūkai's), 32
Sangō Shiki (Kūkai's), 27, 184
Secret Explanation of the A-Syllable
  (Raiyu's), 204
Secret Explanation of the Mind Moon Disk
  (Kakuban's), 208
Secret Key to the Heart Sutra (Kūkai's),
  74–75, 108, 119
Seed syllable (*shuji*), 62
  deity as, 117
Seizon, 202, 210
Sennyū-ji, 49, 50
Sen'yo, 46
Shakumankaen-ron (Nagarjuna's), 70, 97,
  168
Shakuron Myomoku (Innyū's), 97
Shakyamuni Buddha, 5, 6–7, 58, 67–68,
  76, 81–82, 87, 166, 167
  and Dainichi Nyorai, 59, 82
  enlightenment of, 121, 123–124
  as *ōjin,* 59
Shih-hu, 22, 85
Shin (Ch.), 89, 161–162. *See also* Heart

Shinga, 33
Shingachirin Hishaku (Kakuban's), 208
Shingi school, 45, 46
Shingon Buddhism
  and court patronage, 49–50
  definition of, 3
  developments in, 37–42
  fundamental sutras of, 3, 4, 35, 81
  Kukai and, 3, 126–133
  and Shinto, 48, 53
  and Tendai, 34
  two mandalas of, 35, 53, 81, 122, 147, 151
  See also Esoteric Buddhism; Mikkyo
Shingon Glossary (Raikō's), 109
Shingon Ritsu school, 49, 50
  and social welfare, 50–51
Shingon ritual, 152–181
  general format of, 162–163
  implements and offerings in, 163–167
  purposes of, 152
Shingon rituals, 23, 35–37, 42, 62, 152–181
  confession, 169, 170
  fire, 4, 10, 74, 169, 172–175
  initiation, 175–181
  mandala offering, 154
  "post-seventh day," 154
  single deity, 152, 153
Shinran, 40
Shinto, 48
  and Buddhism, 48, 53
  State, 48
Shinzei, 33
Shinzen, 33, 38
Shōbō, 37, 52
Shōji Jissō-gi (Kūkai's), 68
Shōkaku, 202–203
Shōken, 42
Shōryo-shū, 27
Shubhakarasimha, 12, 18, 24, 25, 60, 71, 83, 128, 158, 161, 183, 189, 198
  on stages of samadhi, 100–101
  on the Universal A-syllable Body, 71
Shūei, 34
Shugendō. See Mountain worship
Shugokokkai-shu Darani-kyō, 80, 100–101
Shunjo, 50
Single Collection of the Essential Secrets (Kakuban's), 191, 212, 213
Single deity ritual, 153–154, 172–175

Six great elements
  and Dainichi Nyorai, 69
  universal body of, 64–71
Skillful means, 103–105
  and compassion, 105
  and wisdom, 103–105
Sokushin Jobutsu-gi (Kūkai's), 66, 69, 70, 106–107, 110, 111–112, 124
Soshitsuju-kyō, 21, 35
Srimitra, 16
Storehouse consciousness (*araya-shiki*), 90–92, 94
Stupa, 7, 166. *See also* Pagoda
Summary of the Essentials of the Tai-zō Realm Ritual (Gōhō's), 208–210
Summary of the Precious Mudra (Gōhō's), 88
Summary of the Vajra Realm (Kazen's), 165
Sun metaphor
  Aditya and, 63–64
  Amaterasu and, 53
  Buddha/deity and, 63–64, 111
  Dainichi Nyorai and, 64
  Vairocana and, 63–64
Sutra(s), 7, 24
  esoteric Buddhist, 3, 4, 8, 24–25, 81–86, 120
  fundamental Shingon, 3, 4, 8
  Mahayana, 7–9
Su Tsung, Emperor, 19–20

Tachikawa school, 44
Taimitsu (Tendai Mikkyo) school, 29, 35
Tai Tsung, Emperor, 20
Tai-zō Bonji Shidai (Kūkai's), 207
Tai-zōkai Nenju Shidai Yōshūki (Gōhō's), 208–210
Tai-zō mandala, 81, 125–138, 147–151, 152, 165, 171, 194, 198–210
  concentric structure of, 132–138
  and *Dainichi-kyō,* 84–85
  outline of, 128–132
Takaosan-ji Temple, 36, 47
T'ang dynasty, 17
  Patriarchs, 17–22
Tantra, 10–11
  anuttarayoga, 10, 13
  caryā, 10
  definition of, 11
  kriyā, 10
  yoga, 11, 13

243

T'an-yao, 16–17
Taoism, 16, 17, 21–22, 44
Tendai school, 26, 28, 29, 34–36
  and Shingon, 34
  and Shinto, 48
Ten levels of mind (jūjūshin), 90, 95–98
Three Powers (sanriki), 111
Three secrets, the, 30–32, 96, 106–122
  empowerment of, 70, 107
  union of, 106–107
  See also Universal Three Secrets
Three-secrets practices (concentrated),
  182–198
  A-syllable visualization, 182, 184,
    190–201
  Morning Star meditation, 182–188
T'ien-hsi-tsai, 22
Tien-t'ai (Ch.) school, 60–61
To-ji Temple, 31, 36–37, 42–43, 47, 49
  and "post-seventh day ritual," 49, 154
Tōmitsu (Tō-ji Mikkyo) school, 29, 35
Treatise on the Attainment of Great Wisdom
  (Nagarjuna's), 8
Treatise on Awakening of Mahayana Faith
  (Nagarjuna's), 70
Treatise on Enlightened Mind (Nagar-
  juna's), 70, 102, 105, 168, 193, 198
Treatise on the Exoteric and Esoteric Teach-
  ings (Kūkai's), 58, 94, 96
Treatise on Mahayana (Nagarjuna's), 70,
  97, 168
Treatise on the Ten Levels of Mind
  (Kūkai's), 32, 97, 124
The True Meaning of the Voiced Syllable
  (Kūkai's), 68, 76–77, 79, 116, 194

Unden school, 53
Unified A-UN Syllable Visualization
  (Dohan's), 203
Universal A-syllable Body (aji taidai), 71
Universal Three Secrets, 70
Unji-gi (Kūkai's), 75, 80, 198

Vajra (kongō-shō), 163–164
  three types of, 164
Vajra bell (kongō-rei), 165
Vajrabodhi, 12, 18, 19, 60, 85, 87

Vajra tray (kongō-ban), 164
Vasubandhu, 90
Veda(s) (Skt.), 4, 77
  Atharva, 5
  Ṛg, 4
Vikramsila, 13
Vinaya (Skt.). See Precepts
Visualization, 6, 62, 84, 86, 108–109,
  118–122, 157–162, 182–188,
  190–206, 212–215
  and concentration points, 159, 162
  internal, and secret of mind, 119–122
  three secrets, 159–160
Visualization technique, 154–159,
  160–162, 195–198
  being-protecting, 160, 168, 196
  breath regulating, 196
  circulation, 156, 162, 196
  expansion, 157, 196, 198
  image manifesting, 156, 196
  permeation, 158, 161, 196
  ritual awakening enlightened mind,
    196
  transformation, 156, 196
Void (ku) school, 65–66, 81, 91–92
  Dainichi-kyō and, 66

Wisdom
  compassion and, 105, 111
  definitions of, 103–104
  delusion and, 72–74, 89, 171
  skillful means and, 103–105
Wisdom of All-Wisdom (issai chichi),
  67–68, 84, 99, 125–126
Wisdom-Truth Sutra, 72, 153, 168
Wu-hsing, 83

Yakushin, 36, 37
Yoga school. See Consciousness-only
  school
Yūkai, 43–44
Yūn-gi (Kūkai's), 75, 80, 198
Yün-kang caves, 16–17

Zen Buddhism, 40, 45, 61
  Rinzai, 40
  Sōtō, 40